How to Be an Adult in Relationships

How To Be an Adult in Relationships

in Relationships

The Five Keys to Mindful Loving

DAVID RICHO

Foreword by Kathlyn Hendricks

SHAMBHALA
Boston & London
2002

SHAMBHALA PUBLICATIONS, INC.
Horticultural Hall
300 Massachusetts Avenue
Boston, Massachusetts 02115
www.shambhala.com

9 8 7 6

Printed in the United States of America

♾ This edition is printed on acid-free paper that meets the American National Standards Institute Z39.48 Standard.

Distributed in the United States by Random House, Inc., and in Canada by Random House of Canada Ltd

LIBRARY OF CONGRESS CATALOGING-IN-PUBLICATION DATA
Richo, David, 1940–
   How to be an adult in relatioinships: the five keys to mindful loving/David Richo.—
   1st ed.
     p. cm.
   ISBN 1-57062-812-2 (alk. paper)
   1. Love. 2. Interpersonal relations. 3. Love—Religious aspects—Buddhism.
   4. Interpersonal relations—Religious aspects—Buddhism. I. Title.
   BF575.L8.R53 2002
   158.2—dc21   2001055015

For Annie, Christopher, Elizabeth, and Joshua,
with the love I feel toward you and always have.
May this book help to walk you through a healed past
into delight in yourselves and in your relationships.
Thank you for all you have taught me in our life together.

Contents

Foreword

THIS BOOK BRINGS THE MYSTICAL DOWN TO EARTH, to the world of relationships that we all navigate from birth to death. In *How to Be an Adult in Relationships* David Richo provides an operational guide to effective relationships that's as gentle and precise as his own presence with his students and friends. Through the reliable spiritual practices of mindfulness and lovingkindness, readers embark on a journey that leads to awareness, joy, and deep relating.

Mindfulness is an ancient meditation mode in which we let go of our fears, our attachments to control and being right, our expectations and entitlements, and our judgments of others. Instead of these popular strategies, we learn to simply stay present openly in the moment—with nothing in the way—so we can experience life as it occurs. When we apply mindfulness to our relationships, we can finally see ourselves and others as we are, in all our touching vulnerability and with all our rich potential for love.

In the spiritual practice of lovingkindness, we expand our awareness of others in an immensely tender and caring way. We journey beyond our own personal relationships and embrace the wider world. We learn to extend our love to everyone around us, even those to whom we are indifferent and those we find difficult. Through lovingkindness the romantic union between two people ultimately embraces the world. At one point in this book, David says, "We can expand our consciousness of giving and receiving love." In my experience counseling couples and training professionals, the question always emerges: How can we expand our capacity to handle more love and positive energy so we don't continue to sabotage any advances? We—my husband, Gay, and I—call this the Upper Limits Problem and the ultimate human challenge.

This book shows just how the widening ripple of love can flow more freely within and between us all. David Richo lays down the stepping-stones from personal love to universal love. The spiritual practices in *How to Be an Adult in Relationships* are not adjuncts to psychological work; they fulfill it.

David Richo offers an important new synthesis in the self-help movement, practical spirituality grounded in what the poet Ted Loder calls "treasures / of joy, of friendship, of peace / hidden in the fields of the daily." David's examples, and especially the many opportunities he gives to practice these shifts of perspective and action, deeply support the reader's evolution. We find a new place to stand together in equality. Clear markers guide us toward a compassionate life in which human beings finally grow up to become stewards for each other and our larger home. Not only can our relationships work for our growth but for the world's evolution too. I invite you to be moved by these waves of possibility.

KATHLYN HENDRICKS, PH.D.

Acknowledgments

I APPRECIATE MY EDITOR, Eden Steinberg, for her warm association with me in the production of this book. She was the first to understand what I was up to. She cheered my poetic inclinations. And I noticed, with admiration, that Eden not only sees a project through but also cares that it be the best it can be.

I am indebted to David Reich who ruthlessly edited my book with respect and competence. His questions helped me become attentive to my own inner debates. David was Argus-eyed in noticing and clearing up my inconsistencies, illogicalities, and in perceiving the heart in my book.

My respect and thanks go to Adam Friedson, a dear friend and generous mensch, who believed in this project a long time ago. His elegant bond with his wife Allie instructs me how—and that—relationships work.

I appreciate my many clients and students over these past thirty odd years in whom I glimpsed such intriguing sparks from the campfire of human relationships, their continuity with the past, and their potential for a glittering future.

I am grateful to all the people in my life who have been brave enough to be in relationships with me: family, friends, colleagues, and partners. I pieced together a heart from each of them, especially the ones who have loved me unconditionally and whom I have loved that way in return. The love I received has lasted in me as a *protection*.

Finally, I honor the work of Chögyam Trungpa Rinpoche, my first teacher on Buddha's unsurpassable path, who, in 1971, opened the then newfound possibility of integrating psychological work and spiritual practice. It was through such a radiant doorway that I dared the project of harmonizing psychology, Catholicism, the Jungian perspective, mythology, poetry, my story, and all the cherished gifts that have made my life the curious pageant it has been.

May I and all these assisting forces keep letting the light through.

How to Be an Adult in Relationships

Introduction

To have loved alone will not suffice
Unless we also have been wise
And have our loves enjoyed.
—Sir John Suckling

LOVE IS THE POSSIBILITY OF POSSIBILITIES. Its farthest reach is beyond us, no matter how long we love or how much. It will always remain the mute mystery to whose ecstasy and ache we can only surrender with a yes. There is something cheerful and plucky in us that lets us risk a journey into the labyrinth of love, no matter how hazardous. However, all the love in the world will not bring us happiness or make a relationship work. That requires skill, and this skill is quite attainable. Practice can make us nimble enough to dance together with grace, however bashful we may be at the beginning.

Love is experienced differently by each of us, but for most of us five aspects of love stand out. We feel loved when we receive attention, acceptance, appreciation, and affection, and when we are allowed the freedom to live in accord with our own deepest needs and wishes. These "five A's" meet us in different guises throughout life's journey. In childhood, we need these five A's to develop self-esteem and a healthy ego. They are building blocks of identity, of a coherent human personality. Human experience has a striking and reliable harmony: What we need for the building of a self is also precisely what we need for happiness in our adult love relationships. Intimacy, at its best, means giving and receiving the five A's, the joys and wealth of relationship. These five elements or aspects of love also describe our destiny of service to the world as mature spiritual beings. Great spiritual exemplars such as Jesus or Buddha can be seen as beings who offer this fivefold love to all of us. Through our spiritual practice we come to know a power greater than our ego, and that power nourishes us by granting us the graces of attention, acceptance, appreciation, affection, and allowing.

This is a touching and encouraging synchronicity built into our very being. The five A's are simultaneously the fulfillment of our earliest needs, the requirements of adult intimacy and of universal compassion, and the essential qualities of mindfulness practice. In the splendid economy of human and spiritual development, the same keys open all our evolutionary doors.

Thus, the five A's come to us as gifts in childhood. They are then bestowed by us as gifts to others. They are not the result of effort but are the automatic overflow of love we receive. We do not have to try; we simply notice that we are attentive, appreciative, etc., toward those we love. The same applies to compassion. It is a spiritual gift, a grace bestowed on us as a result of mindfulness practice. It is not a task. We *notice* that compassion *happens* in and through us as we become more mindfully present in the world. This compassion is shown by the five A's that are now five graces we receive and give.

Is there a way to increase our capacity to give and receive these essential elements of love? Yes, we can do it through mindfulness, an alert witnessing of reality without judgment, attachment, fear, expectation, defensiveness, bias, or control. Through compassionate mindfulness we become adept at granting the essential components of love to everyone—even to ourselves—and in the pages that follow I will keep returning to mindfulness as a fast track to successful love.

This book discusses each of the five A's and how they apply to childhood, relationships, and spiritual maturity. It also suggests practices that can help you in resolving childhood issues, in creating happier relationships, and in becoming more spiritually conscious and compassionate. Indeed, the practices are stirred by a spiritual ambition with higher stakes: a more loving you, with the world as your beneficiary.

All this entails taking a journey together—a heroic one because it involves pain and forces you to shift from a focus on ego to a focus on facing the risks of life together. This book walks you along that path, providing the kind of gear you will need to camp out together safely and enjoyably. We will use both Western psychological tools and Eastern and Western spiritual practices, not graduating from one to the other but employing them simultaneously. The main psychological tools are working through personal and childhood conundrums with a commitment to identify, process, and resolve issues so that you may change and grow. The spiritual tools are letting go of ego, increasing mindfulness, and cultivating an ethic of compassion. We achieve mindfulness when reality takes precedence over our ego. That is why mindfulness leads to intimacy, the mutual egoless gift of love. Couples with a spiritual practice have a greater serenity in their life together and increase their chances for happiness and longevity in their relationships.

A relationship can force us to revisit every feeling and memory in the legend of ourselves. In our psychological work of addressing, processing, and resolving emotional blocks and problems, we pay attention to feelings, explore their implications, and hold them until they change or reveal a path that leads deeper into ourselves. In our spiritual practice of mindfulness, something very different occurs. We let feelings or thoughts arise and let go of them. We do not process them, nor do we hold them. Each of these approaches has its proper time, and we need both of them. Paying attention and letting go are the twin tools that will be presented throughout these pages. Therapy without mindfulness takes us only to the point of resolving our predicament. Mindfulness with therapy helps us to dissolve the ego that got us into it in the first place.

The heroic journey is a metaphor for the yearning in the human soul for something that can repair and restore what has been broken or lost in our limited world. The journey of the hero or heroine involves first a leaving of the familiar, then a passage through struggle to a new place, and finally a return home with the gift of higher consciousness that is available to all who want it. Two people find each other in romance and oppose each another in conflict, only to engage finally in a life commitment to one another. It seems we cannot love maturely unless we go through the full itinerary of just such a risky expedition. But this Western metaphor is incomplete without mindfulness.

In short, we need to get up and go, but we also need to sit and stay. By taking a journey without meditation and silence, we might fall prey to a restricting and extroverted activism. By practicing meditation without a sense that we are on a journey, we might fall prey to an introverted quietism. The Eastern voice tells us we are already here. The Western voice calls us to go out in order to get here fully. We arrive nowhere and are nowhere without that combination. Buddha did not sit forever but went out into the world to spread the word. Jesus did not preach and heal every day but sometimes sat in the desert alone.

The human heart holds much more love than it can ever disburse in one lifetime. This book suggests a program for activating that abundant potential. Intimate love is enigmatic and demanding; many of us fear it while still craving it. Thus, it definitely requires an extensive manual. This book explores the tender and scary territories of our psyche and blazes a path through them. It is not too late or too long for any of us.

I am writing as a psychotherapist on a Buddhist path and as a man with a checkered relationship history. I have met with many problems but have found some ways to deal with them. I have discovered that they are not bottomless pits but portals to a richer life. My accent in this book is necessarily on how we get stuck and how things go wrong. But you can also trust me to show ways to make things work better and ways the whole experience can make us better people and create a better world.

Enlightenment can only be embodied in the world by people who love one another. So relationships are not about how two people can survive each other but about how the whole world becomes more capable of love, with all its dim anguish and glowing rapture. The work and practice I recommend here are not aimed at making your life together smoother but at helping you relate to its inevitable roughness with humor, ease, and generosity. An untamed ego cannot pull that off. Only an awakened heart can do it. Then intimacy is best approached on a spiritual path. As a bonus, our limited personal work can heal the wider world.

I hope this book will pose poignant questions like these and help you answer them:

- What will it take for me to find the happiness I always wanted?
- Will I feel loved the way I always wanted to be loved?
- What will it take for me to let go of the past?
- Will I learn to protect my own boundaries, insist that others honor them, and honor those of others?
- Will I ever let go of the need to control?
- Will I ever dare to love with all my heart?

This whole book is a letter from me to you. I am eager to share with you what I have learned from clients, friends, and my own life. At the same time, the book will elicit information *from* you, not just give information *to* you. The truths of love and how it works are deeply and enduringly known by you and every person. My part has only been to type into this Apple the wisdom that came to me from Eden and its exiles.

PART ONE

The Home We Leave

To leave home is half the Buddha's teaching.

—MILAREPA

1

How It All Began

✧

Man is a giddy thing.
—SHAKESPEARE, *Much Ado about Nothing*

W e are born with a capacity to dance together but not with the necessary training. We have to learn the dance steps and practice until we move with ease and grace. The joy in it requires work. Some of us have been damaged physically or in our self-confidence, and we will have to practice dancing more than others. Some of us have been so damaged we may never be able to dance well at all. Some of us were taught it was a sin to dance.

It is exactly the same in relationships. Our early experience forms or deforms our adult relationships. As children, some of us were so injured or disabled psychologically—by neglect, inhibition, or abuse—that it may take us years of work and practice before we can dance a graceful adult commitment. Some of us were so abused that we feel compelled to abuse others in revenge. Some of us were so damaged in the past that we may never be able to relate in an adult way.

Most of us, however, had good-enough parenting—reasonable fulfillment of our emotional needs for attention, acceptance, appreciation, affection, and allowing: the five A's. And so in adulthood, we are reasonably facile at relating to others in healthy ways. This means relating mindfully, without either blind possessiveness or a crippling fear of closeness. Yet no one relates with perfect ease without learning the skill, just as no one dances with perfect ease without instruction. Some people master dancing, and others never quite get it right—though perhaps others do not fully notice. A relationship, likewise, may look successful, but it may not be providing true intimacy or commitment—a real problem if it has led to marriage and children. As dancers we can refuse to improve our skill with little consequence to anyone else, but if we do the same thing in a relationship, someone may get hurt. (*Relationship* in this context means intimate involvement, while living either together or apart.)

Then there are those of us who suffered serious childhood abuse and lack of need fulfillment and thereby were damaged in such a way that we cannot easily be intimate. In time, we too may learn to relate intimately, but only if we work through our early issues. It is our responsibility to expend the energy it will take to practice and become skillful at relating well. It does not come automatically. We will have to learn, be taught, grieve our past, work in therapy, get to know our true self, undo years of habits, practice with a partner, follow a spiritual practice—and read and work with a book like this. The good news is that we, like all human beings, have a psyche calibrated to do the work. Eventually, the awkwardness and missteps give way to harmonious and cooperative movement that reflects the love song behind it all.

We have heard about the harm our childhood wounds can do to our adult relationships, but I take a generally positive view of the childhood phase of our human journey. What happened to us then is not as important as how we hold it now: positively as something we have grown by or negatively as something that goes on wounding us and our relationships. If we can mourn the past and thereby diminish its impact on our present lives, we can then maintain our boundaries while still bonding closely to a partner. As long as we have a program for dealing with adversity, no problem can lead us to despair.

We have heard people being labeled as "codependent" when they cannot leave a painful relationship that has no future. Yet our sense of self is radically embedded in our negotiations with original family members. If a relationship reconfigures an original bond with our father or mother, leaving it may pose a terrifying threat to our inner security. Then all prospects of change—even for the better—represent a threat. We are challenged to be compassionate toward ourselves for the time it takes to make changes. Taking our time does not have to mean we are cowardly or codependent, only that we are sensitive to pressures and meanings from regions of our psyche still in the grip of an old regime. Our failed and failing bonds have preoccupied us all our lives. To repeat is human; to reframe is healthy. As we replace, however slowly, defensive reactions with different ways of doing things, new capacities open and new skills come into play in our relationships. It's not only a matter of breaking out of the enclosing arc of childhood. We humans require the animating sustenance of our fellows. We have to know that an echoing and enthusiastic resonance to our unique existence is available somewhere in this vast and ravaged world. We cannot make that happen, but we can be open to it and welcome it.

If we found total satisfaction in childhood, we would have no motivation to reach out to the wider world. The journey of adulthood begins when we leave, as we must, the secure nest provided by father and mother and try to find a partner in the adult world. Without such a need we might be seduced by the comfort of home, isolate ourselves from the larger world, and thus never find our unique place in it. This also explains why no person or thing will ever be enough to satisfy the full breadth of our human potential. Nature cannot afford to lose any of her stewards, so she has calibrated the heart so it is never permanently fulfilled. But she does grant moments of satisfaction with things and with people, and they can sustain us. Once that happens, we have found ourselves. This was expressed so touchingly by the character of the knight in Ingmar Bergman's film *The Seventh Seal:* "I shall remember this hour of peace—the strawberries, the bowl of milk, your faces in the dusk. I shall remember our words and shall bear this memory between my hands as carefully as a bowl of fresh milk. And this will be a sign of great contentment."

Love from another adult does more than just satisfy us in the present. It ripples back in time for us, repairing, restoring, and renovating an inadequate past. Sincere love also sets off a forward-moving ripple and a resultant shift inside us. We get to the point where we can think: "Now I don't have to need quite so much. Now I don't have to blame my parents quite so much. Now I can receive love without craving more and more. I can have and be enough." Only the person whose journey has progressed to that point can love someone intimately.

A holding environment—the safe and reliable context of the five A's—is necessary for all growth, both psychological and spiritual. We are like kangaroos developing in a pouch. We experience being held within the womb, within the family, within a relationship, within support groups, and within civic and spiritual communities. At every stage of our life span, our inner self requires the nurturance of loving people who are attuned to our feelings and responsive to our needs. They are the ideal sources that foster our inner resources of personal power, lovability, and serenity. Those who love us understand us and are available to us with an attention, appreciation, acceptance, and affection we can feel. They make room for us to be who we are.

Our work, then, is to become the healthiest possible version of who we uniquely are. The healthy ego—what Freud called "a coherent organization of mental processes"—is the part of us that can observe self, situations, and persons; assess them; and respond in such a way as to move toward our goals. We do not let go of this aspect of ego but build on it. It assists us in relationships by making us responsible and sensible in our choices and commitments. The neurotic ego, on the other hand, is the part of us that is compulsively driven or stymied by fear or desire, feeding arrogance, entitlement, attachment, and the need to control other people. Sometimes it is self-negating and makes us feel we are victims of others. This neurotic ego is the one we are meant to dismantle as our spiritual task in life. Its tyrannies frighten intimacy away and menace our self-esteem.

Western psychology places major importance on building a sense of self or ego. Buddhism, in contrast, places major importance on letting go of the illusion of a freestanding, fixed solid self. These views seem contradictory until we realize that Buddhism presupposes a healthy sense of self. It does not recommend abdicating the adult tasks of building competence and confidence, relating to others effectively, discovering life purpose, or fulfilling responsibilities. Indeed, we first have to establish a self before we can let go of one. That self is a provisional and convenient designation but not ultimately real in any enduring, unchanging way. To say that there is no limited, fixed self is a way of referring to the boundless potential in each of us—our buddha mind or buddha nature. We can transcend our limited selves. We are more than what appears in our limited egos.

Great mystics feel the oneness experienced in meditation as soothing at first, but then as a force propelling them into the world with a sense of service. (This is why ours is a heroic—and paradoxical—journey.) This does not mean that all of us have to live a life of constant service to humanity. That is a special calling requiring special graces. *We are fulfilled when we live out our personal capacity for loving. Our spiritual practice is perfect when we show love in every one of the unique and peerless ways that are in us.*

The Power of Mindfulness

> Meditation is not a means of forgetting the ego; it is a method
> of using the ego to observe and tame its own manifestations.
>
> —MARK EPSTEIN

Self-actualization is not a sudden happening or even the permanent result of long effort. The eleventh-century Tibetan Buddhist poet-saint Milarepa suggested: "Do not expect full realization; simply practice every day of your life." A healthy person is not perfect but perfectible, not a done deal but a work in progress. Staying healthy takes discipline, work, and patience, which is why our life is a journey and perforce a heroic one. The neurotic ego wants to follow the path of least resistance. The spiritual Self wants to reveal new paths. It is not that practice makes perfect but that practice is perfect, combining effort with an openness to grace.

Authentic practice combines effort with an openness to grace, a free gift of progress or awakening that comes to us unbidden and unconjured from buddha mind. Bread takes the effort of kneading but also requires sitting quietly while the dough rises with a power all its own. We are not alone in our psychological or spiritual evolution. A higher power than ego, wiser than our intellect and more enduring than our will, kicks in to assist us. Even now, as you read this, many bodhisattvas and saints are gathering to become your mighty companions on your heart's path.

Mindfulness is an elegant Buddhist practice that brings our bare attention to what is going on in the here and now. It does this by freeing us of our mental habit of entertaining ourselves with ego-based fears, desires, expectations, evaluations, attachments, biases, defenses, and so on. The bridge from distractions back to the here and now is the physical experience of paying attention to our breathing. The classic sitting pose plays an important part in mindfulness meditation by encouraging us to stay still and become centered physically. Furthermore, sitting is earth-touching, and earth, because of its here-and-now concreteness, grounds and centers us in the face of compelling mental seductions. We sit as a practice for how we will act throughout the day. Mindfulness, however, involves more than sitting. It is moment-by-moment nonclinging to ego and calm presence in the simplicity that results when we experience reality without the clutter produced by the decorative arts of ego.

The word *mindfulness* is actually a misnomer since the act itself involves mind-emptying not mind-filling. It is the only nonaltered state of mind, the pure experience of our own reality. Meditation is the vehicle to mindfulness in all areas. Mindfulness meditation is not a religious event or a form of prayer. It is an exploration of how the mind works and how it can be stilled so as to reveal an inner spaciousness in which wisdom and compassion arise with ease.

Mindfulness is not meant to help us escape reality but to see it clearly, without the blinding overlays of ego. Meditation is not escapism; only the layers of ego are. To stay with that vision leads to letting go while, ironically, escaping leads to holding on. In the haunted valley of human paradox, *we gain and go on by losing and letting go,* and mindfulness is the good shepherd within.

In mindfulness we do not repress or indulge any thoughts, only notice them and return to our breathing, gently guiding ourselves back to where we belong as a kindly parent does to a straying child. Meditation is entirely successful when we keep coming back to our breathing in a patient and nonjudgmental way. Mindful awareness is the condition of the fair and alert witness rather than the judge, jury, prosecutor, plaintiff, defendant, or defense attorney. We notice what happens in our minds and simply take it in as information. This does not mean stoicism or indifference, because then we would lose our vulnerability, an essential component of intimacy. To witness is not to stand aloof but to stand by. We then can act without compulsion or disquiet, relating to what is happening rather than becoming possessed by it.

There are two kinds of witnessing: compassionate and dispassionate. In compassionate witnessing we observe from a loving perspective. It is like looking at photos in a family album. We are suffused with a kindly feeling with no sense of grasping. We look and let go as we move on to what may appear on the next page. In dispassionate witnessing, on the other hand, we look with passive indifference. We are stolid and unmoved, with no expectancy for what comes next or appreciation of what has gone before. This is like looking at the scenery from a train window. We simply watch it go by without inner responsiveness. Mindful witnessing is compassionate witnessing, a committed presence free of fear or clinging.

Mindfulness is watchfulness more than watching: We look at reality as custodians of its truth. Sister Wendy Beckett says great artists make great paintings because they have learned "to look without fixed ideas of what is fitting." This is mindfulness. It can be either consciousness without content (pure awareness with no attention to any particular issue or feeling) or consciousness with content (attention without ego intrusions, called mindfulness of the mind). Generally, the latter style is the one I mean when I refer to mindfulness in this book.

Mindfulness is thus a courageous venture because it is trusting that we have it in us to hold and tolerate our feelings, to grant them hospitality no matter how frightening they may seem, to live with them in equipoise. We then discover a strength within us that is the equivalent of self-discovery. From that self-esteem comes effective relating with others. Because mindfulness leads us to let go of ego by letting go of fear and grasping, it is an apt tool for healthy relating. It makes us present to others purely, without the buffers of the neurotic ego. We simply stay with someone as he is, noticing not judging. We take what a partner does as information without having to censure or blame. In doing this, we put space around an event rather than crowding it with our own beliefs, fears, and judgments. Such mindful presence frees us from constricting identification with another's actions. A healthy relationship is one in which there are more and more such spacious moments.

Mindfulness is a path to giving others the five A's, the essential components of love, respect, and support. The word *mindfulness* is a translation of Sanskrit words meaning "attend" and "stay." Thus, we pay attention and we stay with someone in her feelings and in her here-and-now predicament. When I accept someone in this serene way, shifts occur in me, and both of us begin to discover the skillful means to more appreciative affection and commitment. To accept is also the first step toward letting go of control and allowing freedom. Thus, this mindful acceptance is our working basis for relationships. *The five A's are the results of and conditions for mindfulness.*

Mindfulness is inherent in human nature. We were built to pay attention to reality. Indeed, paying attention is a survival technique. Over the years, though, we learn to escape and take refuge in illusory sanctuaries built by an ego frightened of reality. We notice that it is easier to believe what will make us feel better, and we feel entitled to expect that others will be what we need them to be. These are man-made chains that look like links to happiness. But once we commit ourselves to experience divested of ego wishes and attachments, we begin to act straightforwardly, becoming truthful with one another. We relax into the moment, and it becomes a source of immense curiosity. We do not have to do anything. We do not have to search in our bag of ego toys for something to face the moment with. We do not have to put our dukes up. We do not have to become the pawns of our fixations or our fixed conceptions of reality. We do not have to find a pigeonhole. We do not have to go on the defensive or devise a comeback. We can simply let things unfold, attending to reality as it is and staying through it as we are. This is a lot more relaxing than our habitual reactions, and we use the original equipment of the human psyche rather than the artificial con*trap*tions concocted by ego over the centuries. This is why mindfulness is also called waking up.

A holding environment is necessary for all growth, both psychological and spiritual. Like kangaroos developing in a pouch, we experience being held within a family, a relationship, or a community—including a community of fellow recoverers or practitioners. At every stage of life, our inner self requires the nurturance of loving people attuned to our feelings and responsive to our needs who can foster our inner resources of personal power, lovability, and serenity. Those who love us understand us and are available to us with an attention, appreciation, acceptance, and affection we can feel. They make room for us to be who we are.

Though it may sound odd to say so, mindfulness is itself a holding environment. When we sit, we are never alone because all the saints and *bodhisattvas* (enlightened beings) of the past and present are with us. Meditating mindfully means contact and continuity with a long tradition. To sit is to be assisted and held. When Buddha sat on the earth, it was as if he sat in a lap. It is the same for us.

Mindfulness is being an adult. It is unattainable for someone who lacks inner cohesion, personal continuity, and integration. Being a fair witness requires a healthy ego, because distance and objectivity are unavailable to someone with poor boundaries, no tolerance of ambiguity, and no sense of a personal center. Meditation may be threatening to someone who is unstable and in need of mirroring, the reassuring and validating reflection of one's feelings by another person (see chapter 2). The Buddha's ruthless commitment to acknowledging impermanence will be terrifying and destructive to someone without a firm foundation as a separate and autonomous and intelligently protected self. Finally, the call to live in the present comes at the wrong time for someone who needs first to explore the past and be free of its stubborn grip. This is why both psychological work for individuation and spiritual practice for egolessness will always be required as dual requisites for the enlightenment of beings as beautifully and mysteriously designed as we.

Meditation is not to be attempted in any serious way if we are not psychologically ready for it. At the same time, we can begin simple meditation daily as an adjunct to psychotherapeutic work. This book advocates working on the psychological and the spiritual simultaneously and in bite-size chunks. This is based on the fact that some spiritual attitudes contribute to psychological health and vice versa. For instance, the spiritual attitude of acceptance helps us bear necessary and appropriate grief, while the psychological ability of assertiveness helps us stand up for justice for ourselves and others and so increases our compassion. The Buddhist social activist and author Ken Jones says: "Systems of maturation like Buddhism teach that it is only through unflinchingly facing our afflictions and opening unreservedly to our feelings that we can come to experience an empowerment that is other than this trembling self [ego]."

When ego is deposed, mindfulness leads to the higher Self, Jung's approximation of buddha mind. This Self is unconditional love, perennial wisdom, and healing power (the very qualities that foster evolution). We are never without it. To find ourselves spiritually is to acknowledge our destiny to use our ego skills to serve the purposes of the Self. Thus, we strive for intimacy with the whole universe, not just with one person. After all, we cannot expect from a partner what can only come from the Self/universe/higher power. This is why pursuing our own spiritual path is so important to the health of a relationship.

Mindfulness does not mean that we have no desires, simply that we are not possessed by them. We may feel fear and desire, but they no longer drive, shame, or stop us. Instead we hold them, without the elaborations our brain so habitually adds. We handle fear and enjoy desire and move past both of them with ease, like Ulysses, who heard the sirens' song and sailed on. As the Tibetan Buddhist teacher Chögyam Trungpa Rinpoche said, "Go through it, give in to it, experience it. . . . Then the most powerful energies become absolutely workable rather than taking you over, because there is nothing to take over if you are not putting up any resistance."

A Positive Spin on How It Was and Is

It may seem like a sign of weakness to have needs. Actually, needs direct us to grow in the ways we were meant to. Childhood yearnings for attention, acceptance, appreciation, affection, and the experience of being allowed to be ourselves are not pathological but developmental. In trying to get a parent to pay attention to us, we were seeking what we needed for our healthy evolution. We were not being selfish but self-nurturing, and there's no need to feel ashamed about it now.

Childhood forces influence present choices, for the past is on a continuum with the present. Early business that is still unfinished does not have to be a sign of immaturity; rather, it can signal continuity. Recurrence of childhood themes in adult relationships gives our life depth in that we are not superficially passing over life events but inhabiting them fully as they evolve. Our past becomes a problem only when it leads to a compulsion to repeat our losses or smuggles unconscious determinants into our decisions. Our work, then, is not to abolish our connection to the past but to take it into account without being at its mercy. The question is how much the past interferes with our chances at healthy relating and living in accord with our deepest needs, values, and wishes.

For better or for worse, our psychic development is the result of a life-long continuum of relationships. The adult goal is to work through each of them. We wrestle with past relationships respectfully, like Jacob with the angel, until they yield their blessing. The blessing is the revelation of what we missed or lost. Knowing that gives us momentum to let go of the past and find need fulfillment in ourselves and in other people who can love us in self-affirming ways. Such love restores or repairs the psychic structures that were lost or damaged in early life, and we begin to get a coherent sense of who we are, which in turn makes it possible for us to love others in the same powerful ways. We receive from others and thereby learn to give, for love teaches generosity. Thus, maturation consists not in leaving needs behind but in recruiting supportive others who can give age-appropriate and generous responses to our needs.

Among childhood habits, defenses in particular have been looked upon as signs of inadequacy and pathology. However, we need many of our defenses for psychological survival. We are defending ourselves from things for which we don't yet feel ready—for example, closeness or full commitment. We learned to stand guard over our unique wishes and needs in early life if showing them was unsafe. We learned to defend the delicate and vulnerable core of ourselves from humiliation, depletion, or distrust. Those were skills, not deficits.

If we feel unsafe as children we may still feel that way and still be using our old defenses. We may run from or defend ourselves against intimacy now for fear of a replay of childhood betrayals that left us crouching behind a wall of fear. On this wall are graffiti that besiege our self-esteem: "Don't let anyone get too close." "Don't commit all the way." "No relationship will ever really work." "No one can love you as you really need to be loved." "Men/women can't be trusted." Our work as adults is to replace these governing principles of behavior with healthy and more optimistic ones. Governing principles that limit our full potential for lively energy—the manifestation of our own unique life-force—are like the governor on a truck accelerator that prevents the truck from ever getting up to full speed.

Most of us have unrelenting longings for whatever was missing from our childhood. Every intimate bond will resurrect these archaic yearnings, along with the terrors and frustrations that accompany chronically unmet needs. But this puts us in an ideal position to revisit those thwarted needs, to revive our energy, and to reconstruct our inner world in accord with life-affirming principles. A solid bond in a relationship—as in religious faith—endures despite the impact of events, so our resistance is the only obstacle to the growth that can emerge from pain. As we mend the broken fabric of ourselves, what was arrested in the past is released. We are back in touch with who we really are and can live in accord with that rediscovered essence.

Every person needs the nourishment of food throughout life. Likewise, a psychologically healthy person needs the sustenance of the five A's—attention, acceptance, appreciation, affection, and allowing—all her life. It is true that unmet needs for the five A's in childhood cannot be made up for later in life, in the sense that they cannot be fulfilled so absolutely, so immediately, or so unfailingly. That absolute, immediate fulfillment of needs by one person is appropriate only to infants. But needs can be fulfilled, in short or long installments, throughout life. The problem is not that we seek gratification but that we seek too much of it all at once. What we did not receive enough of before, we cannot receive enough of now; what we did receive enough of before, we can receive enough of now.

We do not outgrow our early needs. Rather they become less overwhelming, and we find less primitive ways to fulfill them. For example, an infant may need to be cradled and carried, while an adult may be satisfied with a supportive remark and a kindly glance. Sometimes a lifelong need can be fulfilled by just such little moments of mindful love. However, we still need to be cradled at times.

If our emotional needs were fulfilled by our parents, we emerge from childhood with a trust that others can give us what we need. We can then receive love from others without distress or compulsion. Our needs are moderate. We can trust someone to help fulfill our needs while we help fulfill hers. This provides a foundation for a life of compassion and equanimity.

Mothers play the primary role in our growth. In the first phase of development, a mother is the container: She provides the holding environment in which we learn and feel the safety it takes to start to become ourselves. But eventually we need to separate from our mothers to establish an identity. Thus, the first stage of development confronts us with a paradox: The safety it requires is meant to help us go! If a mother's embrace is too seductive or too tight, we might not be able to separate from her. If we heard and heeded the words "Don't go!" we might eventually turn them into "I can't go," so that later, in an abusive adult relationship, we stay where it hurts.

In the second phase of parenting, the mother is a safe base. Now we say, "I can go and come back." From the time we can crawl, we are separating, leaving the warm embrace to explore the unknown, though we still need to know that our mother is nearby, the safe harbor to which we can return. If this stage goes well for us, we don't equate absence with abandonment or departure with loss. This developmental achievement is an expansion of object constancy, whereby we can let someone go and still believe he loves us and is available to us. In adolescence, the need to separate reaches a climax, but we still need the safe base to return to.

In the third phase, the mother becomes a coadult who loves us as a peer and respected advisor. Now we have fully separated and have established our own identity, and we live apart from our mother but still with undimmed mutual respect and support. The goal of the work of becoming an adult is, after all, not to reunite with Mother but to find in ourselves and others as much as we can find of what she was meant to provide: the five A's.

In the first phase, we have no sense of boundaries, of where we begin and where our mother ends. In the second phase, we establish boundaries, which may become rigid by adolescence. In the third phase, we honor one another's boundaries. Interestingly, these phases of parenting resemble the three phases in an adult relationship: closeness in romance, distance in conflict, reunion in commitment. The archetypal heroic journey is an extended metaphor for human development, since it takes the hero through the same three phases: leaving the comforts of the familiar, finding a separate identity away from home, and returning home renewed and interdependent. Returning home is a metaphor for the integration in oneself of psychological and spiritual powers.

The mother with adult consciousness will not only soothe her child but show him how to soothe himself when she is absent or unavailable: "Whatever resources I have, I help you find within yourself." Such a mother will show how her child's natural gifts can be inner resources for self-soothing. For instance, a child who loves to draw can be reminded of the comfort he finds in that activity. (Creating art often soothes us because it offers contact with the anima, the feminine source of nurturance that exists within each of us.) What is found in the healthy style of parenting is also found in adult relating and in mature spirituality. In healthy intimate relationships we do not seek more than 25 percent of our nurturance from a partner; we learn to find the rest within ourselves. Likewise, an authentic spiritual teacher is one who teaches practitioners to appreciate that enlightenment is an interior reality, not something to be drawn from the teacher. Thus, parent, partner, and teacher point us toward our own inner parent, inner partner, and inner guru.

We are all in intense love relationships from birth onward. Love keeps mother nearby. This is how humanity has survived. Baby's love and smiles keep Mother attached to him so his survival can be assured. Thus, our cellular memory equates presence with safety and distance with danger. This is why the prospect of abandonment is so terrifying. At the same time, the play between mother and child is encoded in our memory as an essential ingredient of authentic love. In short, our higher powers and most cherished psychic structures of sensitivity and caring for one another derive from early love and mirroring, not from biological drives.

Can fathers provide the container for the holding and separating experience so crucial to growth? It seems unlikely. Their role is to protect us from being contained too long! Women can provide a safe place for us to express our feelings and make our unique choices. Men can show us a safe exit into the larger world. And if fathers are sometimes so demanding that they undermine a developing child's freedom to be himself, this is where grandfathers can step in to give male nurturance mindfully, without expectation or demand.

We begin in a containing womb and then move to an embrace. Alchemy, the transformation of something into its opposite, also happens in a container. A vessel is required in which the lead of ego can be transformed into the gold of the higher Self. Only then can the giant of fear be faced and conquered. Therapy or a support group might be an appropriate vessel when we face difficult transitions. Alcoholics Anonymous, for example, can play this role for someone moving from addiction into sobriety. Our identity cannot grow in isolation, because we are dialogical by nature. "Only in the arms of someone can the first 'I am' be pronounced, or rather risked," British psychiatrist D. W. Winnicott says.

The original emotional needs of life were fulfilled in the holding environments of the womb, our nursing mother's arms, the warmth of our home, and parental protection, which are the requisite loci of serene development. In such a safe and embracing environment, children feel they are living in a folder of security that is also roomy enough for them to express feelings freely. They feel their parents can handle their feelings and mirror them back with acceptant love—in short, that there is room for their true self at the inn.

If their needs are unmet, on the other hand, they may have difficulty trusting a higher power or acknowledging the need for spirituality in adult life. (*Higher power* is my term for what I believe to be the perfect source of the five A's.) Faith commitments call for trust in an invisible source of nurturance, and when visible sources of nurturance have let us down, we are less likely to trust the invisible sources. Yet Jung says the longing for the spiritual is as strong in us as the desire for sex. We therefore ignore an inner instinct when we totally deny the possibility of a power greater than ourselves. Another face of this same problem is religious fanaticism, or a negative, abusive religiousness that is full of guilt and obligation.

When we did not receive fulfillment in one or more of the five A's, a bottomless pit was created in us, an unfulfillable yearning for the missing pieces of our puzzling and arid past. Mourning an unfulfilled childhood is painful. We fear grief because we know we will not be able to control its intensity, its duration, or its range, and so we look for ways around it. But engaging with our grief is a form of self-nurturance and liberation from neediness. Paradoxically, to enter our wounded feelings fully places us on the path to healthy intimacy.

Is this my problem? Have I been afraid to grieve what I did not get from Mom and Dad and so have demanded it from partners, strangers, and innocent bystanders? Am I unable to find it in myself because I have been investing all my energy in looking for it in someone else?

To retrieve the past and to undo the past are our paradoxical goals in relationships. No wonder they are so complex! Their complexity is not about the transactions between two adults but the fact that such transactions never begin: instead, two children are tugging at each other's sleeve, shouting in unison, "Look what happened to me when I was a kid! Make it stop, and make it better for me!" In effect, we are asking an innocent bystander to repair a problem he has no knowledge of and little skill to repair. And all the time and energy that goes into that transaction distracts us from the first part of our work: repairing our own lives.

The cold ground of our psyche is like a cryogenic laboratory where our unmet needs from childhood remain frozen in their original state, awaiting healing and fulfillment, usually without revealing to us the full extent to which we felt forlorn and bereft. The path to love begins in our own past and its healing, then moves outward to relationships with others.

Even if our childhood needs were met, we may need to work on ourselves as adults. Nurturant parents make sure our childhood environment is safe and soothing, and as adults, we may keep looking for the people or things that can recreate that miracle. The recurrent fantasy of, or search for, the "perfect partner" is a strong signal from our psyche that we have work to do on ourselves. For a healthy adult, there is no such thing as a perfect partner except temporarily or momentarily. No one source of happiness exists, nor can a partner make life perfect. (The fact that this happens in fairy tales says it all.) A relationship cannot be expected to fulfill all our needs; it only shows them to us and makes a modest contribution to their fulfillment. We ask: *Could it be that I would not have learned what I needed to learn if I had met the perfect partner?*

The perfect partner is the mirage we see after crossing the desert of insufficient love. Mirages happen because we lack water—that is, we lack something we have needed for a long time. They are normal, nothing to be ashamed of. We should notice them, take them as information about where our work lies, and then let them go. If we do this, we will come to the real oasis, nature's gift to those who keep going, who were not stopped by the mirage.

Yet it is a given of life that nothing is permanently and finally satisfying. Despite this fact, many of us believe that somewhere there is a person or thing that *will* be permanently satisfying. Such a chimerical belief, and the restless, desperate seeking that follows from it, can become deeply disheartening and self-defeating. In mindfulness we can surrender to reality with all its impermanence and frustration, and from that position of surrender something wonderfully encouraging can happen. We find that we want a partner who walks beside us in the world, not one we hope will change its givens or provide an escape-hatch from them. *We find a pleasing balance between surrendering to the given of the fundamental unsatisfactoriness of life while at the same time maximizing our opportunity for contentment.* This is our discovery of the felicitous pass between the snowy peaks of delusion and despair. From this point of view, moderate need fulfillment, experienced in days or even just moments, becomes satisfactory. Emily Dickinson, making every word count, called this "a glow / as intimate, as fugitive / as sunset on the snow."

"Moderate" is the key word for giving and for receiving the five A's. A nonstop flow of them would be quite annoying, even to an infant. Our fantasy mindset makes us long for just what we would soon flee. Hence, what seems like an unsatisfactory compromise is actually the adult's best deal.

The hospitable sanctuary and the generous waters of an oasis can be enjoyed for one day or many, but not forever. Sooner or later they will cloy, and our hearts will long for what comes next. The desert and what lies beyond it, whatever their mystery and hardship, beckon, and they cannot be evaded or renounced. Journeying is built into us no matter how beautiful our home. The idea of change excites us no matter how pleasing our present circumstances. This may be what the poet George Herbert meant by the lines in which God says of the newly created Adam: "Yet let him keep the rest, / But . . . with repining restlessness, / Let him be rich *and* weary."

> As long as you hold onto wanting something from the outside, you will be dissatisfied because there is a part of you that you are still not totally owning. . . . How can you be complete and fulfilled if you believe that you cannot own this part [of yourself] until somebody else does something? . . . If it is conditional, it is not totally yours.
>
> —A. H. ALMAAS

The Five A's: The Keys that Open Us

We know deep down, and have always known, that need fulfillment and good parenting mean the five A's: attention, acceptance, appreciation, affection, and allowing. As children, we noticed how our parents did and did not fit the bill. We then looked for someone who could fit the bill better or more consistently. This process is like looking at a reproduction of the *Mona Lisa* but noticing it is blurred and the color is not right. We know how it should look, and we keep our eye out for a sharper print with brighter color. As adults we look for the partner who will be just right. At first that means a replica of our parents with some of the better—or missing—features added. So we find the man who controls but is also loyal. As we mature we no longer seek the negative traits, only the positive ones. So we no longer look for controlling men but for loyal men who let us be ourselves. In full maturity we do not demand perfection at all, only notice reality. We access our resources within. A partner who cooperates in that is a gift but no longer a necessity. The five A's begin as needs to be fulfilled by our parents, then become needs to be fulfilled by our partners, and someday become gifts we give to others and to the world.

Because we are dialogical beings, our self-esteem emerges from contact with others who provide us with the five A's. The five A's are not extras. They are the components of the healthy, individuated ego: Attention from others leads to self-respect. Acceptance engenders a sense of being inherently a good person. Appreciation generates a sense of self-worth. Affection makes us feel lovable. Allowing gives us the freedom to pursue our own deepest needs, values, and wishes. When the five A's were not forthcoming we might have felt we were to blame. That may leave us with a gnawing need to make reparation all our life. Such reparation is futile and misleading since the true task is a journey out into the world to find some of what was missing and then to discover it in ourselves too.

We feel something missing when we speak and do not receive attention, show ourselves and are not accepted, ask for love and are not held, or make a choice and are not allowed to pursue it. In contrast, when others grant us the five A's, we feel fulfilled and at ease with ourselves. An adult can unabashedly ask for the A he needs if it is not freely offered. He is only asking for what it takes to achieve the commencement of full humanness. That tender and ever so gingerly ventured bid to be loved is precisely what makes us humans so lovable.

Nature never intended us to find all we needed from two individuals, our biological parents. Indeed, one or both might have died or left us, leaving holes inside. But we were endowed with sockets too. These are the archetypes of mother and father, innate receptacles in our psyches for mother and father energies. These can be filled by stand-ins. The aunt or uncle, the older sibling, the grandparent, the minister, the teacher, or anyone offering even one of the five A's will do. No set of parents is sufficient to fulfill our parenting needs, no matter how nurturant they may be. It is necessary and healthy to receive need fulfillment from other sources all through life. An archetypal longing encourages us to keep an eye out for those who offer it. An adult sensibility releases us from expecting any person to fulfill it totally.

In addition, in an adult partnership, as in childhood, the expression of the five A's changes throughout the relationship. A mother shows attention differently to a twelve-year-old than to a one-year-old. A partner shows a different kind of attention in the conflict phase than in the romance phase of a relationship (more on these phases later). *To expect everything to remain the same is to miss the analogy between adult relating and growing up.* The quality and the amount of all the graces of love change with time. This is not because lovers are less generous in what they offer but because they are more conscious of ever-shifting needs and resources.

The five A's are the essential ingredients of love, respect, security, and support. In addition, they form the essence of spiritual practice: what we cultivate in meditation and the path of compassion. The practices in this book suggest techniques and insights to bring meditative awareness and compassion to relationships. *These suggestions are not strategies to stay together but keys to the practice of love, our life purpose and our fulfillment.* Indeed, we stand to gain so much when we show the five A's. They are given to others but all of them make us more loving as we give them. They are therefore the components of building the virtue of love in ourselves. To love is to become loving.

ATTENTION

It is a joy to be hidden but a disaster not to be found.

—D. W. WINNICOTT

Every mammal feels instinctively that it needs and deserves full parental attentiveness. When a parent is only halfway attentive, the child notices and feels uneasy. The mother leopard does not have her mind on her own grooming while she is feeding her young. Nor does she demand that her young groom her and wait for their dinner. Her single-minded attention gives them healthy priorities later in life. Children's psychic life becomes confused if they have to take care of a parent or make sense of one, because that is the reverse of what children instinctively expect.

Attention to you means engaged focus on you. It means sensitivity to your needs and feelings. Did your parents pay at least as much attention to you as they did to the TV? Did your father notice and attend to your feelings and fears with the same care he showed his car? Did he ever concentrate on you for as long as he did on a ball game?

Watching your every move, even if it comes from a desire to protect you, is not attention but intrusion or surveillance. In truly loving attention, you are noticed not scrutinized. Overprotectiveness is a rejection of your power (and thus of you). Authentic attention comes to you any time, not just when you present a problem. Such statements as "Children should be seen and not heard" are odious to a parent committed to paying attention to his child. "My father turned to me as if he had been waiting all his life to hear my question," says a character in one of J. D. Salinger's novels. *Was I listened to like that? Did I matter that way?*

If we missed out on attention when we were children, we might have learned to attend to ourselves, to become more and more creative, to look for attention from adults other than our parents. In this way, a deficiency became something beneficial, the pothole that became the portal. Likewise, our ability to reach out as adults may be directly proportional to our recognition that what we needed in our childhood was not there to be had. Seeing that deficiency in the past will help us see it in a present relationship and not keep looking for something we need in a container that is empty.

Attunement is mirrored attentiveness from one person to another. Attentiveness means noticing and hearing words, feelings, and experience. In a moment of authentic attention, we feel that we are deeply and truly understood in what we say or do and in who we are, with nothing left out. Likewise, we can attune to others' feelings, needs, bodily reactions, comfort levels with closeness, and degrees of willingness—for example, whether someone is acting out of coercion and compliance rather than true concurrence. We cannot attune if we assume certain feelings are right and others wrong. To attune to someone, we need neutrality toward all feelings, moods, and inner states and the fearless openness of mindfulness. Only with such pure attention can we see beyond his bravado to his terror, beyond his stolidity to his turmoil. This is how attention becomes compassion.

What has failed to find attunement stays folded up within us or becomes a source of shame. Faulty attunement in early life may lead to fear of standing up for ourselves later or keep us from trusting that others will come through for us. Faulty attunement can make us scared and lonely, too. We fear exposing some regions of our psychic topography because of our inbred despair of ever finding the requisite human mirroring.

Attuned attention creates an ever-widening zone of trust and safety. We feel encouraged to look for—rather than wait for—our submerged longings to emerge and our stunted hopes to assume their full dimensions. We believe they will be attended to at last. This is love in the form of mindful attention, and we feel safe in it. Implicit in such attentiveness to our truth is truth from the one providing it. We trust him to say what is true to him; that is where our sense of safety comes from.

The first A is the core of mindfulness. Attention means bringing something or someone into focus so it is no longer blurred by the projections of your own ego; thus it requires genuine interest and curiosity about the mysterious and surprising truth that is you. A parent or partner who has gotten to know you in a superficial way may only be meeting up with her beliefs about you. Those beliefs, or biases, can endure for years, preventing the person from taking in the kind of information that would reveal the real you. The real you is an abundant potential, not a list of traits, and intimacy can only happen when you are always expanding in others' hearts, not pigeonholed in their minds. Our identity is like a kaleidoscope. With each turn we reset it not to a former or final state but to a new one that reflects the here-and-now positions of the pieces we have to work with. The design is always new because the shifts are continual. That is what makes kaleidoscopes, and us, so appealing and beautiful. Parents and partners who give us attention love to see the evolving mandala of us.

The desire for attention is not a desire for an audience but for a listener. Attention means focusing on you with respect, not with contempt or ridicule. When you are given attention, your intuitions are treated as if they matter. You are taken seriously. You are given credit when it is due. Your feelings have such high value to those who love you that they are on the lookout for them. They even look for the feelings you are afraid to know and gently inquire whether you want to show them.

When others give you attention, they also confront you directly when they are displeased, harboring no secret anger or grudges. But they always do this with respect and a sincere desire to keep the lines of communication open. Attention, like the other four A's, is given in a trusting atmosphere of holding.

ACCEPTANCE

In Buddhism there is a phrase, "the glance of mercy," which refers to looking at other human beings with acceptance and understanding. Acceptance means we are received respectfully with all our feelings, choices, and personal traits and supported through them. This makes us feel safe about knowing and giving ourselves to others. Our ability to be intimate grows in accordance with how safe we feel, and that safety is based primarily on how authentically we were accepted in early life. But even after we grow up, moments and months of acceptance by other adults can fill in some of what we may have missed as children, so that intimacy is still an option for all of us. As with all five A's, it is never too late to find acceptance or learn to show it.

If we lacked acceptance in childhood, we might have felt ashamed or inadequate. But we also might have compensated for the lack in a positive way by finding a center of evaluation in ourselves, thus becoming less dependent on others' approval, so now as adults we are swayed by neither criticism nor flattery. We learned early on to ground our self-worth in the depths of our own psyche. This not only builds our self-esteem but also makes it easier for us to accept others. Since we are not trying to get something from them, we can appreciate them as they are. *How much my parents missed out on when they could not let this happen between us!*

To accept their children, parents must be free of preconceived plans or agendas for them. These parental representations can begin before birth and range from "This will be a boy" to "This baby will be a spark plug in our marriage; he will make it work" or "This girl will do what I couldn't do." Each is a subtle rejection of our individuality, with its limitations and potential. Parents can accept us only after they succeed in dismantling their original representation of us in favor of the person we are turning out to be. This means not being disappointed with us for breaking a bargain we never made. Acceptance is unconditional since it means validating someone's choices and lifestyle even when we do not agree with them. It is the opposite of moralizing. Acceptance is a style of pure mindfulness. We see all that is and feel all that we feel about what is, but then we focus only on what is as it is.

Acceptance is approval, a word with a bad name in some psychologies. Yet it is perfectly normal to seek approval in childhood and throughout life. We require approval from those we respect. The kinship it creates lifts us to their level, a process referred to in self-psychology as transmuting internalization. Approval is a necessary component of self-esteem. It becomes a problem only when we give up our true self to find it. Then approval-seeking works against us.

In attention, you are heard and noticed. In acceptance, you are embraced as worthy, not compared to your siblings but trusted, empowered, understood, and fully approved of as you are in your uniqueness. You sense a kindly support of your path, no matter how unusual; of your feelings, no matter how disturbing; of your deficiencies, no matter how irritating. These are not only tolerated but encouraged and cherished. You are perfectly you, and that is enough. Rather than expecting you to meet a standard, your parents eagerly await your full emergence as yourself, no matter how different you may be from them or how divergent from their wishes. *Yes, there really are people who love like this.* Did your parents believe in you? Did they come through for you? Were they reliable? Did they stand up for you? Did they refuse to give up on you, no matter what? The psychologist Heinz Kohut wrote: "The more secure a person is regarding his own acceptability, the more certain his sense of who he is, and the more safely internalized his system of values, the more self confidently and effectively will he be able to offer his love . . . without undue feelings of rejection and humiliation."

APPRECIATION

Appreciation gives depth to acceptance: "I admire you; I delight in you; I prize you; I respect you; I acknowledge you and all your potential. I appreciate you as unique." To acquire the riches of personal worth and self-confidence, we need just such encouragement. Human evolution proceeds from human accomplishments and consequent validations. But it also proceeds from one person's faith in another's value. A parent's belief that a child has great potential actually engenders potential in the child. Long-held and continually affirmed belief gives people the capacity to make it come true. Many centuries of belief in the healing power of faith, for instance, make more and more faith healings happen. In this and in all five A's, fulfillment of the need instills that quality in the personality.

Appreciation also includes gratitude for any kindness or gift we might bestow. Appreciation as gratitude recognizes us and how we extend ourselves. Because intimacy is about giving and receiving, appreciation fosters closeness. When we give, we instinctively await a thank you. This is not a middle-class or selfish expectation but a wish that the transaction be completed in the normal way. We know something is missing in a relationship if gratitude is lacking.

Is the following description of mindful appreciation familiar to you? Someone acknowledged and cherished your unconditional worth without envy or possessiveness, expressing these feelings verbally and nonverbally. The appreciation came as an understanding of what you were capable of or what you felt, validating the mystery of you. It also came as a word of praise, a wink when you did something well, a pat on the shoulder when you excelled, a loving look when you were just yourself, thanks for something you did or gave or simply were.

The ratio of appreciation to complaint in couples that stay together is five to one, according to the research of psychologist John M. Gottman, Ph.D., of the University of Washington in Seattle. Indeed, *behind every complaint is a wish for one of the five A's.* When we blow up or feel dejected, we may be experiencing the lack of one or more of the five A's. "I see you are feeling unappreciated," may be an accurate and compassionate response to a partner who is angrily complaining.

AFFECTION

To give and receive love is our primary need. We express love emotionally, spiritually, and physically. An affectionate touch or hug from someone who really loves us can penetrate our bodies and restore our souls. All our fears, no matter how deep, can be erased by a single loving stroke.

Love cannot be defined in a universal way because our experience of love is ours alone. Just as there is no single, universal signature but only unique, personal signatures, so there is no love in general, only unique love uniquely experienced by each unique person. I learn what love is when I first feel loved. It is then encoded in every cell of my body, and the love I feel later in life may have to replicate that original experience.

If I first felt loved by being held when I was hurting, or by being given credit, or by being paid attention to, or by being given things, my body will remember that all my life, and when it happens again, I will feel it as love. I may perceive loving as receiving things, so I keep trying to get others to help me or give me things. Someone may appear to wink at me, and I may take that as love and cling to him even though he may have only been clearing a speck from his eye.

Love in adulthood is a re-experiencing of the love our every cell remembers. The way we were loved in early life is the way we want to be loved all our lives. Most of us know just what it takes for us to feel loved. What we have to learn is how to ask for it. A partner is not a mind-reader, so it is up to each of us to tell our partner what our brand of love is. And if we have to teach our partner how to love us, we also have to learn how to love him. Knowing this makes it clear that love is not a sentimental feeling but a conscious choice to give and receive in unique and often challenging ways.

Psychoanalyst Heinz Kohut wrote: "The child's bodily display is responded to with a gleam in his mother's eye." Affection throughout life includes being loved as we look—with our body shape, our style of grooming, our choice of clothes, whether or not they conform to the current model of excellence. Our way of being present is more descriptive of what we are about than anything we have done or do. Intimate contact is with a living presence not a set of genitals or words that promise love. As adults, we may see a beautiful body and think: "Having that to myself will make me happy." What happened to us that made us so confused as to think our needs could be fulfilled by a pretty face? So much of attraction is intuitive and a matter of physical and psychic history. It is not to be taken too personally. To let go of ego is to let go of taking things personally.

The word *affection* comes from *affect*, feeling. *Affection* refers to closeness both on the physical and on the feeling level. Physically, it includes the spectrum of touch, from holding to sex. Affection is also a quality of feeling. In this respect it includes kindliness, considerateness, thoughtfulness, playfulness, and romantic gestures like giving flowers or remembering a special anniversary. Affection flows from a genuine *liking* of someone.

If affection is only a strategy for sex, it is not intimate but manipulative. In adult relationships, there is intimacy without sex at times and sex with intimacy always. Affection looks different in the romantic phase of a relationship than it does in the conflict stage. In the former it may have more of a sexual dimension; in conflict it may mean patient working through of mutual concerns. Finally, sex is meant to manifest all five A's. In healthy relationships, sex is attentive, accepting, appreciative, affectionate, and wildly allowing.

As a wise adult, I will know the difference between sex with someone who is doing it the way he does it and sex with someone who does it in a way that arises from our specific bond. Real love does not come off the rack; it is uniquely tailored by the lover to the beloved. Part of the pain of letting go of someone who really loved you is letting go of being loved in that special way.

Affection includes nearness, or loving presence. We receive real affection when someone is committed to being beside us often. This does not mean constant cohabitation but reliable availability. It is the opposite of abandoning and distancing. A child is abandoned every time a parent notices distance and lets it go by without comment or amendment. That child may grow up to say, "I felt abandoned and hurt when Mother saw my pain and did not comfort me." Another adult may say: "In my childhood, I felt something was being taken from me when I was hugged or held. So when I'm touched, I'm afraid of losing myself." Contemplating this pain and the pain that caused our parents to act the way they did leads to compassion for ourselves and the other flawed characters in our touching story.

Mindfulness is the path to loving presence. Mindful contact is unconditional in granting the five A's and unconditioned by the creations of the ego such as fear, demand, expectation, judgment, or control. Is the following description of mindful affection familiar?

You are loved the way you are. The need for affection is fulfilled when you are loved unconditionally all the time and genuinely liked most of the time. This loving and liking is demonstrated both verbally and physically. Such love/liking confers a sense of personal power, as Freud says: "To enjoy a mother's love is to become a conquistador." In childhood physical contact has no sexual component or price. This makes it possible to feel safe and prized for who you are rather than for what you can provide to fulfill the inappropriate needs of a parent. Every cell of your little body knew the difference between being held supportively and being clutched to fulfill a parent's needs. You knew when something was being given and when it was being taken.

Compassion is a form of affection. It is love's response to pain. This means being willing to acknowledge pain and caring about how you feel within it. It is a willingness to be in it with yourself. This empathy has a soothing quality, a sure sign of being loved. In fact, the empathy we receive throughout life is the equivalent of parental nurturance.

Since your parents' opinion was so crucial to you in early life, to be unloved may make you feel unlovable and responsible for it. Love can later be equated with measuring up to another's standards and can be tied to a sense of obligation. You may feel this way toward partners all your life and never know the ancient story behind it.

Finally, as one finger is not the hand, so affection is not love but only part of it. To be held and cuddled but not allowed later to make choices freely and without blame will soon be revealed as inadequate and untrustworthy.

ALLOWING

In a good-enough holding environment in early life, I learn that it is safe to be myself, knowing and showing my deepest needs and wishes. This happens in a family with an embrace wide enough to include all of me. Given such a welcome in the world, I gain a sense of stability and coherence, and I develop a reliable source of self-support, a nurturant inner parent who knows how to tolerate my feelings, no matter how contradictory or painful they may be. I reach out for healthy relationships, that is, those that give me all five A's.

But not everyone has the benefit of such a childhood. Some parents set rigid strictures on eating, sleeping, clothing, and grooming, all to suit their own needs or standards, rationalizing that such strictures are crucial to a child's health. In our childhood home it may have felt unsafe to be ourselves. We may have noticed that to be real meant losing the love of those from whom we needed it most. We may then have become whatever others needed us to be as the price of being loved. The false self that resulted must eventually give way to a truer version if intimacy is ever to work for us. If it was never safe to be ourselves—if we had to conceal what we were—we may not really believe in our talents and virtues now, feeling like impostors and frauds. Trying to live in accord with the needs and wishes of others is like being a cygnet and trying to become a duck just because you find yourself living in a duck pond. The false self is that of a conformist who is a royal heir in hiding.

Psychologically healthy adults come from a background of flexibility, not severity. Early needs (like all needs) are best fulfilled in an atmosphere of joy and forgiveness. In such a garden, crocuses ceaselessly pop up, yielding blooms of personal stability and self-nurturant powers, just the qualities that make intimacy possible in later life. Without healthy allowing in childhood, we may choose a controlling partner and tell ourselves, "I have to do it his way or else." We do not notice others' attempts to manipulate us. We can be fooled by a relationship that looks good but is full of demands and expectations.

Yet even standing amid the ashes of continual submission, we may someday find a personal internal liberty, insisting on agreements made bilaterally rather than unilateraly, on cooperation rather than dominance. Submission is compliance with the deepest needs, values, and wishes of others and not our own. But compliance can become defiance.

We do not allow others to control us once we are healthy, but we do understand and feel their pain when we realize that control is a compulsion. Most controlling people cannot help themselves; they are not in control of the controlling. They are not insulting us by trying to control us; rather, they automatically take charge and dominate people and situations. They do this because of a chilling fear that they cannot handle letting the chips fall where they may. It takes a spiritual program to be liberated from the compulsion to be controlling and to become compassionate toward controlling people. A higher power than ego has to kick in, because ego will not give itself up easily or become so gently tolerant.

Yeats wrote of the special person who "loves the pilgrim soul in you." Mirroring freedom means encouraging the liveliness and passion in others rather than squelching it for our own good or safety. The "pilgrim soul" also implies going. True allowing also means letting someone go. To allow is to stand aside when someone needs space from us or even leaves us. This is an "A" in courage. Emily Dickinson wrote: "They shut me up in prose / As when a little girl / they put me in the closet / Because they liked me still." Her poems tell us "they" did not succeed. Some people just have the pluck to resist control, or they learn it along the path of life, making it impossible for others to prevent their self-emergence. "She won't let me be myself" becomes "She can't stop me." This formula applies to love as well. "He won't let me love him" can become "He can't stop me from loving him." Thus unconditionality is the profoundest key to personal power.

Is the following description of allowing familiar to you?

You instinctively seek the full range of motion and emotion in the course of your development, yet you can feel in the psychological air of your home a heartfelt permission to be yourself, to have your own thoughts and to express them without punishment, to make your own choices, even to step out of line. You have the freedom to accomplish the two primary tasks of maturation: to separate from your parents and to develop as a unique person. The relationship is not at risk no matter what feelings you express. You think: "I always knew I could say or feel anything here." You are allowed by your parents to see; tell; talk; touch; be separate; protect yourself; and pursue your own talents, relationships, and interests.

You do not often hear "You have no reason to be scared," "You had better not get mad or sad (or even glad)," or "How dare you say no?" When love is the life force of a relationship or a family, each member becomes fully complete as himself. This is the alternative to control, which generates a false self.

If you didn't receive the gift of freedom, you may have heard things like "You will never do as well in school as your brother does." As a child, did you feel "There is no way to say it"? Did you have to ask yourself, "What does it take to matter here?" Or did you know deep down that all it took was to be yourself? Did your parents represent the world as scary: "You always have to be careful" instead of "You have it in you to take care of yourself"? Were you not surprised when you first went to school and felt scared and controlled because you had been taught that was how the world was?

What is the difference between control and limit-setting? Control is meant to make you what others need you to be. Limit-setting makes it safe for you to be yourself. Paradoxically, we can't achieve freedom without limits. They are the holding environment in which we flourish. Limits are at first the arms around us and then the word *no*. Even a sanctuary has gates around it. How else can it provide safety?

There is a connection between freedom and self-confidence: When you are kept from expressing your deepest needs and wishes, you lose trust in their validity and in your own judgment. You survive by finding out the rules and following them, thus hiding what you really want. You make it your purpose in life to please others rather than to affirm yourself.

If you felt free within your family, you can more easily trust a supportive authority such as a loving teacher or therapist. This is mindful authority, without blame or unilateral judgment—the elements of ego that create opposition to authority. As we saw earlier, in transmuting internalization parents gradually share their power with us, a process that proves to be a necessary component of a stable sense of self. We discover what Shakespeare referred to in *Measure for Measure:* our own "unknown sovereignty." Human authority and hierarchy are useful and legitimate when they empower us to take our own initiative but not when they subjugate and belittle us. When authority, civil or religious, mirrors healthy parenting, it is honorable and wins our respect.

Unconditional Presence versus the Five Mindsets of Ego

Together, the five A's are the components of unconditional presence. But there are also five major mental habits that interrupt authentic, unconditional presence and may cause others to feel unloved. They are virtually involuntary mental reactions that are common to people the world over. These mindsets are like bullies who enter unbidden and intrude upon our pure experience of the present and of the people we meet in the present. The spiritual practice of mindfulness is a rescue from the siege of these invaders.

Here are the five fundamental mindsets of ego that interrupt our ability to be here now and that distort reality:

- *Fear* of or worry about situation or of this person: "I perceive a threat in you or am afraid you may not like me so I am on the defensive."
- *Desire* that this moment or person will meet our demands or expectations, grant us our needed emotional supplies, or fulfill our wishes: "I am trying to get something from this or you."
- *Judgment* can take the form of admiration, criticism, humor, moralism, positive or negative bias, censure, labeling, praise, or blame: "I am caught up in my own opinion about you or this."
- *Control* happens when we force our own view or plan on someone else: "I am attached to a particular outcome and am caught in the need to fix, persuade, advise, or change you."
- *Illusion* overrides reality and may occur as denial, projection, fantasy, hope, idealization, depreciation, or wish: "I have a mental picture of or belief about you or this and it obscures what you are really like." (The central illusion in life is that of separateness.)

Any of these five interpretations by the editorial board of ego may be accurate but they still interfere with our experience of the present. Each is a minimization that imposes our personal dramas upon reality and makes fair witnessing impossible. In this sense, they are causes of karma. The gate to enlightenment opens when mindfulness closes down the show, even for a moment. The gate to empathy and compassion opens when we see human experience, no matter how unsavory or disfigured, without the mindsets of judgment and fear. At both gates we pronounce the "open sesame," the unconditional "yes" to reality.

The five mindsets are not to be construed as bad. Each of these pirates is full of energy that can be recruited for the invincible ship of mindfulness. The task is not to disown the mindsets but to redirect their energies so they can serve us and others. Thus, fear can be mined for wise caution. Desire makes it possible to reach out. Judgment includes intelligent assessment. Control is necessary in most daily activities. Fantasy is the springboard to the imagination and creativity. When we find the useful kernel of these mindsets, the trespassers can become our bosom buddies.

We cannot provide the five A's as long as these five mindsets are engaged because they distance us from authentic contact and suspend or disable direct perception of reality. *Throughout this book, these five mental defenses are referred to as the layers or overlays of ego.* We cannot stop our minds from engaging in these distractions, but mindfulness reduces their impact and helps us catch ourselves in the act. Mindfulness is the watchdog or rather the seeing-eye dog of the psyche, watching for the raiders of reality and walking us safely past them.

When we come *to* others with the five A's, we are profoundly present and closeness happens. When we come *at* others with the five mindsets, we are caught in a personal agenda and distance happens. The commitment to intimacy is a journey from the ego's favorite resorts to the paradise of mindful love.

The unconditional presence of someone who loves us hearkens back to the past and repairs our childhood sense of being unwanted. At the same time, no human being can or is expected to be fully and unconditionally present all the time. An individual can only offer moments and hours of presence without mindsets. Only pieces of presence can come from beings like us, "kings of shreds and patches." If any one of us were whole and totally satisfactory, we would not be motivated to go on the journey that makes our life so wonderful. Adults have always known this. Religion has responded with a comforting assurance that there is an eternally and unconditionally loving presence, not in pieces but whole. The mature religious view finds that reality deep within our own souls. Thus, even in the spiritual world, we are hurled back to ourselves, and others are partners not providers.

Finally, keep in mind that it is always acceptable not to know what something is or means. This ability to endure mystery is what Keats called "negative capability," or "being in uncertainties, mysteries, and doubts without irritable reaching after fact and reason." It is in mindfulness that we act in just that way: enduring our unknowing and yet sitting serenely. From that position a unique meaning is allowed to ripen over time, in its own time. This is an alternative to the ego's frenzy to impose a makeshift meaning from its lexicon of standard mindsets.

Mindsets are minimizations, since every reality and person is actually an infinite field of potential, a vast open space beyond limit. Without mind-conjured limits, all is perfect and exuberantly provocative just as it is. Joy is the energy that happens in freedom from mindsets. We no longer feel *obliged* to figure out what people are up to. We are finally free to be fully mindful.

Practices: Our Skillful Means

Practice does not mean forcing yourself to improve but trusting your potential to open. All the suggestions for practices that follow have a single purpose: to provide a program of skillful means for you. To become a psychologically healthy and spiritually conscious adult alone, in one-on-one relationships, and in and for the world. In these practices, psychological and spiritual work are meant to be done not sequentially but simultaneously. As we do our psychological work, we become more spiritually enlivened. As we engage in spiritual practices, we become more psychologically adept. Couples who work things out together with the help of therapeutic tools can greatly improve the psychological health of their relationship. But spiritual practice together deepens their bond at the level of the soul. Soul mates, after all, are those whose spiritual paths have met. Sitting together in meditation makes as powerful a contribution to bonding as holding one another in a sexual embrace, because mindfulness is the best tool for communication and for processing issues that arise in a relationship. So to sit is relationship practice, not just spiritual practice.

The practice sections in this book consist mainly of leading questions meant to challenge you to face and admit your own truth. They are meant to be answered in your journal and, when appropriate, aloud to your partner. If specific agreements for change can emerge from the responses, so much the better. But do your own work only. Do not attempt to design your partner's program of change or even judge what she should do or say.

You may want to discuss your practices with one person you trust in addition to your partner, looking for ways to apply what you are learning to your friendships and to your dealings with all people. This program is not only about making your intimate relationships more effective but also about lighting the way to an efficacious love of everyone.

Psychological work and spiritual practices are not ruggedly individual enterprises. Effort is important, but so is grace, the assistance of forces beyond you. Enlist and acknowledge the aid of higher powers than ego as you begin each practice. When you trust that your efforts are in the embrace of larger purposes, you feel supported, sustained, and held.

The practices show us our vast potential to be healthy adults who know how to love. They also show us where our constrictions in and resistance to love may be lurking. The practices raise our self-esteem as we observe ourselves activating our potential for love and letting go of our barriers to it. No matter how inadequate or flawed we imagine ourselves to be, we have it in us to find wholeness. The words and practices in this book offer moments of repair and new adjustments that can make pain less impinging or intimidating.

The practice sections expand on the ideas and themes that have been explored in each chapter and should be read whether or not you choose to try the exercises themselves. These sections complement and enhance the text. But also note that you do not need to do all the practices. Some practices are designed for introverts and some for extroverts. Some are tailored to specific problems and therefore do not apply to everyone. But I believe you will find the whole experience of this book much more exciting if you try some practices from every chapter. Choose those that appeal to you, challenge you, or fit your circumstances and personality. You will notice your relationship—and yourself—being enriched in powerful and touching ways as a result.

Finally, be sure to notice your bodily sensations as you read this book and work through the practices. They tell you so much about where your work may be, what holds you back, and what holds you.

DAILY MEDITATION • The first practice is to meditate daily. Begin with a few minutes a day and increase to about twenty as an ideal minimum. It is best to sit together as a couple, but sitting alone is certainly appropriate and valuable also. Sit in a quiet space with your eyes open or closed, your back straight, and your hands on your knees or thighs. Pay attention to your breath. When thoughts or anxieties enter your mind, simply label them as thoughts and return to awareness of your breathing. Do not attempt to stop thinking. The practice requires only that when you notice thought, you return to consciousness of your breath. When your meditation ends, try to get up slowly and see if you can maintain the same sense of awareness throughout the day. Eventually, breath becomes more real, and more interesting, than our stories.

There are a variety of meditation techniques and postures, and you should find the meditation style that works best for you. Some good introductions to meditation are *Zen Mind, Beginner's Mind* by Shunryu Suzuki (New York: Weatherhill, 1993), *The Path of Insight Meditation* by Joseph Goldstein and Jack Kornfield (Boston: Shambhala Publications, 1995), *What Is Meditation?* by Rob Nairn (Boston: Shambhala Publications, 1999), and *Thoughts without a Thinker* by Mark Epstein (New York: Basic Books, 1995).

LETTING GO OF CONTROL • Healthy control means ordering our lives in responsible ways—for example, by maintaining control of a car or our health. Neurotic control means acting on the compulsive need to make everything and everyone comply with our wishes. Control is what we decided to seek when we noticed the implacable givens of our existence and felt helpless in the face of them. We were not yet able to say, "I will stay with this predicament and see what it has to offer me. I notice I seem to get stronger this way." Saying yes to our experience in this mindful way leads to empowerment. Can you make a decision, a commitment to be less controlling and to dedicate yourself to this as your present project?

OPENING UP TO FEEDBACK • When you are committed to the work of making yourself a more loving person, you no longer rely on your own brain for all your information. You are happy to learn about yourself from your partner or anyone else you trust. You are open to finding out how you appear to those who see your shadow or dark side. You want to be ex-*posed* so you can drop your poses and let your authentic self emerge. You welcome feedback about how others are affected by you. A commitment to working on yourself—the whole point of these practices—includes this openness to feedback. Zen Master Wuzu reports: "The ancients were always so glad to hear of their mistakes." If you find that your ego cannot tolerate being called to task or shown to be inadequate or wrong, then the work begins here. A sine qua non of the work is a willingness to let go of ego. *I commit myself to find some truth in any feedback I receive.*

As a step toward achieving this willingness, ask your partner to describe something that has been upsetting her and notice when you are judging what she says, wanting to control her reactions, feeling afraid of her, wanting to fix her, and so forth. Acknowledge each of these reactions as ego distractions and return to listening openly. When your partner has finished, tell her what distractions interrupted your mindful hearing of her story and acknowledge them as ego. Make a commitment to notice them in future conversations. You can commit yourself instead to listening with your heart, where the five A's are. How can that happen? By the mindfulness habit you are building in meditation, by returning to your breath undistracted by mindsets.

Here is a practice that uses mindfulness for responding appreciatively and yet self-protectively when someone gives you critical feedback:

- Approach any person who has an issue with you with a conscious intention to give her the five A's. Say this aloud to her and maintain it in your heart as she speaks; it describes a profoundly loving way to listen, useful at any time of life and in all communication:

  > I am paying close attention to you now.
  > I accept you as you are in this moment.
  > I allow you to be yourself.
  > I appreciate you for what you have been and are.
  > I have real affection for you, no matter what.

- Establish eye contact while really listening mindfully, without defensiveness, anger, or plans to retaliate or prove the person wrong.
- Acknowledge the impact you have had on the other and the feelings you aroused in her. Do not use denial to protect yourself. Do not minimize or discount your impact by contrasting it with your good intentions. The impact matters more than the intention.
- Commit yourself to taking what the other person says as information, not as censure.
- Speak up, however, if the feedback includes blame, insult, ridicule, or put-downs. You will not permit that when you are taking care of yourself.
- Make amends when appropriate, design a plan to change, and ask for support.

This practice instills the virtue of humility and makes you more open and endearing.

ATTENDING TO NEEDS • In the film *The Sixth Sense,* the main character, a young boy, was released from his fear of the ghosts that haunted him when he finally asked them, "What do you need from me?" Focusing on other people's needs allows us to stop fearing them. Needs come from the heart and are heard by the heart. To listen with the heart is to listen for what someone needs without fear, judgment, criticism, moralism, contradiction, or projection. That is successful communication, and it results from mindfulness. We are present in the here and now without mental interferences. With a mind free of bias, we can really notice when another person needs our attentiveness, acceptance, appreciation, affection, or allowing. Philosopher Martin Buber spoke of the "empathic connection," which cannot happen when we are judging, only when we are witnessing. Write out these sentences in your journal and complete each one with as many particulars as you can think of:

> I see my partner in these same old ways: _____.
> I believe s/he will never change these behaviors: _____ .

As long as we believe a partner to be the same as always or to be what we imagine her to be, we operate from that image and not from consciousness of her needs. We can change this mental habit by giving her the five A's and really hearing her needs. A person who knows we have pigeonholed her in our minds will not trust us and will therefore not show us her needs. Then communication fails, and defensiveness or arguments take over.

Using the five A's as guideposts, ask yourself what you need most from a partner or a friend. Ask your partner or a friend what he needs from you. Be careful not to confuse needs with requests, plans, or remedies. For example, to say "I need you to listen" describes not a need but a request. To say "I need more space in this relationship" describes not a need but a plan. To say "I need a drink" describes not a need but (your idea of) a remedy. Tell your partner your present desires, plans, and ideas for remedies. Then identify the need behind each of these and ask him to hear it. For instance, behind the desire to be listened to may lie the need for authentic attentiveness, an undistracted focus on your words and feelings with respect and sincere appreciation.

FEELING LOVED • Begin this exercise by recalling memories of feeling loved in childhood, and notice any connections to the kinds of love you seek as an adult. Then ask your partner what feels like love to him and share what it feels like to you. You may not feel loved by someone who truly loves you because she shows it in ways you do not understand as love. This is like hearing a foreign language and presuming it is gibberish. Ask for a translation: The challenge of intimacy for adults is to expand our original concept of love to accommodate a partner's unique way of loving. We can still ask for what we want while trying to accept an approximation of it and opening ourselves to new versions of love.

Consider these questions in your journal: What feels like love to me? Who makes me feel that way? Do I feel loved in bodily resonant ways by my partner? Who was the first person in my life to make me feel loved? Have I thanked him/her enough? Can I tell my partner what feels like love to me? Can I ask her the same question? What will I do with the information? Is the love I offer childlike, parental, or adult? Is the love I seek childlike, parental, or adult? When we feel little or no love coming our way, we may look for proof of love. The more proofs we seek, the more our partner feels threatened, tested, and on the spot. Am I in either of these positions?

THE TOUCH • Becoming an adult does not erase or cancel our fundamental needs. We all feel a need to be held at times, no matter what our age. This comes from an instinct for personal validation. We are always on the lookout for the mirroring and holding that may have been inadequate or missing in early life. When someone loves us, cares about us, and respects us, that person's body becomes a resource for repair of the neglect or abuse in our past.

Some of us fear, quite reasonably, the letdown of finding closeness and then losing it again. We want to be sure a potential partner deserves our trust, and it is always a gamble. If we can get past the inhibiting fear, we may open ourselves to the touch of others, however limited, and find it holds a healing power. Being held with tender attention—for example, in someone's lap or side by side with arms around each other—supplies the mirroring love that may have been missing in our childhood. It feels embarrassing only at first; once the ice is broken, it feels natural. Try this kind of holding sometime with your partner or a close friend. You may offer to hold a partner on your lap or cuddle side by side and read a part of this book to him or her. We do not outgrow the need for such comforting forms of childhood closeness and there is no shame in it.

OFFERING SUPPORT • Emotional support means a generous giving of the five A's. Yet, how do we know exactly what kind of support a partner needs in a given moment or situation? For instance, our partner is weeping. Will it help most to hold her or to give her space?

The Little Prince acknowledged: "It's such a secret place the land of tears." There is sometimes a recondite, unreachable, unnamed feeling in a person's experience. She herself does not know what she really feels or needs in the moment. Support may consist simply in honoring that inner mystery. We may not find out how to help. Then, like Hamlet, we can only say: "Sit still my soul."

At other times sensitivity may take the form of inquiry. When your partner seems distressed and willing to communicate, practice asking her what kind of help she needs. This is a way of honoring—and encouraging—her comfortableness in asking for support from you, another contribution to intimacy. Here are some examples of how to ask: "I see your pain. Please tell me how I can be here for you now." "I want to support you in this moment. Please let me know what will work best for you." "I am available in any way I can be. How can I nurture you best at this time?" "If you do not know what you need right now, I can simply be here with you."

NOTICING MINDSETS • Loving presence takes five forms: attention, acceptance, appreciation, affection, allowing. Mindfulness is the path to such loving presence. Mindful contact is unconditional in granting the five A's and unconditioned by the mindsets of ego such as fear, demand, expectation, judgment, or control. Look at the chart below and journal examples of how you find yourself on both sides in your way of relating to a partner. Show your results to your partner and ask for feedback in making changes and for a compassionate response too.

The Five A's (based on mindfulness)	*Their Opposites* (based on mindsets)
Being attentive	Ignoring, refusing to listen, being unavailable, fearing the truth
Being accepting	Trying to make someone over to fit our specifications, desires, or fantasies
Being appreciative	Criticizing
Being affectionate	Acting selfishly or abusively
Allowing	Being controlling, demanding, or manipulative

SPIRITUAL COMMITMENT TO THE FIVE A'S • The five A's are purposes, or ends in themselves. Giving and receiving them are not only the ways we are fulfilled but also the spiritual practices by which we fulfill our heroic destiny of bringing the world the benefits and treasures we find on our path. Viewed in spiritual terms, they can be explained like this:

- Attention means consciousness of the interconnectedness of all things.
- Acceptance means saying an unconditional yes to the sobering givens of existence, the facts of life.
- Appreciation means the attitude of gratitude.
- Affection means the love we feel for others and for the universe.
- Allowing means that we grant to others and protect in ourselves the right to live freely and without outside control.

Turn these five needs/purposes into affirmations and commitments, which you can then repeat daily or more often if possible. Use the following as examples:

- I feel unity with all human beings and with nature. I notice their pain and their joy. I make decisions that make me feel more connected and closer to them.
- I accept the givens of existence, both those that seem positive and those that seem negative. I surrender to what cannot be changed and trust it to be useful on my life's path.

- I am thankful for all that has been and open to all that will be. I show appreciation for everything I receive.
- I show my love in my every thought, word, and action.
- I cherish my right to live in accord with my own deepest needs, values, and wishes. I respect that right in others.

Finally, practice this meditation style: As you breathe in, think or say one of the five A's as an adverb (for instance "attentively," "acceptingly," "appreciatively," and so forth). Move from one word to the next with each in-breath or simply repeat the same word. An adverb modifies an adjective, verb, or another adverb. To use an adverb on its own in this way creates an automatic sense of incompleteness in the mind—we naturally seek an object. That object might be a difficult emotion or experience you're going through, or it could be the next person or circumstance you meet.

An alternative is to breathe in and out with two words, one from the five A's and the other a virtue you are working on, for instance, "attentively compassionate," "appreciatively generous," etc. Or you can imagine a particular immediate issue, concern, or person occupying your thoughts, and, while breathing consciously, you might say: "I hold this _____ compassionately or attentively," etc.

2
Love and Less

Mirroring Love

> A person wishes to be confirmed in his being by another person. . . . Secretly and bashfully, he watches for a Yes which allows him to be and which can come to him only from one human person to another. It is from one human being to another that the heavenly bread of self-being is passed.
>
> —Martin Buber

We were born with the capacity to feel the whole panoply of human emotions, but that capacity requires activation before we can use it fully. We all have what it takes to feel, but to experience our feelings fully and safely, they have to be "installed," in a sense, by someone through mirroring. Mirroring involves the unconditional positive regard for our unique needs, values, and wishes shown by someone who mindfully provides the five A's. The element of mindfulness means that we feel loved without the ego's artifacts of fear, attachment, control, expectation, clinging, biases, defenses, or judgment. For instance, if we feel fear and it is met with mindful attention, acceptance, appreciation, affection, and allowing, then the fear is in effect installed; that is, we are able to acknowledge it and feel it safely thereafter. The opposite of mirroring is shaming. The less mirroring we have received, the more ashamed of ourselves we may be.

Here is an example of mirroring and its alternative: A child is afraid to go to school for the first time. His mother says, "I know it's scary, and it's OK to have that fear. I'll come to school with you today and stay with you for a while. When I come home, I'll be thinking about you. Then I'll come and pick you up right on time, and we'll go for ice cream. You can be afraid, but don't let it stop you from having the fun you will have at school and after school!" This child, and later the adult this child grows into, will not be likely to abandon himself later. He will trust his ability to survive fear. Fear will not mean "stop," but only "proceed with pluck and with support from others." The feeling of fear has been legitimized, installed safely and permanently, because it has been mirrored with the five A's.

Compare the response of the mother who mirrors the fear of her child to that of the mother who says, "Stop being a crybaby. You're going to school whether you like it or not! None of the other kids are afraid. What's wrong with you?" The first mother mirrored the fear and walked her child through it collaboratively. Trust in oneself results from this approach. The second mother ridiculed the fear and associated it with inadequacy, resulting in shame. With no supportive container for his feeling, this child/adult will have to find his mirroring and safety that results from it elsewhere.

Mirroring can also come in response to joy. You run into the house excitedly, and tell your parents about your success at gymnastics. They respond with full attention, excitement, hugs, praise, and a plan to come and watch you. The opposite response is "Now, don't get all excited. Take it easy. Let's wait and see if you still like it next month." Your enthusiasm is squelched. The first approach leads to a future of self assuradness and exuberance, the second to a future of self-doubt and shame.

Shaming is a kind of abandonment, and holding on to our own shame is self-abandonment. Now we begin to see why we fear abandonment so much. It is the absence of mirroring, and we need mirroring to survive emotionally. We also see why we fear the loss of our partner. To grieve is to feel keenly isolated and bereft of mirroring. To grieve with supportive others, however, is mutual mirroring. This is why funerals are public events: Our fellow mourners mirror grief to us and we to them. Grief is healed by letting go and by contact.

Allowing the mirrored partner to have her own story presents a major challenge for those who want to offer mirroring. When we are mindful, we are not fixing but rather supporting another in her distress or in her choices. We respect her freedom and yet stand by if she needs a hand. This is the same protocol we follow in parenting older adolescents. We do not stand by and let them be hurt; we inform them of possible consequences. Yet once they have the information, we do not stop them from making choices that may hurt them. A mother cannot prevent her daughter's mistakes but can help her deal with their consequences.

Mirroring helps us survive emotionally—that is, to experience the events of our life with the power to handle them and without being devastated or embittered by them. If we receive no or poor mirroring, we may believe we have to attune to the other or lose our tie with her, a tie that feels so necessary to our continued existence. Our unconscious is therefore not just a sea of repressed memories or unacceptable drives, as Freud suggests. It contains a host of feelings that failed to attract validating attunement and so had to be scuttled or submerged. If, on the other hand, we received mirroring in early life and now let ourselves feel fully and appropriately, we have a safety net, a place to fall into when we face a crisis. Sometimes in life we may make choices that find no mirror of acceptance from anyone. Then, for the sake of our psychological and spiritual health, we need either to seek out a support system from which to receive mirroring or to stand alone and trust ourselves when there is no support to be found. *Can I stand in the moonlight and feel its reflection as nature's mirroring and let that be enough for now?*

Healthy adults appreciate those who mirror what was left unmirrored in childhood. Unhealthy adults try to siphon what they need from others. In mature relating we find people who mirror us; we discover the same mirroring powers within ourselves and then show them to others as well. *As you mirror me, I learn to assume your function.* It is like copying a tape and still having the original of it.

Some parents fear their children's feelings. When a son says to his father, "You don't understand!" he may mean, "I can't show you my feelings because you can't handle them." He is protecting his father from ever having to face those frightening feelings. We may stay in this role all our lives, implicitly believing that men or women are too fragile to receive our feelings. When we despair of mirroring and of the possibility of trusting in others, we despair of the very things that make intimacy possible. Intimacy is mutual mirroring.

The five A's, it is now clear, address one essential need and that is the need for mirroring. This is attunement, the perfect pitch of emotional acceptance and support. When our feelings as children are minimized, proscribed, or disregarded, we can't hear the full range of feeling tones, and a part of us becomes inert and numb. Imagine the joy we feel when someone comes along who welcomes and loves us with all our feelings. A relationship with such a person opens and releases us; in other words, it works. It supports and enriches the insights of self-psychology, which focuses on the healing power of sustained empathic attunement, mindfulness in relating.

On the other hand, how crushed and disappointed we feel when we attach ourselves to someone whose love turns out to be a hoax, who shows no real acceptance of what we feel or who we are. Who can blame us for numbing ourselves again? Ultimately, our fear of intimacy may be a fear that our reaching out will be met with the same rejection we encountered in childhood. Who would not be afraid of that?

It does not seem appropriate to seduce or trick another person into mirroring us. A healthy alternative takes two forms. First, we may ask for mirroring directly from those we trust: "Would you listen to my story? Would you hold my hand as I say this? Can you appreciate what I have done?" Second, we can open ourselves to mirroring that comes to us as grace, a free spontaneous gift from others and from the universe. Yes, nature mirrors us too. It is holding us right now. Since we inhabit a generous universe, we are indeed receiving mirroring, and our challenge is to notice it. The kindness of the universe is reflected in the Buddha's teachings of universal compassion. When we realize that mirroring is often a form of grace, we are freed from the despair that we will not find it.

Contemplating an image of the compassionate face of the Buddha, we see all our sorrows and joys mirrored there. This type of mirroring also takes two forms: a deactivation of our clinging and fearing ego and compassion for our plight as humans. It is the equivalent of an assisting force in facing life's conditions. The presence of buddha mind means we may be separate but we are not alone.

Mirroring engenders a sense of self in us. So does what self psychologist Heinz Kohut called "transmuting internalization: oneness with an idealized source of strength and calm." The child competes with his parents for power and is frustrated in the attempt. He then internalizes his parents' power rather than competing with them, and as a result he develops a sense of mastery and self-esteem. In adult life, he knows how to internalize others' support and thereby gain the power to support himself. Transmuting internalization provides us with an inner nurturant parent, a coherent adult self that can protect the inner child.

Saying "I am Buddha" is a spiritual form of transmuting internalization. In the practice of devotion to Avalokiteshvara, the bodhisattva of compassion, the initiate begins by honoring the bodhisattva and ends by acknowledging that there is no distinction between herself and himself. A shrine can be seen as a mirror of what we are in our essential nature—that is, our buddha-nature, Christ consciousness, the breath of God, the higher Self.

We are mirrored by the divine because our humanity includes divinity that can never be damaged or diminished. This is another implication of mindfulness, which frees us from a limiting identification with our ego and awakens us to our richer identity with all nature and all divinity. The equivalent of the divine in Buddhism is *bodhichitta*, the enlightened mind of Buddha in ourselves.

When We Deny We Were Deprived

It would have starved a Gnat—
To live so small as I—
And yet I was a living Child—
With Food's necessity

. . . .

Nor like the Gnat—had I—
The privilege to fly
And seek a Dinner for myself . . .
—EMILY DICKINSON

During my inner-city childhood, I spent several weeks each summer at my Aunt Margaret's farm. At age forty-two, I suddenly had a vision—in a Reichian body therapy session—of the inside of Aunt Margaret's refrigerator, which was always full, while ours at home was usually mostly empty. I realized in that moment that I had often been hungry in childhood. My mental memory had no available record of this, but my body remembered it: abundance at the farm and scarcity at home. In childhood, we may have denied to ourselves that our needs were not being fulfilled, and this kind of denial can persist all our lives. Is food my metaphor for emotional nourishment, which also was scarce at home? Is this why I always keep many extra cans of food in the pantry today? Is my body still caught in the past and acting out its fear of scarcity in the present? Is this what stinginess is about?

"My parents did the best they could" is what our denial of deprivation may sound like. But our bodies cannot be fooled. We know viscerally and instinctively that what we needed was not there or was being withheld. In an adult relationship, we may go on denying how deprived we feel and never address, process, or resolve the deprivation. It wouldn't be surprising, considering just how difficult such tasks are. I may have decided in the midst of the unalterable deprivation in my past: *I just won't need what isn't there.*

Beneath denied deprivation, though, is a silent scream, a stifled cry. Our rational mind minimizes the impact of what happened to us physically, emotionally, or sexually, but every cell of our body knows and feels the true impact. Our body is the only part of us that cannot lie or be lied to. Such phrases as "They meant well" or "It wasn't intentional" mean nothing to the body. It only understands words like "This hurts" or "I am so scared"—or angry or sad or powerless.

If our mental appraisal of an abandonment or betrayal now includes excuses for the perpetrators of them, this is another subtle way of avoiding our grief work, which addresses not the other's intention but the impact of his actions on us. However, forcing memory or grief work can retraumatize us. Part of our response to being abused is learning to dissociate, and we may still need to do that for now. In the work of mourning, once we are ready, we reassociate with the occluded vision of our pain. The readiness is the key, and only we know when we are ready.

The child part of us may have a split desire if we were abused or neglected as children. The healthy half of us wants to recover from the past, and the other half wants to repeat it, to reenact the past compulsively and thereby continually broadcast the unaddressed needs. When a crisis or accident befalls us, we feel compelled to tell people about it not once but many times. Such repetition is a way of absorbing the shock. Yet only grieving the past truly frees us from it. The work is complicated because both halves may be at work until one gains ascendancy. Yes, I really have something inside me that wants to sabotage my happiness. How can I give it space, comfort it, and thereby lay it to rest?

What Hurts Us Comforts Us

When our primal needs were left unmet, we might tolerate abuse in adult relationships. We keep going back for more where there is only less. ("You keep hurting me, and I can't leave you.") If we woke up every morning in childhood thinking, "Someone here hates me, and I can't leave. Someone here will hurt me today, and I have to stay. Someone does not want me here, and I have nowhere else to go," how can we go easily now? Sadly, the lesson that we are powerless is reconfirmed each day we stay in a painful situation.

Exploitive love from our parents leads to the belief that *we* are defective not that they are inappropriate for abusing us. "They did it for my own good" is collaboration in the abuse. Such conformity and surrender to unfair authority engender a self-hatred that is then expressed in violence, either overtly or covertly. The origins of retaliation are here. We can decrease our self-hatred by tuning into it fully in a mindful way— without shame, fear, censure, and so forth—and meeting it with compassion, directed both toward ourselves and others.

In childhood we learned self-protective strategies. We found mental and physical ways to acclimate or inure ourselves to the pain. We conditioned ourselves to escape while staying. Now these same strategies only keep us stuck in untenable situations. Look at the irony: We are protecting ourselves by denial and dissociation, thereby succeeding only in remaining at the mercy of the abuse.

As mirroring (acceptance of us by another) gives us power, so abuse takes away access to our power. In an abusive relationship we may believe we cannot let go because things *might* get better. Our power is thereby deflated in two ways: by the belief that we can't extricate ourselves from abuse and by clinging to an unfounded hope that the abuser will change. These are the lies we learned when we became accustomed to unhappiness and hurt. As Shakespeare said, "I weep to have what I fear to lose."

In some abusive relationships we feel we cannot live without the other. When drama is all we know, we imagine that's what relating is all about. We may train our partners to play our unique game of drama and uproar, which may take the form of continual abandonments and reconciliations, seductive and then withholding behavior, argumentativeness, triangulation, infidelity, addiction, and so on. When things are quiet and running smoothly, we may feel bored, even insecure. If our childhood home was stormy, we may see stress as normal. It is almost as if we are compelled to recreate the parched landscapes of our desert past. Something inside us wants to be done with it, but we only succeed in restoring it.

Sometimes, the abuse is so subtle that we fail to notice it. Sarcasm, ridicule, teasing, "kidding," or continual criticism, for instance, start to feel less like abuse and more like a part of the background noise. Sometimes one partner does not meet the other's needs, but since he also does not do anything major to upset the apple cart, Adam and Eve go on in the relationship without thinking of options such as change or separation: *He will never be so bad that you will leave him but never so good that he will satisfy you.* In either case, we may fool ourselves into hoping for change rather than working for it. If hope doesn't include a plan for change, it is actually hopelessness and avoidance of change. What we do not change, we choose. Is this the message we get from the partner of our distress: "Stay with me and I won't give you what you want" or "Come back and I still won't give you what you want"? We cannot be fooled forever. One day we allow ourselves to know and then take action. Emily Dickinson writes:

The Southern Custom—of the Bird—
That ere the Frosts are due—
Accepts a better Latitude—
We—are the Birds—that stay.

The Shiverers round Farmers' doors—
For whose reluctant Crumb—
We stipulate—till pitying Snows
Persuade our feathers Home.

To be "the birds that stay" in wintry New England when wisdom would send us to Mexico is a cruel fate to impose upon ourselves. We can use it as a metaphor for a relationship in which we stay with someone who does not nurture us: We need a loaf and beg for a crumb from someone who's afraid to give a loaf and hardly willing to give a crumb.

To live in Massachusetts winter after winter and then say "enough of this" and move to California takes some pluck and then yields warmth. However, we may be conditioned to accept that our lives are not supposed to be comfortable. Likewise, we may believe that relationships will never work for us, that we are meant to be unhappy and unfulfilled. With that perspective, we may not be able to muster an "enough of this" when we find ourselves in pain. Instead we may ask ourselves, "Why bother?"

Yet to live with abuse is dangerous because it can make our wish to die equal in strength to our will to live. We think, "Nothing I can do will stop him from hurting me" or "Nothing I can do will make her love me." A frightening conclusion can result: "Nothing matters, and I don't care." Such deep despair can take the form of poor self-esteem, disease, distortion of the body by overeating, self-abuse, addiction, risky jobs or hobbies, accident-proneness, anorexia, the belief that we can't improve our lives, and so on. These all boil down to a wish to die.

We might even seek relationships that guarantee protection against having to look at or process our issues. A partner may be appealing to us precisely because he implicitly promises that we will never have to confront, process, and resolve any issue very deeply, never have to change a self-defeating style. We think, "He is superficial and just as scared to confront things as I am, so I am safe here." In such relationships we forge a tacit bargain to be the "shiverers 'round farmers' doors."

Mindfully loving partners never consciously engage in hurtful behaviors toward one another. They police themselves and place under arrest all the pilferers from the ever so pregnable hope chest of intimacy: vendetta, violence, ridicule, sarcasm, teasing, insult, lying, competition, punishment, and shaming.

How Good for Me Was My Family?

Our American myth of rugged individualism ignores how much of our identity is grounded in and derived from family. If identity means that which is identifiable about us, we are definitely branches of a family tree. I look in the mirror and see my father's eyes; I scream at my wife and hear my mother's words; I caress my child and feel Grandma's arms; I scold, manipulate, control, or make demands on my children, and I remember how I was treated as a child; I deal with a disturbing neighbor and lo, I find that familiar upstart ego that characterizes so many males in my family. My name is my family name; my grave already waits beside my family's graves. I came here with ancestral traits, and I will leave those same traits behind. My life is a chapter not a book.

However, there are differences between my parents and me: I apologize when I hurt others; I have more resources for I dealing with interpersonal problems; I have become more conscious and softer thanks to all the self-help books I have read and all the healers I have met. My immigrant ancestors never had the chance to do those things.

No family is perfect. The best we can hope for is a family that is functional most of the time, makes allowances for some dysfunction, and when things break down, finds a way to mend them. In my view, the functional family is one that grants the five A's most of the time and does not abuse any family member.

In addition, feelings and deprivations are expressed every time they are noticed or felt, both between parents and between children and parents. Parents in such a family are not afraid or too proud to apologize to their children (and vice versa) when that is appropriate. Life events are patiently and caringly processed by inquiry into each person's reactions, intuitions, and feelings. Family members get ample time and permission to feel fully and to resolve things in their own way. Crises don't become secrets to be kept. There are no limits on free speech. *Did anyone ask me how I felt when a family crisis occurred?*

How much stronger we all might feel if our parents had candidly shared their feelings and fears with us: "Jane, this is the letter your father sent from Vietnam. He feels fear and despair often, but when he thinks of you and me, he gains some hope. I feel sad to read this. How do you feel?" This kind of invitation to dialogue exemplifies the mindful and mirroring attention that makes feeling less isolating and disempowering and therefore less scary.

Frustration does a child no good, but struggle is different from frustration. A child struggles to get his jacket on. A parent stands by without helping. Thus, the child learns to stay with a process and reach a successful conclusion: The jacket is on. But when the child is frustrated because a task is truly too difficult for him to manage and he is ready to give up in despair, the good parent steps in and helps. In healthy families there is struggle and assistance when necessary, not frustration and shame about failure. This is how antidotes to despair are installed in our psyches.

In a functional family, parents separate if one of them is an addict or an abuser and refuses help. The other parent does not let abuse go unnoticed, and the children never become objects of inappropriate need fulfillment by either parent. A caring parent is protector of her children and herself. She does all she can to cocreate conditions of safety and need fulfillment and moves on, with her children, if that is impossible.

In becoming an adult, we learn to play for ourselves the roles the functional family was supposed to play for us. Becoming more adult means having an inner nurturant parent who supervises our unruly inner child, protects our endangered inner child, and comforts our scared inner child. Issa was a Japanese poet born in 1763 and abused in childhood who wrote: "Fear not, / Puny little frog! / I'm here to back you up." Often the feeling of loneliness results not from a lack of people to entertain us but from the absence of an adult self to nurture our inner child who feels abandoned in some way. (Loneliness is also an appropriate way to feel as we make transitions, take a stand, become more spiritually awake, or find ourselves.) We may take our loneliness literally and look for company in all the wrong places. When the child within cannot depend on our inner parent, she attaches to something or someone—anything or anyone—as a surrogate. A reliable inner nurturant parent keeps our scared child company in a tender and powerful way, helping us steer clear of inappropriate attachments. While not eliminating loneliness, this reduces its wallop. These words of writer and teacher Natalie Goldberg are helpful: "Use loneliness. Its ache creates urgency to reconnect with the world. Take that aching and use it to propel you deeper into your need for expression—to speak, to say who you are."

The ancient Romans knew how difficult family life could be. They realized that human agency alone could not keep families safe and sound and that it takes heaven and earth to make a human group truly functional. They therefore acknowledged and invoked gods appropriate to each area of difficulty. (Gods are personifications of grace, a special gift that comes to us unbidden and helps us transcend the limits of our ego and will.) Vesta was the goddess of the hearth, around which the family gathered for warmth and companionship and at which their food was prepared. The Lares were the spirits of the ancestors, invoked as an acknowledgment that parents alone are not sufficient as sources of nurturance; we also need help from earlier generations. The Penates were the little angels of the table and of the cupboards. Janus, who had a face on each side of his head, protected the family's front gate from the outside world, with one face looking in at the family property and the other looking out toward the rest of the world. There were also three gods of the doorway: one for the door itself, one for the hinges, and one for the threshold. Juno, the goddess of marriage and family, protected the psychic and physical well-being of everyone in the family. All these invisible presences helped make the household work. Religious images in homes today make the same appeal that the Romans made to sources of nurturance and protection beyond the merely human.

The ancient Greeks also saw a close connection between the family and the gods. In the play *Agamemnon* by Aeschylus, the title character is stabbed and killed by his wife while he is in his bath. He cries, "I have been struck a mortal blow deep within," words that portray how we suffer our deepest wounds of betrayal and separation in the context of the family and relationships. Plays in ancient Greece were shown as part of religious feasts, and the subject of the plays was psychological, usually familial, for the Greeks made no distinction between the psychological and the religious. Agamemnon's murder, for example, which happens in the water at the hands of a woman, uses the archetypal theme of dissolution in water of an arrogant ego by female spirits such as mermaids and lorelei. Similarly, in alchemy, dissolution in water is part of the process by which the leaden ego becomes the gold of the Self. Myth and ritual continually mirror the design and destiny of the psyche, another reason that our work is both psychological and spiritual.

Light on the Hurt

> Our greatness will appear
> Then most conspicuous, when greater things of small,
> Useful of hurtful, prosperous of adverse
> We can create, and in what place soe'er
> Thrive under evil, and work out ease of pain...
> Majestic though in ruin...
>
> —MILTON, *Paradise Lost*

Since the five A's are the components of emotional support, when we don't receive them, we feel physically, emotionally, and spiritually disconnected and isolated. The lack of any of the five A's feels like a gap in our psyches, a hole, a deficiency. Yet each unfulfilled A is more than a hole. If we stay with the pain of the emptiness, it opens a spacious chamber in our psyche. To be human, after all, is to be deficient, to have some holes, and yet deficiency can have a positive side.

Lack of this from others	*Can be a door to*
Attention	Looking within myself
Acceptance	Exploration of both positive and negative aspects of my shadow self
Allowing freedom	Finding my own deepest needs, values, and wishes and taking responsibility for living in accord with them
Appreciation	Cherishing myself and the Self that embraces me and all the world
Affection	Unconditional love for myself and others, the generosity to love before I am loved— in other words, true initiative

Viewed this way, our unfulfilled needs turn out to be gravitational forces, pulling us into the depths of our adult self. *When we apply the five A's to our own deficits, they take us to the very place in our soul where fulfillment is guaranteed.* We find our depth when we go directly into the hole, as Alice did. Wonderland is really the depths of the human soul, with its defiance of logic and all its radiant possibilities.

Mindfulness provides the technology for transforming our gaps into soulful potential. When we are mindful, we enter the pure awareness of our predicament and cradle it without judgment, fear, blame, shame, or expectation. This loyalty to what is allows us to turn unfulfilled needs into self-knowledge. *Mindfulness shows that a hole is a tunnel not a cave.* Our emptiness turns out to be a transitional space like the dark passage in a concerto, a movement rather than the whole piece. Emptiness means we have no sense of being held, no net in which to drop safely. Our practice is a net, a parachute, a catcher in the rye. So are our healthy relationships. *What do I need by way of support as I look into the holes in myself?*

The work of healing the past is not to recall past hurt and fix it but to stay with it, in it, until it starts to shift and open on its own. To stay is to find the inner Beloved, our deepest personal reality. To stay in a painful situation and be abused is to accept our victimization; to stay with our pained self is a spiritual victory. The hurt becomes a doorway into our vulnerability, and in that raw place we find our most tender self. When we make the commitment to stay, we are respecting our wounds as shrines that heal us just by being visited and lingered in. We are pilgrims not carpenters when we do this work. If we were hurt because we didn't find love, we paradoxically can find it simply by sitting mindfully in the sense of longing we once felt. We resolve our original loss not by entirely filling it with someone else's response to us but by also relocating it in ourselves. Our ego searches for love, but we are meant to find love within ourselves first. Once we have done that, we can reach out to others as rich people looking to share the wealth, not as paupers seeking to commandeer it.

The hero of myths and legends is fearless, yet every heroic story has an interlude in which the hero is powerless, for example, Robin Hood in the dungeon, Jack in the giant's wife's cupboard, Jonah in the whale, Dorothy asleep in the poppy field. All these incidents serve as metaphors for the times of calm abiding in mindful sitting. They acknowledge the legitimacy of powerlessness and inaction as useful stages of any human journey.

In recent decades, the self-help movement has put far too much emphasis on how we should never be victims. We have perhaps become one-sided and forgotten the dynamic interplay between such complementary opposites as defenselessness and resourcefulness. To be solely a victim is admittedly dangerous. We should never accept being victimized by violent abuse. But falling victim to depression when others betray us is appropriate. Occasional lapses into powerlessness help us let go of ego and control, and every real hero welcomes them.

It is even true that losses, hardships, disappointments, hurts, and betrayals seem necessary to encourage our growth from childhood to—and throughout—adulthood. The mother dog snarls at pups that want to suckle when it is time for them to be weaned. This way, they learn to fend for themselves. In all nature, self-nurturant powers evolve from anguish and separation. When parents say no to us, we feel the pain of not getting our wishes met, but something else is afoot developmentally. Prohibitions give us the power to negotiate. The mother who always gives us our way will not help us build character. Like Cinderella and Snow White, we may need some time with the "wicked stepmother" to integrate our orphan archetype and prompt us to move on to our adult destiny. (Although *orphan* is generally taken to mean anyone abandoned or rejected by one or both parents, the word also can refer to the part of us that survives an abusive or neglectful family intact.)

As war hero Tom Daly said, "Often, the events we regard as our deepest wounds are in fact initiations that break us out of the unhealthy enchantments of innocence, grandiosity, passivity, violence or addiction." We need such initiations, for without them we may resist growth and change or even deny our responsibility toward others and our destiny to transcend personal ego. Even early abuse and betrayal, albeit reprehensible, have a positive side for beings like us who benefit from initiatory ordeals. Every disruption, interruption, and failure at empathic attunement from our parents helps us gain the power to face the future, with all its separations, disappointments, and defeats. All it takes to access this power is a willingness to visit the past and stay with its pain long enough to receive its boon.

Opposites continually rendezvous in the unfolding human world. For instance, joy requires us to open ourselves to experience, and that results in letting sorrow in, too. When a child becomes able to hold the apparent opposites that appear in a parent, he is maturing: "This same mother is at times responsive to me and at times unavailable, and I can love her in both moments and trust that she loves me in either case." All of us had some good and some bad experiences with our parents. When, as adults, we look back into our childhood and see only the abuse—or only the good times—we know we face the challenge of becoming adults who can hold opposites with equanimity.

Without betrayal we would have no stimulation, no incentive to leave home, to strike out on our own, and consequently, to find self-reliance. Without it, Joseph would not have sold himself into slavery and thereby walked the path to his special destiny beside Pharaoh. We stumble onto such paradoxes at every turn of the human story: Dante had to be exiled from Florence, the city he loved, before he could write *The Divine Comedy*. Homer and Milton went blind before they wrote their thrilling epics. Beethoven went deaf before he composed the great quartets. In each instance, the artist produced the great work he was destined for after pain and loss. We are artists, too, and our fate—and challenge—is much the same. *We cannot unlive our painful history, but we do not have to relive it. We cannot let go of it, but we do not have to hold on to it.*

In Egyptian myth, Osiris is cut into pieces by his dark brother Set. Thereafter Osiris becomes immortal when his sister/spouse, Isis, does the work of finding the pieces and re-membering him. Repeated assaults on our sense of self cut us into pieces. We live in pieces for a while and then, through our feminine powers of searching and sewing, we are re-collected and find our way to wholeness. The ancient shamans initiated men by ritual dismemberment. As with Christ, Dionysus, and Osiris—and us—fragmentation is often a necessary phase in the transition from humiliation and abuse to self-assurance and compassionate love. Wounded heroes redeem others only because they themselves have experienced both fragmentation and restoration. There is a path to love among the ruins.

We think we are the sum of all the bad things that have happened to us, but that is only true if we have not worked on ourselves. Actually, all that has happened to us *and* our work on it provide the necessary ingredients for us to emerge as what we were meant to become. In a healthy relationship we can safely say, "Join me in my chaos not to help me eliminate it but to help me tolerate it." Sustained, empathic self-staying, which we accomplish by granting ourselves the five A's, mobilizes powers once buried in pain. This does more for us than any of our attempts to root out our problem. It is the difference between an aggressive attack and nonviolent love in the face of an attack.

Behind all our wounded sensitivities, flawed inclinations, and regretted mistakes is a reliable growth-fostering milieu inside us that remains alive, no matter what. We never lose our unconditional love of light. This is what we build on. Challenges and betrayals are the afflicting forces that greet us at the thresholds of growth, as they awaited the mythic heroes on their journeys. If there is an afflicting force at every threshold, there must be a threshold in every afflicting force. There is no initiation without a scar. Among primitive people, such scars are given by parents and elders. Young people today do it with tattoos and piercings.

For our heart to yield without revolt to the hard law of creation, is there not a psychological need to find some positive value that can transfigure this painful waste in the process that shapes us and eventually make it worth accepting? . . . Dark and repulsive though it is, suffering has been revealed to us as a supremely active principle for the humanization and the divinization of the universe.

—TEILHARD DE CHARDIN

A Heroic Journey

The archetypal heroic journey is not a move from point A to point B as in football, where the purpose is to go from the line of scrimmage to the goal. It is a movement from point A to point A to the thousandth power, as in baseball, where the purpose is to go from home to home with a point made—that is, something to show for the journey.

The phases of the heroic journey exactly match those of intimate relationships. The hero leaves familiar surroundings; passes through a series of trials; and returns home with a spouse, treasure, amulet, or healing power. Relationships likewise begin by leaving the family, the familiar; passing through a series of conflicts in unknown territory; and returning to one's full self, but this time within a committed partnership. Since childhood needs turn out to be the same needs we have in adult intimacy, the journey takes us back to where we began, but without the fear of loneliness that initially drove us to leave home. The obstacles that lie along the journey to intimacy, which take the form of conflicts that arise in the course of a relationship, become a bridge to true communion and commitment when successfully negotiated. What seems to be in the way *is* the way. Adult love is the goal of the human journey. The hero is meant to become the lover of a partner and then enter a partnership with the world. There is no exclusively personal work. Every practice, both psychological and spiritual, readies us for enlightening and serving the world. Love is indeed a journey *from* aloneness *through* closeness and opposition *into* communion.

The journey's final stage, like the culmination of a healthy relationship, is to return to where we began and bless the place with love, wisdom, and healing—gifts we received en route so we could give them away at home. The path of the personal and the intimate journey goes beyond the inflated ego to the generous and wholesome ego, readying us for the higher task of being couriers from the Self to all our fellow humans. The gifts we bring back are the talents we were endowed with at birth now activated personally and in relationships. In addition, bringing good works and compassion, we make the world a better place than we found it and fulfill our evolutionary destiny.

Practices

CHECKING FOR SAFETY • Take whichever of the following questions strike a chord in you and write your responses in your journal. Can I chance being myself and let love happen with you? Can this relationship provide a zone of security where the submerged parts of me can surface? Will I still be held and cherished even if I show you all my worst traits and most unappealing feelings?

MIRRORING • In every phase of life we see the influence of our earliest longings. Our work is not to renounce our childhood needs but to take them into account, work on them, and enlist our partner to help us do this, if she is willing. Our goal is not just to cut our parental ties but to unite with a partner who can join us in our work. As Shakespeare says in *King Lear*, "Who alone suffers, suffers most."

Ask these questions of your partner: I was derailed in some of my development. Can you help me in my efforts to get back on track? Are you the person with whom I can safely welcome and revive my earliest unmet needs and redirect my thwarted strivings? Can I work with you on mutual mirroring? Do I sometimes make you feel the things I couldn't bear to feel, so that you can help me identify it and then hold it with me? Do you make me feel the things you couldn't bear to feel? How can we challenge ourselves on all this and move past it? Which of my feelings do you mirror? Which of yours do I mirror? Which feelings do we fear in one another?

ADULT SEEKING • Mature adults bring a modest expectation of need fulfillment to a partner. They seek only about 25 percent (the adult dose) of their need fulfillment from someone else (100 percent is the child's dose), with the other 75 percent coming from self, family, friends, career, hobbies, spirituality/religion, and even pets (dogs are expert at giving the five A's!).

In meditation, according to Chögyam Trungpa Rinpoche, 25 percent of our attention goes into technique, 25 percent into relaxing, 25 percent into self-befriending, and 25 percent into lively expectancy. He uses the analogy of our experience in a movie theater: 75 percent of our attention is on the movie, the rest on popcorn and the person with us. The divided attention makes for a pleasurable experience, not possible if all our concentration were on the movie only. It is said that half a loaf is better than none. Accepting a quarter of a loaf may be one of the secrets of successful relationships.

Respond to these questions in your journal or together with a partner: What are my sources of need fulfillment, and what percentage of my needs get fulfilled by each source? What are your sources and percentages? How do I react to this quip from Chekhov: "If you fear solitude, don't get married"? Do I present an adult-size need for the five A's? Has it moderated since childhood (like my need for milk)? Can I receive a moderate, adult amount of attention and be happy with it? Or do I have a gnawing sense that I did not get what was coming to me? Am I insisting on it now? Was I rejoicing on our wedding day when every cell in my body was poised to cry about what went on in early life? Can I join Henry David Thoreau in saying, "I will come to you, my friend, when I no longer need you. Then you will find a palace, not an almshouse."

FACING OUR OPTIONS • How does the chart on the next page fit your experiences? Which phrases describe you?

The unmirrored inner child may either	*Or*
Seek relationships that mirror and build trust	Seek relationships that fail to mirror and that break trust
Understand trauma as a bridge	Experience trauma only as an obstacle
Recover from the past and move beyond its pain	Repeat the past and cling to it
Risk what is different	Do only what is familiar
Wish to transcend an experience	Feel compelled to reenact an experience
Expect success in relationships	Expect failure

SELF-CARING • Early abuse can affect our adult capacity to take care of ourselves, especially when it comes to our health. How do you take in warnings about life-threatening behavior? Reading the warning label on the cigarette pack may lead us to stop smoking. In this case the warning is received in an adult way. But the warning can also fall flat in the deep, deaf "I don't care" of the despairing inner child who has found yet another way to die. Answer this question in your journal: Where am I on the spectrum?

REFUSING ABUSE • Intimacy entails openness to others' feelings. However, it does not mean allowing ourselves to be abused. We speak up and say "ouch!" directly to someone who hurts our feelings. If someone is physically abusive, we immediately get away and get help. In the case of long-term discomfort in a relationship, here is a practice that may help: We can commit ourselves to suffer no more than thirty days of unhappiness and emotional pain with a partner before telling her about it directly or bringing it to therapy. *Am I on the thirty-day plan or the fifteen-year plan?*

At the same time, there are some instances in which we do not have to confront others, but we also do not have to tolerate abuse or lack of courtesy. For example, we might be at a family dinner where a tipsy relative is saying sarcastic things to us. We do not have to stop him, but we do not have to stay there either. This rule may also work at a party when the group's level of alcohol intake has reached the point at which intelligent conversation is no longer possible. In both instances we leave. We do this not to punish or judge anyone but to take care of ourselves.

Tell a therapist and/or a close friend about any abuse you are suffering in your relationship and ask for suggestions on how to proceed. Involve the police if the abuse is physical. Ask for help if you cannot see the seriousness of the abuse but others can.

REVERSING MESSAGES • Recall the parental message you heard most often in childhood. When does it come up now? For instance, perhaps the message was "If something good comes your way, you will lose it." Now when you are promised a job, you worry: "They will change their minds and not offer it to me after all." You feel that this kind of happening is an old pattern in your life, but the record does not confirm your feelings. You are simply operating out of a fear/belief that was installed in you early on. The undeserving child still hides in you and emerges whenever something good comes your way.

The fear you feel now can be reconfigured as a call for your attention from that child. Welcome him and hold him, reassuring him that he is not powerless anymore; you will handle his losses and rejoice in his gains. You may say, "The adult I is here for the child me. I know how you still feel those fears. I am with you now. I have many resources, and you can rely on my protection. I will simply sit with what I/you feel in a mindful way." This metaphorical active-imagination technique ends the child's sense of being undeserving and increases his trust in himself/yourself.

Most of us have internalized many messages by which we judge and insult ourselves. But when we notice a censorious self-debasing voice within, we do not have to submit to it. We can focus on it as an assault by an inner enemy who is caught in a habit of self-defeat. We can patiently redirect the judgmental voice, converting it to a new avuncular voice— one with feisty compassion for our frightened inner child; one that speaks kindly to us; one that responds to us with attention, acceptance, appreciation, and affection and allows for error. This is how we self-soothe and keep from giving up on ourselves.

The loving voice of the inner ally accepts us as we are, and we feel stronger and more lovable. What works is patient redirection of the judgmental voice to a new avuncular voice, one with feisty compassion for our frightened inner child. A new adult driving force is at work when we work on ourselves in ways like this. Our new inner voice is not to be construed as a soliloquy. It is being listened to by the enlightened companions of grace who assist us on the path. We are not alone in our practices. Love is all around us.

We are all lovable because there is an enduring wholeness in us, our buddha nature, a capacity to love that remains uncompromised no matter what has happened to us in life. This basic goodness *is* the core of our being. It does not have to be conjured by effort but is a grace given to all of us, abiding intrinsically in human nature. We access the gift dimension—grace—when we look with friendliness upon ourselves.

Our ego defenses arose in reaction to unfriendliness toward us from others. They thus originated in a frustrated longing for love. That is why our puffy ego deserves compassion not insult. We can choose compassion for ourselves—be a buddha to ourselves. The Buddha's first words upon enlightenment, as he looked at the world and the human heart, were "Wonderful, wonderful." Or we can campaign against ourselves—be a Luther who nails onto our hearts his ninety-five theses of what is wrong with us.

Imagine yourself a missionary when you hear those critical voices inside. Gently but indefatigably work to convert them to a more compassionate form of spirituality. Then, when next they speak, they will be fellow practitioners of mindfulness and lovingkindness.

Finally when the desperados of the neurotic ego—fear, grasping, expectation, judgment, control, attachment, and so forth—threaten our psychic domain, it is time for mindfulness. Sit quietly or walk slowly as you contemplate each stressful assault and let go of it with a label such as "just a thought" or with an affirmation such as "I let go of control in this predicament and let the chips fall where they may." Then expand your personal concern into universal lovingkindness, mature love: "May all beings let go of whatever stands in the way of their happiness." This is how we move from ego-love to eco-love!

ALLOWING BOTH SIDES • Read these questions and statements to your partner or to yourself and ask how you can act on them:

> Will there be losses in my life? I've been there and back.
> Will there be wonderful gains? I found them before and trust the universe to give them again. It will not be all pleasure or all pain, all hope or all despair. It will be some of each, and I have it within me to handle the pain and enjoy the pleasure.

> Was my mother always kind to me? Was my father always tender toward me? No, I found that consistency is rare in human relating. With such a history, I will never expect anyone or anything to be perfectly consistent, perfectly pleasing, or perfect at all. My accommodation with the givens of my existence makes me a healthy adult. Could I have come to that accommodation if I had spent all my time on only the bright side of the river?

BEING AWARE OF FULFILLMENT • In your journal list specific ways the five basic needs (attention, acceptance, appreciation, affection, and allowing) were fulfilled and/or neglected in your past. Since these five needs are also the five central qualities of love and support, list what you have been looking for in your adult relationship, and draw lines connecting similar entries on both lists. Are your most desperate needs the very ones that went unfulfilled in your childhood? Ask your partner and/or children how good you are at receiving and responding to their needs. If you feel brave and clear about yourself, make a careful list of all your unmet needs, show this list to your partner, and say, "Here's what I *don't* want you to provide because this is my work."

FINDING THE HOLES • It is painful for us to find ourselves fully. We avoid the holes that were left in us by the disappointments of early life and adult relationships. But we launch ourselves into them and through them. Here is an empowering practice to be done in a quiet, meditative way:

1. Find the holes in yourself, the places where the five A's have been unfulfilled.

2. Think of all the times you have tried to fill these holes with someone or something else.

3. Make a commitment to climb into these scary craters and sit in them on your own, with no attempt to fill them. The only tools you bring in with you are the five A's. Simply stay in each of your deficiencies attentively, acceptingly, appreciatively, and affectionately, fully allowing it to be there without protest, shame, or blame. The five A's are the only true fulfillment of the needs. By giving them to yourself, you are healing wounds you received because you didn't get them from others in your past.

As you stay with your empty places again and again, you will gradually see them open into lively spaces. Our gaps are not covered or cancelled but exposed by the five A's.

Alice, by herself, followed the White Rabbit into a hole that led to the parts of herself that were confusing and scary. Ask yourself if your various partners were meant to be just such rabbits that kindly tried to show you the way into your deepest self. Now you are finally willing to enter. (A soul mate, by the way, is a partner who is willing to take this journey with you carrying the same tools.)

WITNESSING THE PAIN • Early or throughout life, your partner or you may have suffered abuse and/or betrayals and hurts. Offer your partner the experience of mindful witnessing of the pain that still remains. Mindful witnessing means listening with complete attentiveness, acceptance, allowing, affection, and appreciation to what the other person reveals and to the feelings behind the person's story. As a mindful witness, you do not give advice or try to fix anything but simply take in what is said and felt in a respectful and encouraging way. Keep what is said completely confidential, and do not talk about it later unless the other person asks you to. One caution: Do not try this practice if one of you feels unready to face pain, for the practice may bring up pain that has been repressed and controlled for years.

LOCATING THE PEARL • Consider this commentary on the pearl as a metaphor for pain and its potential to be changed into something beautiful. Then write a poem in response (exploring your memories of pearls or how they figure in your life) or answer the questions I've supplied below.

> In reaction to an irritation caused by a parasite or a grain of sand, the self-healing power of the oyster covers it with layers of aragonite. After several years, a pearl is created, composed of the same materials as the inner shell of the oyster. A pearl thus achieves its beauty and value from deep within its own protective shell. The unique luster ("orient") of pearls depends on the refraction of light from their translucent layerings. The iridescence that some pearls emit is caused by the overlapping of many successive layers that disperse the light as it hits them. Unlike other gems, pearls are not cut or polished. They can easily decay, and their softness makes them vulnerable to acids and heat. Pearls like to be worn against human skin, which is the best way to maintain their luster.

There are many layers of metaphor in this description. Journal your responses to these questions: What is the grit in you that awaits attention or has already been covered? Do you trust your inner resources to provide the layerings that will make grit into pearl? Notice the phrases "self-healing power," "from deep within its own protective shell," "their softness makes them vulnerable," "against human skin . . . to maintain their luster." How do they work for you?

GRIEVING THE PAST • Turn to the appendix and read the introductory section. When you feel ready, begin the steps of grieving for childhood losses and abuses. Continue with the steps according to your own timing as you read this book, perhaps working on one step with each of the following chapters. You may also opt to begin the steps after reading the entire book. Respecting your own timing is an essential element of success in any practice.

PART TWO

Struggles along the Way

Zeus ordained that only in sorrow and in
suffering do we find wisdom's way . . .
by suffering we shall gain understanding.

—AESCHYLUS, *Agamemnon*

3

Choosing a Partner

✡

Perhaps the best partners come to us when we neither seek nor avoid the possibility of finding someone. We simply live in accord with our deepest needs and wishes and notice people we meet. We trust the universe and its miraculous power of synchronicity to bring us just the person who is best for us. But even more important than finding a partner is taking care of our hearts in a dating game that can be a devastating enterprise of broken promises and disappointed expectations. Caring for ourselves while dating means not betraying our true nature in a desperate attempt to get someone to want us. We have to retain our boundaries intact if the process is not to end in self-abandonment and self-deprecation. We cannot allow anyone to take advantage of us or put us down for trying. Looking at ourselves from this perspective, we think: "I want a partner, and I am taking care of myself as the first step. I remain the sentry over my vulnerable inner self during this process, which may be quite dangerous to my self-esteem."

Yet we cannot be overcautious, for our sense of aliveness is directly proportional to how much we allow our longings to have their full career in our hearts. Longing is a source of motivation and thus of achievement. In a profound way, longing *is* our capacity to love. Our goal as healthy people is not to give up longing for a relationship but to let it be fulfilled moderately by others and following a model of mutuality rather than neediness. After all, relationships are not meant to fulfill us completely but to provide us with ever-changing and ever-evolving resources as we move through life. This happens when our feelings are welcomed and supported with the five A's and when more and more of our shadow side is perceived by the other, who meets it with the five A's as well.

In early life, we may have had to hide our deepest selves in order to maintain the bond with our parents. We may have become used to paying that price, and so we went on paying it in relationships, too. We stayed where we had to hide. That changes as we become healthy adults. We still have needs, but they no longer have us. *When we tolerate not having our needs met fully, fear turns to vulnerability and a more generous love awakens in us.* A healthy person looks and longs for an open, caring, daring partner capable of attuning to and holding his feelings. This grants unprecedented permission to the frightened child within to release old hurts and trust new ties.

Am I Cut Out for Close, Intimate Relationships?

An adult commitment is a thoroughly truthful enterprise of ongoing love. It entails an unremitting willingness to keep agreements and handle obstacles by addressing, processing, and resolving conflicts. Happiness and mutual respect result. True love cannot be fooled, nor does it attempt to fool others. As mature adults, we can no longer be charmed by looks or sweet talk. All that matters is enduring mutual commitment.

Some people confuse attachment with love. We may feel attached to someone and imagine we love him; someone may be attached to us, and we imagine he loves us. But mindful love is bonding by commitment, not attachment by clinging. Being attached will immobilize us; love, on the other hand, helps us achieve a progressively effective and joyous evolution. We can also mistake dependency for connection. Insecure people may try to create a connection with us by fostering dependency through the offer of riches, humor, flattery, indebtedness, and so forth. The five A's, especially allowing, offer the reliable alternative path.

Of course, not everyone is cut out for a fully committed relationship. Someone can work diligently on all the practices in this book and still not be able to fulfill the needs of another adult in an intimate bond. He may not be relationship-oriented, or he may simply have no interest in doing the work a relationship requires. Some people are more comfortable with—and only psychologically calibrated for—light relationships or friendships. They are driven not by fear of intimacy but by truthful recognition that intimacy is not for them. There is no shame in not wanting a relationship. A healthy person is not one in a relationship but one in his own skin.

So many of us married out of social convention rather than out of a choice that reflected our deepest inclinations, readiness, and personality. People who have it in them only to be friends, never spouses, want the rhythms of distance *and* closeness that friendship provides. They prefer absence alternating with presence rather than continued presence. This is a legitimate option. But social pressures—once internalized—may push such a person into marriage and the result is two unhappy people and perhaps unhappy children.

In the conventional view, living together is considered the logical goal of relating and an indicator of success. But the reality is that some people do not do well in mutual living situations, and they are better off in separate quarters even when the relationship becomes more intimate. Neighbors might have a better chance at stress-free relating than live-in partners. It is up to both partners to make the uniquely appropriate plan that fits for them. A primary goal in a relationship is to make sure it has the best chance of surviving—and that may not happen under one roof.

Marriage and family are a special vocation not meant for everyone. It is an individual not a collective choice. It is for those who will enjoy a commitment to lifelong working through, working on, and working within a context of family. It is equally legitimate to choose a celibate life, a gay life, serial relationships without children or marriage, or any variation of these. The issue for a healthy adult is not which choice she makes but whether it reflects her true desires and is carried out with integrity. This book, including the practices, is meant for straight and gay readers, marrieds and unmarrieds, friends, companions—anyone trying to love someone and be happy.

How do you know whether you are cut out for a relationship? Look at the following categories and see which most accurately describes you.

Essentially not: Some hard-wired trait prevents me from succeeding in relationships. Examples: introversion so extreme that I cannot tolerate togetherness for very long, mental derangement, active addiction, misogyny or misanthropy, criminal maliciousness or dangerousness.

Existentially not: Some of my traits keep me from succeeding in relationships, but these are changeable—it will take a commitment of time and work. Extreme and mild examples: I have had no success at relationships, and each one is worse than the one before it. I have to have things just so. I am in an intimacy-defeating cycle and do not seem able to break it, for example, as you get close, I run. My buffed and bantam ego reigns supreme; I cannot be wrong or corrected, let anyone else be first, or let anyone hurt me without severe reprisals. I cannot—or choose not to—be faithful to one person. I become stuck; my unhappiness in a relationship leads neither to changing nor to leaving. I prefer the pain of staying together unhappily to the pain it takes to end the relationship. I have a low desire for sex or require such unusual forms of sexual satisfaction that normal sex does not interest me. I seem to have a low or no capacity to forgive. A relationship does not truly, consistently, and enduringly fulfill my deepest needs, values, and wishes but is a choice I make in reaction to societal or family pressure. I am just as glad to see a partner go as stay. As of now, I require 75 percent of my waking hours to be spent alone.

Some people see this issue in extremist terms: we either are or are not cut out for relationship. In reality, we can combine apparent opposites. We can know our own comfort level and design our commitment level to match it. We do not have to fear that someone will take over the oval office of our life and mind. We can decide the size of the foothold a partner can have in our psyche. This happens in two ways: we know and respect our deepest needs, values, and wishes, *and* we find a partner who agrees with them and willingly joins us in them. The words "consenting adults" says it all: two people who are truly adult and truly agree can work out a pleasing plan.

Qualified Candidates

Once we make our relationship choices in an adult way, a prospective partner who is unavailable, nonreciprocal, or not open to processing feelings and issues, becomes, by those very facts, unappealing. Once we love ourselves, people no longer look good to us unless they are good for us.

A person is a candidate for a relationship when he is able and willing to give and receive love, to handle feelings, to make a commitment, and to keep agreements. He can show the five A's in ways that are pleasing, satisfying, and noninvasive. He can forgive and let go of his ego long enough to work problems out amicably and fairly most of the time. He follows a reconciliation (not retaliation) model in his interactions. He loves you for yourself not as the latest woman to fill the slot in his life marked "female." (Rebound relationships are especially dangerous in this regard.)

A suitable candidate will probably meet the following additional criteria:

- Lives reasonably close by
- Has no distracting ties that make true commitment impossible, such as another relationship in progress, an old relationship unfinished, a divorce pending, a parent to be cared for or consulted (children do not represent an obstacle unless they require or are given so much attention that he is tied codependently to their needs and has no life of his own)
- Has no active addictions
- Has no overpowering political or religious obsessions
- Wants children if you do or does not want them if you do not
- Has the sexual capacity, accessibility, and interest to satisfy you or can work on it within the relationship
- Has no disability with respect to money (e.g., cannot earn, spend, share, save, lend, contribute, receive)
- Is your friend and not just your sex partner; loves your company and is compatible
- Shares interests with you

- Is on a fairly close intellectual par, so you do not have to play down your vocabulary or acumen
- Is not looking for the ideal woman/man (To need the ideal woman is not to want a real woman—the only kind out there!)
- Does not appear to you to be ideal; you are not so infatuated that you cannot see his shadow side
- Has done at least half the work it takes to be healthy in life and relationships
- Satisfies the ruthless criterion that applies to all significant choices: that a relationship with him reflects and fulfills your deepest needs, values, and wishes
- Can and loves to focus on you in an engaged, lasting way (*How do I know this is happening enough?* You can remember the last time it happened.)
- Meets with the welcoming approval of your personal trio—your head, your heart, and your gut

Do these criteria fit your prospective—or current—partner?

What Are We Up To?

Every day the real caress replaces the ghostly lover.

—Anaïs Nis

It is now clear to us that completed transactions from childhood settle into a state of rest in our psyches. By contrast, unmet needs and incomplete transactions, like unfulfilled dreams and wishes, clamor for completion all our lives, hovering over most of our relationships. Thus, we have to learn how to finish our old emotional business on our own when a partner will not finish it for or with us.

What are we up to when we look for a relationship? Our apparent agenda may be the opposite of our real agenda. We have a conscious agenda when what we say we want matches what we set out to do. For instance, we say we want a relationship and we mean it, so we are willing to make a commitment. A secret agenda, on the other hand, is usually unknown to us. We have a secret agenda when we actually want the opposite of what we say we want. For instance, a woman who says she is looking for a partner becomes especially interested if a man seems unattainable. Once he becomes attainable, however, she loses interest quickly. The clue to a person's true agenda is always in how the transaction ends. In this example, the woman's real agenda—genuinely unknown to her— is not to find a partner but to conquer one and then to no longer have to want him.

Here is another example: Piers presents himself as looking for an intimate partnership. His secret agenda, however, is not to find adult intimacy, which scares him deeply. His fantasy of intimacy is to be held and cared about physically, but he is not so concerned about what his partner gets from him. Interestingly, when Piers locates someone, either she is just right and not available or she is available but not quite right. This makes him seek further. He is disappointed but fully convinced he is looking for intimacy and not finding it. In reality, though, he is spinning his wheels.

Piers's agenda is secret even to Piers. He may be terrified of closeness. He may feel compelled to repeat an original and now habitual disappointment with women. His actions and frustrations show him where his work is, but will he ever do it? How many women will be blamed, how many relationships will go sour before he sees? If he doesn't acknowledge his pattern, Piers will never know his own agenda, how it disables him from intimacy, how it relates to issues in his early life, or how to do the work that will free him from self-defeat.

Peter, unlike Piers, has a sincere, open agenda and no secret agenda. His fantasy is to hold and be held by someone who does not have to be perfect. When he locates a prospective partner, he asks himself, "Is she available, does she approximate what I want, and are we warming up to one another?" If she is unavailable—no matter how attractive—he doesn't waste his energy but passes her over. Peter bases his level of responsiveness on his intuitive powers of assessment. In a partnership, when beset with obstacles and conflicts, he works through them with his partner, the way an adult in a committed relationship does.

Piers and Peter illustrate the distinction between willing and wishing. To will is truly to want something, to choose both the goal and the means to goal. This means accepting the work and the risks involved in seeing something through. To wish, on the other hand, is only to be enamored of the goal. Piers wishes for intimacy; Peter really wants it.

Both Piers and Peter may marry. Peter chooses a partner wisely; marriage truly suits him. Piers eventually marries someone with whom he can continue the game of hide-and-seek. He marries because that is what one does, making the big decision before he really knows himself. Finding a match is usually easy for people like Piers because more people are drawn to apparent openness and availability than are drawn to authentic openness and unavailability. Piers, then, will have many more candidates to choose from than Peter will. This is not because the candidates are foolish but because they are afraid. After all, the real thing can make demands and hurt, and it is certainly unfamiliar.

There is one final quality to assess in determining availability. A writer needs to know whether his computer is equipped with enough random access memory—RAM—to hold the volume of material he has to work with. Likewise, processing conflicts in relationships can take a great deal of emotional energy, so we need to know whether we have enough random emotional energy to work on the kinds of conflicts that arise in a relationship and whether our partner does also. For example, if your prospective partner has deep issues of sexual confusion and inhibition because of incest in her past, this will require serious, long-term work on both your parts if you want a happy sex life. Are you willing to do this work? Is your partner? If not, you are undertaking a project you cannot finish. Working in personal therapy or in a support group may help, but if you cannot carry the freight of your personal issues, no amount of love will create enough wind for your voyage. *The commitment to work through problems as they arise is the only sign that we truly want full intimacy.* Only that commitment makes a difference, not good looks, not empty words, not what we seek, not even what we find. An adult knows his limits, addresses them, and expands them wherever possible. That is the equivalent of candidacy for an intensely real relationship.

Even if we did not find the five A's in childhood, we can find them— and give them—in a truly intimate adult relationship that allows a no-holds-barred exchange of feelings. Not all healthy relationships offer this, of course. Some partners want only a light, undemanding companionship, while others want to share their deepest feelings and experiences both past and present. Both styles are acceptable, but it is important for us to know whether a prospective partner is seeking the same style relationship we seek. Conflict happens in both kinds of relationships, but in the former it is dealt with lightly and passed over as are the gruesome dramas of one's past. In the latter, however, conflict is addressed with ruthless directness and processed with what might be unpleasant, messy feelings. We grew up seeing both models in the movies of the 1940s and 1950s: The light and lovely companionship of Cary Grant and Myrna Loy in *Mr. Blandings Builds His Dream House* was quite different from the blood-curdling, storm-and-truth intimacy of Marlon Brando and Kim Hunter in *A Streetcar Named Desire.* If we want Mr. Blandings's dream house, it would be best not to board the Desire streetcar.

One way to know whether someone is open to working on a relationship with you is to give him this book. Notice whether he even reads it, reacts negatively or positively, and most of all, wants to discuss it and even practice its suggestions with you. Reading and working on this book together is also useful if you are concerned that your partner has stopped growing.

Full Disclosure

> I snore loudly, drink exuberantly, work excessively, and my future is drawing to a close. But I am tall and Jewish and I do love you.
>
> —DAVID O. SELZNICK *proposing to Irene Mayer*

The first requirement for trust and commitment is telling the truth. We sometimes do not share our feelings and reactions with a partner because we sense that she cannot receive the truth from us. Only when the relationship is over do we let go fully with all we have stored up and always wanted to say or show. Then we find out how inhibiting the relationship was for us and how afraid we were of the full truth, ours and others'. We feared saying what the other was afraid to hear. We were missing out on the five A's but putting up with the deficit to maintain the bond and avoid winding up alone.

But we can say and hear anything when we trust the loving intent and loyalty of another. In the holding environment of intimacy, we can allow the truth to emerge without fear, shame, or embarrassment. Such trust flourishes when partners are committed to working on themselves. The personal information we exchange then is not scary but becomes grist for the mill. Thus, commitment to personal work is the equivalent of commitment to intimacy. And since self-disclosure entails letting go of ego, a spiritual practice figures in, too.

In the meantime, we may want to make a disclosure of some kind so a new partner may know what she's getting into—but only if we are open to the partner's feedback, because it will certainly lead to that. The paradox is that self-disclosure leads to more self-knowledge. What follows is a somewhat humorous example of how truth-telling might sound:

> Our relationship seems to be getting serious now, and I'm happy about that. In the interest of keeping everything clear between us, I would like to share some things about myself. I'll begin with the qualities that are less appealing and then go on to others that may be more encouraging.
>
> I want so much to love and be loved, but I have to admit that my fears make me fight it tooth and nail once it gets close to happening. I can only be loved by someone flexible enough to allow for such inadequacy. In fact, I can't be depended on for perfection in any area.
>
> If you can only love someone who meets your specifications as a perfect mate, you won't want me. If you have a rigid definition of love, I won't fulfill it. I don't have a history of getting it right.
>
> Most likely, I will not come through for you as often as you would like. I am often combative, especially when I notice that intimacy is beginning to happen. I may not always listen or even try to understand. I may not always be there for you when you need

me. I may not accept you as you are. I may seduce you with my looks, my charms, my words, or sex, and then I may not deliver!

I look self-sufficient, but that is a facade. Underneath I am needy, scared, bereft, and lonely. I may lie or hide my true feelings; I may run from yours.

I may try to get you to do things for me or give me things. Those are my ways of getting you to prove that you love me.

I may want a relationship for narcissistic reasons: to have you there for me when and as I want you. I may not be available for a true exchange. I may not welcome someone who comes with personal requirements. I will have to learn how to honor them, and it may take time. Do you have time?

I have noticed that with my distressed childhood background, the hill of relating slants quite steeply. I may be seeing one or both of my parents in you and may try to get you to give me what they gave me or could not give me.

I may try to control you. You will have to be on your toes to catch me in my many slippery ways of manipulating you. And if you do catch me and confront me about it, I may be so scared that I lash out at you for standing up to me. I may not be able to handle your freedom or your choices. I am jealous and even paranoid at times. It may be intolerable to me that you have close friends.

If you require someone who won't ever make you cry, I'm the wrong one for you. I could hurt you.

You can only love me as I am, not as you need me to be. I'll disappoint you again and again as long as you expect me to meet your criteria. You can only love me unconditionally and with no guarantees that it will pay off to do so.

On the other hand, I can also offer you some valuable things, more valuable than what money can buy (which I may not always have much of). In each of these, I acknowledge my limitations and my commitment to work on them.

I know who I am, and I'm not ashamed to admit what I know. At the same time, I know it's in me to lie or hide to protect myself.

I'm working on myself. I'm looking for ways to love more authentically. I do this by trial and error, by asking and doing, by falling and rising, by busting myself and letting myself be busted, by being and becoming.

I want to love you the way you want to be loved, and I welcome your telling me how.

I'm always scanning my behavior to see exactly how I am controlling and demanding. And though I often don't notice, I welcome your saying "Ouch!" When I see how I offend, I make amends. I may hurt you, but it will never be with malice, only through oversight or because my scared ego is strangling my wish to be kind.

I'm trying to feel safer with vulnerability, with letting the truth come out, no matter how threatened it makes me feel. This is a work in progress, nowhere near completion. Perhaps you can even hear me opening right now in this honest—and embarrassing—presentation of myself. I'm not trying to look good. I want to be good enough to love honestly. I want to be transparent so that you can help me know where my work is.

Go by my performance not by my promises; review my history by calling my former spouses, partners, lovers, and friends. Then look for signs of change. Decide with your eyes wide open; give an informed consent.

I won't disappoint you if you know me as a fallible human being with love to give and not much practice in giving it consistently but with a commitment to keep practicing. I can only be loved with all my faults, my efforts to amend them, and my failures to amend them. Accept me as I am, and love can happen between us.

I can only be loved by someone who loves me for my frailty, the extent of which will keep surprising both of us. I can only be loved by someone who loves me with my arrogant ego, with my shadow, and with all the scar tissue of my childhood. I can only be loved by someone who, like me, has let go of the belief that anyone can be perfect for anyone else.

It will take guts and perseverance to be with me. You will need arms that can hold a frightened inner child without losing respect for the outer adult. You will need eyes that can glimpse the terror that sometimes hides behind a mask of rage. You will need a heart that can bear pain and loss without losing trust in the love that is trying to find you.

I have lived too long in the past of "not enough" and the future of "not yet." I feel readier than ever for love in the here and now. I've fallen in love before, usually with an image of an ideal or a projection of a fantasy partner. But this time, I'd like to rise and stand in love with the real you. This time I will be working for a grade report on the five A's. Perhaps this is how we will not miss, you and I, love's many-splendored thing.

I close with these favorite words from *Twelfth Night*: "I have unclasped to thee the book even of my secret soul."

P.S. Don't be fooled by my eloquence. Sometimes I can be pretty rude.

I have come to recognize that being trustworthy does not demand that I be rigidly consistent but that I be dependably real. . . . Can I be expressive enough as a person that what I am will be communicated unambiguously?

—CARL ROGERS

Sexualizing Our Needs

Players and painted stage took all my love
And not those things that they were emblems of . . .
Now that my ladder's gone
I must lie down where all the ladders start
In the foul rag and bone shop of the heart.

—W. B. YEATS

St. Thomas Aquinas was once asked if Adam and Eve had sex before their fall in the Garden of Eden, before ego became the driving force of human choice. He answered, "Yes! The intensity of pleasure is not excluded from the state of innocence; only the fever of lust and the restlessness are." Perhaps from this thought we begin to see what sex with the five A's might be like: the primary motivation for each of us is to bring pleasure to the other; there is no goal; we allow for shifting levels of arousal throughout the lovemaking; we continually check in with one another through eye contact, smiles, and hugs.

There is actually a physical basis for a connection between nurturance and sexual fulfillment. The pituitary hormone oxytocin is released in the cuddly moments following sex. Oxytocin works on the mammary glands to stimulate the release of milk in nursing mothers. It seems that nature intended sex to be connected with nurturant tenderness, as if, in love, we breast feed one another's hearts.

Needy sex carries that delectable charge, the thrill of involuntary sensation and irresistible force, the anticipation of ecstasy, *la forza del destino*. The lust with a must exploits our unconscious habits and longings. It is sensation (physical autonomic reaction) not feeling (physical, emotional, intelligent response). Sex based on charge is stimulating and sensational but does not include the authentic depth of feeling requisite to intimacy.

We sometimes seek a sexual relationship not to share an adult passion but because we believe that a sexual response from another person fulfills our unmet emotional needs or even grants us a sense of security. We may feel we are simply looking for sex when we are actually seeking to be personally received and confirmed with the five A's. When we sexualize our needs in this way, we are recruiting our genitals for tasks they are not designed to fulfill.

Sex is a trickster. It can feel good no matter how unfulfilling or troubled the relationship. Sex can even survive unscathed in the midst of abuse or anger. This is not a skill but may signal a severe disability and confusion in self-nurturance. As Euripides sardonically writes in *Medea:* "If your life at night is good, you think you have everything."

Because sex leads to bonding, problems with sex in a relationship may increase with the fear of intimacy. Anyone who fears commitment will run when he senses the growing bond that forms automatically as sex matures. The running can take the form of a breakup or an uproar (anger, infidelity, addictive behavior, and so forth).

A relationship based solely on sex, rather than on a fulfilling friendship that includes sex, can turn to ashes in the years to come. Such relationships can endure thirty years of marriage, but they will be stale, non-nurturant, and sorely regretted. *An adult makes the transition from attraction as charge to attraction as choice.* He does not repress the charge; he enjoys it. But he does not get hooked into a melodrama because of it. The duller the inner life of people in relationships, the more sophisticated their search for thrills—for sensation without feeling. Some people have only had sex as sensation. Perhaps this is the definition of superficial.

As we become healthier and more adult, we no longer seek sex for joy but share sex because of joy. When there is happiness in our inner world, we give up the frantic search for happiness in sex. In fact, we give up desire for anything outside ourselves because there is nothing outside ourselves anymore, only ever-expanding oneness. We allow sex to be ordinary, taking up no more room in our life than our genitals do on our body. All this is exemplified in the story that follows.

Walter, age forty, is a contractor happily married to Wanda, age thirty-six, with whom he has three children. Wanda is everything Walter has ever wanted in a wife: sensible, solicitous, faithful, nurturant to their children, financially careful, immaculately clean, and undemanding in sex; she even makes stuffed cabbage exactly like his mother's. Their home life is tranquil and stable, notably free of alcoholism, abuse, gambling, debts, or marital disputes. Walter and Wanda have a strong and permanent bond. Neither of them has thought or would ever think of divorce or separation.

But unbeknownst to Wanda, Walter has, for the past two and a half years, carried on a torrid affair with Wilma, age twenty-nine, one of the secretaries at work. They share late-night, muffled phone calls, afternoon assignations at motels two towns away, and surreptitious rendezvous on desolate beaches. The excitement of their liaison is fueled by a sexual abandon neither of them thought possible, which they intensify further with the occasional use of recreational drugs.

Wilma sometimes cries and rages about her subordinate role in

Walter's life, and she sometimes threatens to reveal their secret, striking an agitating fear into Walter. But he also stokes the flames under the cauldron with his possessive and paranoid jealousy about her. The high drama of it all makes their every moment together adrenaline-rich. It makes Walter feel that he can't be as old as his actual forty years. For her part, Wilma feels her presence in Walter's life as a never-ending thrill—a fact brought home to her even more clearly the night he recited an Emily Dickinson poem to her that he heard in a class on relationships that he is taking with Wanda:

> Wild Nights—Wild Nights!
> Were I with thee,
> Wild Nights would be our luxury!

Unbeknownst to both Wanda and Wilma, Walter has, since his army days, found himself mysteriously drawn every few months (or sometimes at shorter intervals) to the porno movie arcade where he will stare with rapturous fascination at the images of the beautiful but slatternly women on the soiled screen showing and doing their all for him. He masturbates compulsively during these furtive moments, always apprehensive that he may be recognized upon entering or exiting this "palace of dim night," as Shakespeare says.

Walter, it turns out, is protected from deep feelings by a well-trained body. At the first sign of loneliness, dejection, or fear, his hormones come to his rescue, producing an urgent inclination toward sex. Walter imagines this to be true sexual desire, but it is actually a conditioned reflex, a response to the scary stimulus of an unwanted feeling. All Walter has to do is choose. He can writhe in Wilma's fiery embrace or slink into the sleazy anonymity of the arcade. Walter has a magic wand that rises to any occasion.

Walter's split-level house of relationships shows how deeply unintegrated his sexuality is with the rest of his life. But he does not see it this way. He congratulates himself for still having so much libido to burn—a sign to him of unaging manliness. Wanda fulfills his need for legitimacy; Wilma fulfills his need to feel youthfully virile; his porno princesses give him a quick fix. All three of these needs feel absolutely real and urgent to him. No matter how much Wanda offers, she cannot cancel his other needs. No matter how much Wilma offers, she cannot make him break his marriage commitment. Walter knows this and blames neither Wanda nor Wilma for any inadequacy. Deep down, he knows he has what he wants—all the way around.

When Walter attends family gatherings, he feels lucky to have a wife as wonderful as Wanda, but he also feels guilty about his secret betrayals of her. When he falsely signs the register at a motel, he feels lucky to have such a passionate lover waiting, but he also feels ashamed. When he enters the arcade and sees the lonely desperadoes who lurk and linger there, he feels lucky that he, at least, has real relationships to go back to, yet when he leaves, he feels self-disgust as well.

But Walter swallows back the guilt and shame and never thinks of himself as inauthentic because, for him, okayness is a balancing act. As long as he can keep all three of his worlds separate and two of his women happy, he is in control. And since for him mental health is all about control, he thinks he doesn't need help or have anything to process. He can live on for years as he does today—untroubled, in his three-story house of cards.

An interesting note about this story: I have read it to my classes over the years, and every time, without exception, most of the men in class see Walter's arrangement as perfectly justified and enviable, whereas the women find it unacceptable. Where do you stand? Read this story to your partner and friends and compare your reactions to the story.

Such Longings

We may feel our life is meaningless if we are not in love with someone or not in a sexual relationship. If so, we discredit ourselves and miss out on all the rest of what our life is about. When we feel the absolute need for a one-to-one love relationship, we are really meeting up with a strong need for personal work on ourselves. Our longing for that special someone, the be-all and end-all of our lives, also distracts us from our spiritual practice of compassion, the broader love that is our real focus and destiny as enlightened beings.

It is not that erotic and intimate love are not worthy human pursuits, only that they seem to work better if we approach them with mindfulness. We *relate* to our desire for love mindfully by feeling it fully, witnessing how it changes and where it leads us, and accepting that it may or may not be fulfilled soon. The painful alternative is to become *possessed* by our desire, so obsessed by it that perspective deserts us and we see only the inside of our own head, like a prisoner who sees only the walls of his cell and takes them for a four-cornered world. Then we are unconscious of how desire works or how it can serve as a means to psychological and spiritual maturity.

To reveal our longings to a partner is to trust that he will understand, hold, and mirror them as perfectly legitimate. That validation is what we long for even more than fulfillment. Sometimes our longing is so strong and the partner of our dreams is so long in coming that we settle for sex as if it were love. Fortunately, copious touch with scant love will cloy quickly. Such cloying may be a gift that directs our psyche back to the path of wholeness.

The healthier we become, the more we want only the combination of love and holding, not the ruptured abridgments that come from strangers who offer one-night stands or sex for money. The more respect we have for our own sexuality, the fewer chances we take that will stunt or blunt it. When we save sex for love's purposes and for as long as love takes to get to us, it serves us and others as a means to more love.

> Sex is not a game. It gives rise to real enduring emotion and practical consequences. To ignore this is to debase yourself and to disregard the significance of human relationships. . . . An active sex life within a framework of personal commitment augments the integrity of the people involved and is part of a flourishing liveliness.
>
> —EPICTETUS (translated by Sharon Lebell)

Destiny Plays a Part

> I will prepare myself and someday my chance will come.
>
> —ABRAHAM LINCOLN

Synchronicity is meaningful coincidence that directs us toward our destiny. Something, we know not what, is always at work, we know not how, but we do know why: to assist us in becoming free of fear and open to love. Thus, finding a partner does not entirely depend on our efforts. Other forces over which we have no control come into play.

James is a young man who ardently wishes he could meet the woman of his dreams. He thinks he is doing all the right things: frequenting singles bars, answering ads, joining dating services, and approaching bridesmaids at his friends' weddings, where he has often been an usher or best man. But nothing works. Frustrated and disheartened, he decides to give up for a while and let nature take its course.

In another part of town, Jamie wishes she could meet the man of her dreams: one with tender feelings, interests similar to hers, a sense of humor, reasonably good looks, and basic sanity, which nowadays seems to mean not being a chain saw murderer. She sometimes goes to singles bars with her female friends, briefly joined a dating service (with no luck), and has often been a bridesmaid at her friends' weddings, but recoils from wedding-party members making liquor-brave advances. Like James, Jamie has given up the search and is letting the universe take over, though she is peeved that it is taking its own sweet time.

James is a cyclist who follows a routine path along the beach each day. One day, for no apparent reason, he decides on an alternative path through the botanical garden. Although he usually rides hard without stopping anywhere, on this occasion he allows himself to stop and smell the flowers.

Walking his bike through the garden, James is absorbed by the beauty of a single file of cactuses between two footpaths. He suddenly notices that one of the cactuses has bloomed with a stunning white and gold flower. He knows that this species blooms only once a year for one day, so he is drawn to the flower with an instant and intense focus, and he spontaneously bends down to savor it.

At that same moment, on the parallel path, unnoticed by the fragrance-intoxicated James, a young lady who works in the botanical garden also bends over to experience the blossom's sweetness. Their heads crack together painlessly but resoundingly, and they find themselves suddenly staring into one another's eyes with only the fragrance of the cactus between them.

James says, "Well, we really put our heads together for that one, didn't we?" Jamie responds with a smile, "Yes, you might say it was a true meeting of minds!" They soon discover they have more than just a sense of humor in common. They both love cactuses, grow them at home, know all the Latin names of the various species, and are clumsy enough to have been stuck often by the cactus needles—a sure sign of readiness for relationship.

A year later, James and Jamie finally make it to a wedding at which they are neither usher nor bridesmaid. On that joyous occasion, with no prior knowledge of how they met or of their mutual botanical interest, the poetry-loving minister quotes these lines from Gray's "Elegy": "Full many a flower is born to blush unseen / And waste its sweetness in the desert air." That sweetness is not wasted on James or Jamie. It lasts beyond their extraordinary romance, through their normal conflicts, and into their soul-mated lives.

The events in this story are all coincidences, but they are also an example of synchronicity—that is, a meaningful coincidence or opportunity—because they further and fulfill the personal destinies of two people. Is it a coincidence that both James and Jamie have similar bad luck at dating? Or does that happen to preserve them for one another? Is it a coincidence that James, "for no apparent reason"—that is, not because of left-brain logic but because of stirrings from a deeper, intuitive source—takes a different path and decides to stop where Jamie works. Or was it "Something always at work, we know not what"? Did Jamie take this job because only through it would she meet James? When James took an interest in cycling, was he gearing up to meet his future bride? Is it coincidence that both of them loved cactuses from childhood? Or did their relationship invisibly begin many years before they met, with events repeatedly lining themselves up to make a meeting possible? Was something unknown at work carefully and mysteriously incubating a union that would be good for two good people? Is the universe so reliably on our side, and to such a minutely calibrated degree that it makes a cactus bloom on precisely the day two people might see it and thereby meet? And how did the minister, who knew many poems, choose that one for the wedding ceremony? A great poem benefits a long list of people in future generations. Does a poet write his poem for them?

Reason and logic pronounce all this mere coincidence. But something fearless and boundless deep in the psyche honors it all as part of a larger design of the universe, articulated in and for the fulfillment of individual lives. Notice how in the story, a personal fulfillment required nature's participation. Human methods—dating services, ads, and so forth—had failed, so something greater than what ego could construct stepped in. It is easy to see why people in all ages have believed that love rules the universe.

Synchronicity means that nothing and no one exists in isolation. The pasts of James and Jamie met in the present and initiated their future. The series of coincidences that led to their meeting unite the layers of time; indeed, synchronicity means that times coalesce. Notice also how synchronicity is visible only in retrospect. We cannot anticipate or plan it, and we can disregard it.

The names of our young couple sound similar, but that is not synchronicity. It is simple coincidence since it is not something that leads them to their destiny. Synchronicity happens when events, nature, and people come together to make what was hidden manifest, what was unconscious conscious, what was in us come through us, what was beyond the scope and grasp of ego become fully and easily accessible. It can be the single event that makes all the difference. And it even makes flowers bloom in the desert.

Practices

COMPARING WISHES • Do you have (or want) a face-to-face lifestyle or a side-by-side lifestyle? If you hold your hands so that one palm faces the other and then hold your hands side by side so that both palms face

utward and your thumbs almost touch, you see an illustration of the
two styles. If both partners agree on either style, life can proceed
smoothly. If one partner wants one configuration and the other wants the
opposite, conflict arises. Keep one palm facing inward and the other outward, and you will see the problem. Then hold your hands back to back,
with your palms on the outside. Now you see an example of distance.
Which fits your situation?

If your relationship is "palms outward," are the hands still touching at
the thumbs, or have they drifted apart so that now you and your partner
do less and less together? This happens frequently in relationships in
which the accent is on individual freedom. Compromises in the course
of a relationship are healthy. When the compromises favor autonomy,
distance may grow. When the compromises favor bonding, intimacy
grows. Where do you stand in this relationship? Meditate on these questions and bring your answers to your partner in a way that implies no
censure. Make a plan to align yourselves more satisfactorily. If you cannot do this, consider asking a therapist for assistance.

Adults design a lifestyle in keeping with the percentages of their needs
for alone time and for togetherness. For example, if each of you want to
spend 50 percent of your time together, that logically necessitates outside interests. Ask these questions in your journal: Do you have interests
and hobbies in place? Do you resent your partner for having an outside
focus? Has all this been figured into the equation of your relationship?

CAN YOU ANSWER YES TO THESE QUESTIONS? • Can your
partner focus on you and respond to your needs? Is your partner working on herself? Does your partner love you sanely—rather than need you
desperately? Does she keep agreements? Does she collaborate with you
to handle obstacles together? Are you happy together more than half the
time? Can she handle your strength, your feelings, and your freedom?
Do you feel loved in that special way that is unique to you, and do you
feel it bodily? Can you share with this person what troubles, excites, or
delights you?

If you can see the difference between a good partner and a not-so-
good one but cannot let go of someone who is wrong for you, if you make

the same mistakes with one partner after another, or if you are the victim of—or the volunteer for—one predator after another, ask a friend to be your *relationship sponsor*. (We all need consultants, advocates, and sponsors throughout life.) A relationship sponsor bird-dogs your relationships and has to pass on every prospective partner, since you have admitted that your powers of assessment are weak. This unusual suggestion may make more sense than it first appears.

USING THE "EVEN THOUGH" TECHNIQUE • Answer yes or no aloud: Would you eat strawberries you knew to be deliciously sweet if you were seriously allergic to them? Would you eat mushrooms that looked delicious if you knew they might be poisonous? Would you attempt to read a book you knew to be interesting if it was written in a language you did not understand? Would you stay in a relationship with someone you loved if you were unhappy?

Would you blame the strawberries for your allergic reaction, the mushrooms for poisoning you, or the book for confusing you? Do you blame your partner for your unhappiness?

Let's look closely at the questions. Each object offers advantages but with one serious deficit. Adults can let go of the good things if the one bad thing outweighs them: "Even though I'm crazy about you and you're a great provider, I can't stay with you while you are such a liar and refuse help." Are you seduced by the advantages of a partner while you disregard, deny, or lie to yourself about his disadvantages? Or do you act according to the full truth, even though you wished it were not so? How much self-nurturance and tolerance for grief it takes to disregard that "even though"!

Here are the words of an adult: "Even though you please me sexually, even though we have been together so long, even though I don't know whether I will ever find someone else, I have to let you go because you do not meet me at my soul/adult level."

Here are the words of a codependent: "Because you please me sexually, because we have been together so long, because I don't know whether I will ever find someone else, I can't let you go—even though you do not meet me at my soul/adult level."

Come up with your own "even though" statement using the adult formulation: "Even though . . . since . . . I therefore . . . " Apply this technique to having nothing in common, for example. We may love someone and know she loves us, but if she is not a peer or even interested in the things we are passionate about, an unremitting loneliness will eventually strangle the relationship. Would you dare to say, "Neither in soulful friendship nor in authentic intimacy do you offer what I need. So even though you meet many of my needs, I have to give you up because you do not provide the essential ones."

VOWING/DISAVOWING • Ask yourself: Am I making a vow of commitment to my partner while disavowing an essential partnership with my inner Self? Ask these questions of one another: Can we find ways to work separately on the inner discoveries we both need to make before we can fulfill one another's needs adequately? Can you grant me that space? Can I allow you that space? Can I trust that you will still be there for me when I come back intact and ready to be in touch? Will I be there for you also? Or will our own urgent childhood needs or our desire for drama be so intense that we will vitiate or scuttle this whole soulful venture? Are we genuinely committed to doing the work it will take to safeguard our relationship?

TAKING A SEXUAL INVENTORY • In your journal write an inventory of your own sexual behaviors over your lifetime and ask yourself if you are satisfied with them. How did and do you find or give mirroring in sex? In your present relationship, do you look for and offer fusion without intrusion—closeness without possessiveness? Have you done so in the past? Do you sexualize your need for love? Are you looking for the one who can take you to the outermost limits of pleasure or the one with whom you can mutually touch an innermost core?

OPENING WINDOWS • Draw a square room, seen from above, with a picture window in each wall. Mark the windows with the directions of the compass. Under the word *east,* where the dawn appears, write three things in your life that are now arising. Under the word *west,* where the sun sets, write three things in your life that are now ending. Under the word *north,* write three things in your life that stabilize and guide you, as does the North Star. Under the word *south,* write three things in your life that evoke your spontaneity and creativity—the kind of opening up that can happen when facing a warm southern exposure. You have drawn a picture of a healthy human mind, a clear space that opens in all possible directions without obstruction, distraction, or fear.

Picture yourself sitting mindfully in the center of the room, alternately turning toward each of the four windows. The challenge is to face your east with a willingness to take hold, to face your west with a willingness to let go, to face north by staying with your spiritual practice, and to face south with an ever-enthusiastic creativity in the reinvention of your life.

Now ask yourself if your psyche is a room with openings like this. How do you look out of each of the windows? Who helps open your windows and who attempts to close them? Who says "Whoa!" when you say "Whee!" and who says "Go!"? Journal your responses and share what you discover with your partner—and with whatever guardian angel or bodhisattva who stands beckoning outside each window.

4

Romance:
The First Phase
of Relationship

✦

Einstein once said that if we were to look deeply into nature, we would understand our human story. Nature is fashioned of cycles and our lives are part of nature. Yet we try so hard to make love stay put, to make it stay the way it is or the way we want it to be. This is like expecting a rose to always be in full bloom, with no phases of budding or fading. Nature's style, by contrast, is simply to stay through changes and trust in rebirth. Our human goal is much the same: to stay with love in all its vicissitudes, from bud to bloom to barrenness and then back to bud. "This bud of love, by summer's ripening breath, shall become a beauteous flower when next we meet," says Shakespeare's Juliet. The rose of relationship grows petals in romance, thorns in conflict, and roots in commitment. *We can accept this rose with all its petals folded and unfolding and with its thorns that pierce but also open us.*

All our experiences and levels of interest follow a bell-shaped curve: ascending, cresting/flourishing, and descending. This geometric figure asserts the given of human existence: that all things change and nothing is permanent. Thus, rising interest in someone crests in romance, descends into conflict, and finally reposes in commitment. Love is authentic when it stays intact through all the phases of change. Relationships based only or mainly on physical or sexual attractiveness cannot negotiate such curves.

The rising phase, by definition, leads to a pinnacle, the crest/flourishing phase, which beguiles us into an illusion of immutability. Mindfulness is suspended in favor of attachment. That sets us up for the conflict stage. The dialogue and processing that happen in the healthy resolution of the conflict stage pave the way for commitment. One phase naturally evolves into the next. The curve resumes and rises again in new ways.

It is comforting to know that relationships go through stages. If they always stayed the same, wouldn't all of us be bored and boring? The phases of human relating involve passages of origin, change, loss, grief, and renewal. They are not linear; we drift in and out of them, and their order varies. The purpose of relationships is not to endure (which in Latin means "to harden"). When we try to hold on and endure, the relationship changes and leaves us behind. When we accept and work through changes, we evolve along with the relationship. Our goal, then, is to enjoy changes and grow because of them, to use them as a crucible for personal transformation. Not working through changes together makes the relationship a cauldron instead of a crucible.

Stages characterize all human experiences—not only intimate relationships, but also the parent-child bond, friendships, and religious affiliation. The model of the heroic journey is based on the same phases: departure, struggle, and return. The hero departs from—breaks out of—containment. He separates and, after a struggle, seeks reunion at a more mature level. Unless we disrupt the process, we instinctively go through these same stages. They are blueprints in our psyches. When one stage is omitted, we are left with a lacuna inside. Later in life this lacuna becomes a vacuum that demands filling. For example, everyone seems to need a period of obedience during childhood. It is a feature of healthy attachment. Children reared with total freedom from limits enter adulthood with a "limit lacuna." They may later join cults or movements with rigid rules because a vacuum inside them has long needed filling. The vacuum affects their judgment so that they may not see that the cult's extremism, like anything that discourages growth, is dangerous.

Why must the journey of love go through the three phases to be complete? That is what it takes to be able to give and receive the five A's fully.
They have to bloom with intoxicating fragrance, be blown about by the
winds and become more firmly rooted, and then reseed themselves for
an ongoing future. Thus, in romance two egos meet two ego ideals in an
ideal love. In conflict, two egos meet one another in conflicted love. In
commitment, two persons meet in egoless love.

Rising in Love

Romance is one of the high points of a human life. It is a deeply moving experience of joy, to be cherished and appreciated with gusto. The
reason for the joy is simple: the five A's are flowing in both directions. We
are giving and receiving them at the same time and with the same person.
This is what makes romance so tender and sweet and so desirable no
matter our age or history. The trick is to enjoy it as Ulysses enjoyed the
sirens' song, with full pleasure yet safely. We want to be thrilled but not
wrecked as we sail into it. This means enjoying romance as a full and un-
inhibited participant but also as an amused and sober witness. We fall,
notice how we are falling, and catch ourselves all at the same time.

Romance is real but temporary. We are in love but only with a projection of ourselves, not with a true other. It is not yet an I-thou relationship, only an I-mine relationship. The shadow side of the other has not
yet appeared at this point. We see only the mirror side; the ego has found
its ego ideal. As psychiatrist Irvin Yalom says, "In romance you see the
reflection of your own beseeching gaze." A mirror can only give us an
image not a reality, after all. This is the origin of the expression "Love is
blind." But love is not blind; it sees and faces all. It is romance that can
be blind, when it sees only what it needs to see. Thus, we can be in love
without really loving—without being committed to giving the five A's,
which we can only do with a real person we know fully.

But none of this represents a fault in us. This is how humans love.
Projections are established precisely to be transformed. Images are road
signs to reality. The shadow does not have to come before the light. Most
important, *in romance, however blind, we are being seen in our full po-*

tential for lovableness. Romance gives us the chance to be appreciated in all our grandeur. This is as normal and legitimate as it was in our infancy when so much fuss was made over us. A lover's ideal view of us is not false: It reflects who we really are deep within. If romantic love is healthy, we are mirrored in a way that can enrich our self-esteem.

On the other hand, our first romance may make us a seductive promise: Our original unmet needs, the five A's, can at last be met! This is probably the cruelest illusion of romance: "I can get off scot-free. I do not have to mourn what I missed in the past; I can slip by that stage and find what I lost right here in your arms!"

There are two ways to approach romance. I can meet you in love while we both remain standing or I can fall for you. To fall is to get hurt or to be in danger. Falling in love sounds like falling into quicksand. The Romance languages do not say it this way; English does. We also say fall into a coma, fall from grace, and the market falls. To speak of falling in love implies powerlessness, permission to go out of control, to be foolish, to become the slave of emotions, to be carried away as if no longer in possession of one's faculties. Love is a conscious tie not a bewitching trance.

Yet real love does not happen by accident. Neither are we its passive victims. It requires a choice in response to an attraction. Granted, we have no control over the attraction or our initial reaction to it. But thereafter we choose one response after another, and for those choices we are accountable. We always have the power to make them responsibly and consciously. Strong emotions lead to strong transformations if they can be experienced mindfully. This means relating to a feeling rather than being possessed by it. Attraction simply happens, but love is a process that requires our participation, a unique way of fulfilling ourselves through giving and receiving at the same time. It is a form of rebirth.

Romance blooms in wish, love in will. In romance, we think: "I am contained by you and you by me. We are finding—or rediscovering—the five A's we sought in our primordial relationship. I always wanted to be loved like this. Now that I have found it, I never want to let it go, and I believe I will never have to because of how powerfully I feel it flourishing between us. It feels so strong it must be real and will never change." Actually, the heart of the illusion is contained in this last statement: *strong* does not mean changeless, only emphatic.

Romance is an exuberant and valuable experience to the extent that we can enjoy it without becoming addicted to it. Romance is the best way to begin a relationship and is a bridge to a more mature commitment. But we should not be surprised that it does not last. It is a phase that builds a bond, but it is not a mature bond in itself. Nature designed romance to bring couples together to mate, to propagate the species, and to support one another. In this phase the sexual energy is high, and so is the adrenaline. However, continued high adrenaline levels lower our immune response and eventually undermine our health. Thus, in the best interests of our health, romance lasts only as long as is needed for sex and procreation to occur.

"I know he can be affectionate and close because he was that way at the beginning" is a statement that fails to take into account the power of romance to suspend our fears of closeness and occlude our shadow side so that nothing gets in the way of sexual union. We can be fooled by how things look during the romance phase and feel betrayed when the glow fades and our partner returns to his original fears, priorities, addictions, and basic instincts. Our partner was not lying, only falling *in* love and falling *out* of his usual character. He will revert back to character after the ball is over. It also follows that when someone is afraid of closeness even in the romance phase, he has a fear stronger than his instinct. Here we have to be doubly wary.

As adolescents, we were taught that the way to tell we are in love is by our loss of control, our loss of will, and a compelling sense that we could not have done otherwise. This falling in love contrasts with the reality of rising in love with conscious choice, sane fondness, intact boundaries, and ruthless clarity. We were taught that some enchanted evening we would feel fascination and fall head over heels for someone special. But that kind of reaction is actually a signal from the needy child within, telling us what we need to work on, not directing us to our rescuer.

We may strongly believe in the specialness of our exciting relationship. We say, "It's never been this thrilling," "I've never had sex like this," "We have a lifelong bond," "You are like family, and we will never split up," or the now popular "We were together in a former life." These are all the bells and whistles we thought meant, "It's true love so go for it!" Actually sentiments like these are the alarms that tell us to be careful and point to where our work is rather than to a shortcut through our work. How much we can misunderstand when confronted with the chance to have all five A's fulfilled!

But we can also feel the excitement of romance without deluding ourselves or setting ourselves up for disappointment. How do we tell the difference? Healthy relationships lead to interdependence and unhealthy ones to dependence or domination. The electricity of the false lead takes the form of a shock. The electricity of the true lead is a steady current. A shock leaves us depleted. A current keeps moving through us.

None of this denies the splendor of romance and being in love. Being in love is a highly charged spiritual state. It makes for contact with the higher Self because it forces us to let go of control, makes us love unconditionally, and gives us ease in forgiving. Such an atmosphere makes a heaven here on earth, something like the holding environment we knew or missed in early life. The sense we get of the otherworldly, of an irresistible force, of time standing still, of something afoot that is not in the ego's control are all signs of the numinous. The words we use to describe romance, like religious words, come from the vocabulary of the supernatural. Phrases like "His face glowed" or "I never saw her look so beautiful" speak of a spiritual reality that simultaneously transcends and embraces our sensibilities. Even the trite expression "together in another life" gives a clue to our intuition that something powerful and full of grace is happening within us. Romance transports us to the world of soul, so it is no wonder that a partner may be called a soul mate.

To feel grief at the end of this phase is appropriate, but we usually fail to address, process, or resolve it. Often when "the thrill is gone," it turns into blame and disappointment, or even anger. Paradoxically, when couples grieve together, they strengthen their bond, and the first grief they confront together may very well be the ending of romance.

Gratitude to one another for support in handling and negotiating the stages leads to growing commitment and mutual respect. Letting go of one stage and shifting into another establishes an adult connection to a basic condition of our human existence, the ever-changing and ever-renewing nature of reality. "The biggest risk: to trust that these conditions are all that I need to be myself," said Taoist sage Han Hung.

There is actually a phase preceding romance. It is *investigation,* the subject of the previous chapter. This is the time to ask for disclosures of all kinds, to ask about past relationships and what worked or did not work in them. A wise gold miner wants to see what pans out before he yells, "Eureka!" No one would think of hiring someone for a job without checking references and carefully interviewing the candidate. Yet we often hire on a partner without much inquiry except from parts of our body that do not always make the wisest assessment or from feelings that say more about our neediness than about another's gifts.

Here is a paraphrasing of a scene in the 1938 film, *The Adventures of Robin Hood:*

> MAID MARION: How do you know you are in love?
> BESS (*her servant*): Your legs is weak as water. You lose your appetite.
> MAID MARION (*later, to Robin Hood*): I do love you, but for now, I'll remain here to be of service to England rather than come with you.

Bess describes the romance that disregards everything except sensation. Maid Marion describes the love that respects both passionate feeling and sensible priorities. She has not fallen in love and become less conscious of her life purposes. She has risen in love and become more conscious of her deepest needs, wishes, and values. Love is our identity, and healthy loving is how we put it into practice.

When Romance Is Addictive

> I may not hope from outward forms to win the passion and
> the life, whose fountains are within.
> —SAMUEL TAYLOR COLERIDGE

On first glance, relationship addiction looks exactly like the romance phase of any relationship. The difference is that romance is phase-appropriate, whereas addiction defies flux and attaches itself to the crest of excitement and drama. Romance moves on; addiction halts and para-lyzes us. Addiction is unsatisfiable because, ultimately, satisfaction flows from moving over the curve of exhilaration to repose while addiction tarries at the crest of excitement.

Addiction also feels exactly like unconditional love: "No matter how she betrays me, I still love her even after all these years." ("All these years" is a clue that there has been an interruption of the natural cycle.) But in addiction we are hooked rather than bonded. Remember *Wuthering Heights*? It is thought of as a great love story, but it is really a great addiction story. Kathy cannot let go of Heathcliff though he hurts her so often; Heathcliff cannot let go of Kathy, and yet neither can he stay with her.

We bond in adult relationships the way we did in early life. If there was dysfunctional bonding then, we may be sitting ducks for an addictive bond later. A cellular memory from childhood triggers a cellular reflex in our adult selves. From the empty seascape of our past we peer out, looking for an island paradise. We find it and overvalue it, thus undervaluing the authentic needs of our marooned selves. Those needs are the five A's, which are meant to be fulfilled in mindful love. In addiction, we are seeking a gross version of one of the A's, for example, a need for affection or touch that feels like a need for sex.

There is yet another problem with addiction: *Both rejection and acceptance fire up our adrenaline, so both are equally exciting to the addict.* Thus, adrenaline hooks us both coming and going; we are still hooked when we are breaking up. We can get a fix from our partner even as we leave him. Addictions of this kind often follow the pattern of "seduce and withhold." First I attract you to me and then I withdraw from you. Next, you do the same to me. In any addiction, we feel fear and desire at the same time. Freedom from these is spiritual enlightenment, so addiction is a spiritual illness, especially since it involves seeking that which is beyond change. How well this line from a poem by Rumi expresses it: "My erotic delights with my special someone weave every veil in my life."

Relationship addiction is built on projection. In *Gone With the Wind*, Scarlett O'Hara says, "I loved something I made up. I made a suit of clothes and fell in love with it. And when Ashley came along I put that suit on him and made him wear it whether it fitted him or not. I would-n't see what he really was. I kept on loving the pretty clothes and not him at all." At the end of the story she adds, "I've loved something that does-n't exist." By saying this, she is courageously implying "I was not the vic-tim of a projection. I take responsibility for creating and maintaining it."

However, Ashley was in on it. A sex or relationship addiction is never one-sided. One party may be more strongly attracted than the other, but the more desired one is, the more loved he feels and the more control he has over how much he will or will not respond. In such a painful bond (or rather bind), one person takes the direct approach and the other resorts to the indirect pattern of seduction and with-drawal. We are never alone on stage. The other cast member is always playing his part.

The object of our addiction becomes our higher power: We have turned our will and life over to a partner. Such reverent focus on one per-son and his story and/or on how to fix him can occupy our mind for years. All the time that could have gone into a spiritual practice or en-gaging in creative pursuits or dancing freely is instead absorbed by the great fixation. This is how the "rapacious creditor" of addiction plun-ders our potential and can drag us into "an incomprehensible demoral-ization," as the Alcoholics Anonymous program puts it.

In healthy relating, we connect but do not attach. We can only really possess what does not possess us. This leads us to the great irony of ad-dictive relating: We attach and thereby do *not* have. The second irony is that the more we rely on someone for security, the less secure we feel. It is sometimes frightening to realize how much impact a partner has come to have on our life and thoughts. We may react in counterphobic ways like getting even closer! Men addicted to women can ask, "Have I been using women to hold up a part of me that I doubt can stand on its own?"

In the mysterious trajectory of our lives we may go from one focus or crisis or fascination to another. Eighteen years of focus on our children, twenty years on a career, fourteen on a physical addiction, seven on an obsession with a man or woman—perhaps each of these periods, some overlapping, serves to keep us safely away from our own inner life. We fear having nothing between us and ourselves. Our inner life feels like a terrifying void when it is actually a tremendous spaciousness. Mindful meditation opens us into that space and shows us it is not so scary after all. Mindfulness is freedom from the fear that drives addiction.

Addictive longings do not have to signal weakness, illness, or inadequacy. All of us are candidates for them. The fact that unrequited love increases our desire is a given of relating. In fact, the archetypal theme of addictive attachment recurs all through history. We are not alone in the mystery of joy-with-pain. Compassion for ourselves and viewing our predicaments with amusement and without shame, remorse, or malice will give our human drama a happy ending.

Addiction seems to have very little to recommend it, yet it has many positive dimensions. Through our addictions we find out where our childhood losses are, where our needs were unfulfilled, where our pain is still unhealed. We find out just how needy, bereft, and forlorn we are. We uncover our true condition and become quite humble. This is another way addiction can be a path to spiritual awakening: It helps us let go of ego, that habit of believing that we control our emotions, wishes, and needs. The pain of the addiction is not bad or useless then. It initiates us into greater depths of self-understanding. A synchronous universe recruits just the person to make us fall hook, line, and sinker if that is the only way we will go on the journey. It is the same universe that concocted a tornado so Dorothy could find her powers.

Finally, addiction reveals our perseverance, our stamina in going for what we want. Though its object is inappropriate, our single-minded focus on it shows that we have it in us to pay close attention and to reach out. These are wonderful skills for intimacy that simply wait to be relocated.

What a poignant paradox about us humans: We seek what we cannot receive from those who are unable to give it. We hold on desperately and ineffectually to that which cannot provide what we think we need.

> In pain with you, and yet I could not go.
> I stayed since nothing better came along.
> I loved you by default or just for show,
> My life a whistled flat unechoed song.

I groped for notches in our dun abyss,
And looked for more in lonely only less.
I shunned the path adorned with signs to bliss,
And stood the loyal ground of wait or guess.

It took the tender you to shift the scene,
Bold arsonist beneath our tinder stage!
I then in friendly fire to earth careen
And from our props and ashes disengage.

I begged you long with such a silent ache
In fear of, wish for mercy for my sake.

What Love Feels Like

Every [adult] relationship recreates the original relationship.
The discovery of love is a re-discovery.

—SIGMUND FREUD

Love can be confused with clinging that is welcomed by the other,
sexual desire that is satisfied by the other, or neediness that is fulfilled by
the other. Love can even be confused with dependence, surrender, con-
quest, submission, dominance, gratification, fascination, pain, or addiction. I may feel that I love you because you love me, or will not leave me,
or will not let me feel lonely, or will not make me feel anything. I may feel
I love you and say it with passion when I am mostly reacting to the way
my own needs are being met through you. I may say "I love you" and
simply mean "I am attached to you and it feels good."

We can mistake love for the good feelings that arise in us when we are
in love or because we believe that we posses the other. The five A's are
antidotes to such motivations. They are authentic gifts, difficult to give
sometimes, that require and create a caring heart, an other-directed love
free of narcissism. In real love, I feel and show an unconditional regard
for you, and I love you even in the times when you do not fulfill me. My
love can survive the periods when you have nothing to give. Such love
reflects not my own neediness or expectations but a commitment to a
path of giving and receiving.

We may expect or demand all through life that people show us love in just the way we first felt loved: making a fuss over us, standing up for us, showing physical affection, and so forth. One of my earliest recollections is of Grandma and how I felt loved by her simply by the way she stayed with me while Mother was at work. She sat beside me as I worked on my Dick Tracy puzzle; she listened to the radio show *Baby Snooks* with me. Unlike Mother, she had nowhere to go. All my life, at family gatherings, I find myself sitting in the midst of my elderly aunts, seeking that uniquely familiar comfort that comes to me only from older female presences. My rational mind tells me they are old and not so mobile and that is why they stay so long in their seats, but no mind can dissuade the cells in my body from what they feel. On my trip to England, I loved tea time, when no one gets up and goes away. Even that felt like love to me. I know I have sometimes importuned friends to spend an evening at home rather than go out. *I am always trying to arrange for the love I remember and want. Am I still equating greater fuss with greater love?*

When our demands for love become compulsive or insatiable, we have a clue that we doubt our own lovability. For when we doubt that we are lovable, we often need to see it proved over and over. This seems narcissistic on our part, but viewed from a more compassionate perspective, it may suggest that we have a low opinion of ourselves. Indeed, the need to be seen as special can be a compensation for feeling unloved.

How can we overcome our self-doubt? Through a simple practice: act lovingly. *Lovability is actually the other side of the coin of loving. People who believe they are lovable are people who love.* This involves letting go of ego, but it also requires a unique frame of mind: When any conflict or issue arises between ourselves and someone else, we ask not how to win but how to summon up a loving intent and how to act on it. Our immediate question is "How can I be as loving as possible in this circumstance?" When we show the five A's to others, they feel loved and at the same time see us as lovable. To shift our focus from concern for personal victory or vindication to an attempt to be more loving brings us bliss, and that bliss is the best context for letting go of ego and releasing the five A's.

When excitement comes from learning to invent love in every thought, word, and deed, we soon realize that we are lovable. Because of our new manner we love ourselves more, and this leads others to love us more. Then we stop insisting that others show us how much they love us. The bottomless pit inside has been filled at last, or at least it has become less annoying. An exuberance replaces our neediness. When we give what we miss, we no longer miss it as much. Letting love through us makes *us* the path love takes. Then we can ask for love in return rather than demanding it compulsively. We may find ourselves receiving what we need when we no longer have to have it.

One result of our freedom from neediness is that our love expands to touch all people. We love others because we and they are intimately connected to one another. There is not a separate self anywhere in sight. Compassionate love is the natural response to the human predicament of suffering and the human truth of interdependence, and it lightens the burden of finding a special someone. We are less needy as we grow more responsive to others' needs. As Alexander Pope said: "Man, like the generous vine, supported lives; / The strength he gains is from the embrace he gives."

Practices

SIMPLY NOTICING WHERE I AM • In commitment two healthy egos relate. Three stages characterize most human enterprises, including intimate or family relationships, educational and religious affiliation, and any long-term interest. See if you can locate yourself in one of these three phases of relating, which correspond to the heroic journey:

Attachment	*Detachment*	*Integration*
ROMANCE: TWO EGO IDEALS EMBRACE	CONFLICT: TWO SHADOW EGOS COLLIDE	COMMITMENT: TWO HEALTHY EGOS RELATE
Mutual dependence	The struggle to assert personal needs and wishes	Interdependence, with ease and compatibility in need fulfillment

Enmeshment, no boundaries	Establishing boundaries and independence	Mutual honoring of boundaries
Hero leaves	Hero struggles	Hero comes home

To be fixated in the attachment phase makes for regression, clinging, or addiction. Am I there? To be fixated in the detachment phase makes for problems with authority and distancing. Am I there? To move from phase to phase makes for serenity and opens us to concern for the wider world. This is how healthy relationships heal the world. I choose to be here.

What do the five A's look like in your current phase?

COMPARING ROMANCE AND ADDICTION

Romance	*Addiction*
A phase	Ongoing
Need fulfillment with a sense of contentment	Neediness felt as a bottomless pit
Desire for contact	Desperation for contact
Proportional	More is given as less is received
Usually egalitarian	Often hierarchical
Reciprocal	One-sided
Has a future	Has no future
Feelings of satisfaction and joy	Feelings of not being able to get enough
Secure	Always in doubt
Anticipation for the next meeting	Painful or intolerable absences
Increases self-esteem	Lowers self-esteem
Loose boundaries	No boundaries
Both partners relating to each other	One partner being possessed by the other
Begins the challenging journey to love	Becomes a vicious cycle of pain

Use this chart to find your present way of relating. If you seem to be addicted, write journal responses to these statements: You keep chasing someone who does not want or respect you. You stay with someone with whom problems are unworkable or who is abusive. You are with someone who depletes you. You keep going back for more where there is only less. You can never get enough of what you do not need. You forget that if you can't get enough, you don't need it. You are trying to redo and undo a parental bond simultaneously. You are in an addictive bond with someone who is also addicted to you. You are the object of someone's addiction.

Is the following something you might say? "When I cannot let go, I do not even know whether I really want to stay. As long as I am infatuated, I lose my boundaries and sometimes even my self-respect. I will take anything just to have my fix (him or her). That is what I lose in my addictive attachments."

UNCOVERING DENIAL • In romance we want what the other can give. In addiction we crave what the other, and anyone, cannot give. Recovery from a one-sided addiction can begin with freeing ourselves from denial: "I don't want to know what you are unable to tell me. I cannot see that what I want is not what you offer. I am not really looking at you at all but at my own neediness." Freedom from the addiction will mean ending our confusion. Speak up first in your journal; then when you are ready, to a friend; and then face-to-face with the object of your addiction.

DEALING WITH OBSESSION • An addiction is an obsession in our minds and a compulsion in our behavior. We feed the addiction when we let the obsessive thoughts spill over into compulsive actions. To allow the thoughts and not act on them is a crucial part of letting go. Thus I can think about you every minute while driving on the freeway, but I do not have to swerve off at the next exit and call you just to hear your voice. To free ourselves from addiction is to pass up the chance for a fix.

It takes work to see what we are really up to. Say this aloud if it applies to you: "Actually, every thought about the person who loved me or left me is really a plea for attention from the wounded non–grown-up part of me now reexperiencing its original pain through this newest version of the Dad or Mom who abandoned me, either physically or emotionally. Obsessive thoughts about this present man are actually urgent pleas from my past. Great pain in present relationships gives me a perhaps unwelcome clue to the family ties broken long ago. This person only triggers the old—but ever-current—predicament."

SEDUCING AND WITHHOLDING • When a person assumes the style of seduction and withholding, she seduces because of her terror of being alone, abandoned. She withholds because of her terror of being close, engulfed. She is at the mercy of a panic that creates a reflex response. In the context of such dread, the seduction is not a lie nor is the withholding a punishment. We can respond to a person who acts this way toward us with compassion rather than retaliation. Ask yourself silently: Can you stand aside as a nonjudging witness and support her in finding help to work through her fear? If you are the one seducing and withholding, how about seeking help in a twelve-step program or in therapy?

FINDING THE PROGRAM • In my practice as a therapist, I keep finding that addictions almost always have to run their course. Marcel Proust seems to support me in his comment that obsessive love is "like an evil spell in a fairy story against which one is powerless until the enchantment has passed." Therapy and spiritual practice help, but they cannot compete with an active flow of adrenaline. An addictive relationship promises and delivers an excitement that most people interpret as true aliveness. It is hard to let that go, especially when so little comes along to take its place. Addiction is ultimately a form of pain, as old songs say: "Who can give me what you give me?" "Who can make me feel this way?" "Who, oh who, can hurt so good?" "There will never be another you!" "Why must your kiss torture me like this?"

At the same time, are there tools that work? A twelve-step program is a powerful spiritual tool for people addicted to relationships, to romance, or to a specific person. By working through steps adapted from the Alcoholics Anonymous program and having a sponsor, one can free oneself from addiction. Recognize that all your efforts are not quite enough to deliver you from this kind of pain. You will have to turn yourself over to a power greater than yourself. Who or what is that for you? In Buddhism, it is the buddha mind, that consciousness in and beyond us that transcends ego. In Judaism, it is the breath of God. In Christianity, it is Christ consciousness. In the Jungian view, it is the archetypal Self. These are all archetypes of the assisting force of grace, help that comes to us from beyond our effort or control. A twelve-step program helps us form a link to that power that's higher than ego, a refuge from the snare of addiction.

Spiritual practice can thwart the ego's frail but stubborn attempts to control others and make the world obey our wishes. What is required is meditation on the three marks of our existence: impermanence, suffering, and the fact that a solid self is ultimately an illusion. We cannot see any of this without someone else's help, especially while we are addicted, which is why we need a program with a sponsor, a spiritual practice with a teacher, and a course of therapy.

Approach addictions not with shame but with a spirit of inquiry, wanting to know how your mind got caught in desire. This means finding a way to accept yourself without the mindsets of judgment, fear, blame, attachment, biases, or defenses—that is, mindfully. See the other as a buddha, here to show you where your work is, just how far astray you can go from the path, and how you can return to it.

DEALING WITH AN UNREQUITED CRUSH • Someone becomes powerfully attractive to us and may not feel the same way toward us or even notice us. At first a crush feels enjoyable and encouraging. Then the pleasant fantasies become tormentingly obsessive, and the bashful desires become fevered needs. The joy of longing gives way to the anguish of longing. An urge becomes an ache. Before we know it, we are so thoroughly hooked that our life is hell without contact and heaven with it. We find ourselves manipulating the other or our circumstances to satisfy our craving for contact. We lose our self-respect. This self-diminishing progression of addiction is described in Alcoholics Anonymous literature as "cunning, baffling, and powerful." We are baffled by how fast and intensely we were swept away. Our happiness is now entirely in the hands of the one we have to have. We are stuck wanting things to be other than they are and powerless to make them so. Addiction is the trickster that gives the ego its comeuppance.

Thus, it is a spiritual issue in that it transcends the powers of ego, as well as a psychological issue in that it suspends the powers of the healthy ego. Both spiritual and psychological work are required in response.

In your journal examine these questions: Which of the five A's are you seeking? How did you fail to take care of yourself in this drama? What are your feelings, and are these the very feelings you have been avoiding for a long time? How can you feel them now in ways that are safe and cathartic? Is this a time for therapy?

If you are presently in an addictive relationship (or on the spectrum from crush to infatuation to possession), consider these statements and affirm the ones that may apply you: I admit I can no longer control my thoughts, feelings, or behavior in anything related to him. I keep acting as if I can be my normal self around him while noticing I cannot. I am scared all the time. I try to act normal when I do not feel normal. I *act*. He is bringing me, by his presence and by his absence, into direct, unavoidable contact with the extent of my neediness for the five A's. He won't let me get away with self-evasion any longer. This is not about how much I need a man but about how much I have abandoned myself. I use the image of the needed man to get me off the hook so I won't have to face the challenge of self-nurturance, my only legitimate goal. Everything about me and everything I ever did only serves to make me think I have lost or disappointed him; that is how much I distrust and deny my lovability. And all the while, I do not dare show him the most lovable thing about me, my honest vulnerability. I believe or guess he cannot handle it. I might scare him off if I reveal my feelings. I am afraid of his fear because it might make me lose him, so I stifle myself.

Here are some practical hints for people with unrequited crushes: Do not suggest elaborate plans for time together when he only wants to chat occasionally. Do not propose carefully crafted plans and invitations that seem innocent or polite but are meant only to induce more contact. More contact is more distraction from the only healthy focus for an addict: your own work on yourself. Use affirmations such as "I am letting go of my craving for contact with Jim" and "I am letting go of my attachment to Jim." Join a twelve-step program.

DISCOVERING WHAT AM I LOOKING FOR • Answer these questions silently as you read them: Do I have the empowering adult agenda of finding someone who grants me the five A's? Or do I have a disempowering agenda in which I seek someone to take care of me or be taken care of by me, to do things for me or for whom I can do things, to give me things or to whom I can give things, to control me or to be controlled by me, to flatter me or even to hurt me? Which of these models or parts of them describe your present way of being in your relationship? Tell your partner what you discover.

BEING LOVINGLY PRESENT • Love is not so much a feeling as a way of being present. We show love through a sustained and active presence *with* an unconditional expression of the five A's and *without* the conditioned overlays or mindsets of ego, such as judgment, fear, control, and so on. We receive love the same way—with the five A's and without our ego interferences. In other words, love happens best in the context of mindfulness.

We can expand our consciousness of how giving and receiving love is our life purpose and the true fulfillment of our human yearnings. We can commit ourselves to a life of universal love. One way is by adopting the "with/without" style described in the preceding paragraph. It may also help to say the following affirmation each morning and throughout the day, concentrating on each word and picturing yourself acting this way. It can be especially powerful as a silent mantra, a prelude to interacting with someone or to facing a scary situation: "I am fully present here and now with all my unconditional attention, acceptance, appreciation, affection, and allowing. I am happy to let go of judgment, fear, control, and demands. May this be the way I show my love to everyone. May I be ever more open to the love that comes to me. May I feel compassion for those who are afraid of love. May all beings find this path of love."

EXPRESSING INTIMACY • Here are some qualities of an intimate moment: warmth, physical closeness, respectful touching, eye contact, unconditional presence with nothing held back, vulnerability, openness, candidness, relaxedness, humor, a glowing joy, freedom from tension or demand, full availability, hanging out together effortlessly rather than in a planned way, no concern about time or schedules, the sense that someone wants to be here and nowhere else, and finally, that none of the mindsets of ego are engaged. Everything in such a moment is "off the record" and, as such, is immensely permissive.

In your journal, answer these questions: What are the qualities of intimacy that you experience in your relationship? What is lacking? Some people act in these intimate ways only when the relationship is threatened. Ask yourself when intimate moments happen for your partner and when they happen for you. Share your realizations with your partner without making him or her wrong in any way.

5

Conflicts

I n hero stories, enlightenment is followed by a descent into the underworld. Our journey in a relationship goes down from the summit rather than up to it. The second and usually longest phase in relationships is conflict, as the light of romance is replaced by the shadow of tension. In this phase the romantic image of you gives way to the reality of you. We do not know ourselves, nor can we integrate our experience until we meet our own shadow and befriend it by struggling with it. How can we know our partner until we do the same with her? How can we love what we do not know? *If we truly know ourselves, nothing anyone else does is ever entirely strange or unforgivable.*

Romance shows the love object's bright side, her positive shadow— the untapped potential for good that we project onto those we idealize. Conflict exposes her darker sides, her negative shadow—that is, our own proclivity to meanness, abuse, or selfishness, which we project as strong dislike of those who display such behavior. Once blinded by romance, now we are free to see all sides of the partnership. We confront pettiness, lack of consideration, self-serving choices, and the arrogant ego with its need to be right, to get its way, and to avenge itself. We notice all the things in our partner that we cannot abide or hide. What was cute in romance may become acute in conflict.

This phase is a totally normal, necessary, and useful part of the process of building a lasting bond. Without the struggle it entails, we might be lost in one another and thereby lose ourselves. We need conflict in order to evolve from romantic projection to mature self-affirmation. It is the phase of love that corresponds to the detachment phase of the heroic journey.

Human experience occurs only in a relational context, and specific conflicts from our past are excavated in relationships. As a result of relating to an adult partner, we can remember our life with our parents more vividly than we ever thought possible. In the conflict phase, in fact, we cannot help but meet up with the revenants of early life. This is the phase in which we hear ourselves saying to our partner and our children the very words we heard our parents say to us long ago. This is when we carefully train our partner to help us reenact our earliest and most bitter disappointments, hurts, and losses. In this phase we instinctively bring up the issues we are now ready to grieve and reenact the past to show what happened to us and to master it with the mirroring help of someone we trust. Every passing moment in a conflicted relationship dispossesses us of our illusions, as the psyche continually adjusts itself to newly revealed truths.

The way to the center is through the extremes. We move from the extreme of romance to the extreme of contention in order to reach the center of commitment, according to the cycle of thesis, antithesis, and synthesis. Nature, too, moves from the lushness of summer to the dead of winter so that we may exult in the liveliness of spring. We can now see that relating to someone or something rather than being possessed by him or her or it is equivalent to acknowledging that the relationship will inevitably go through phases.

Finally, it is useful to realize that in the journey from romance to conflict, we move through three modes:

Ideal	*Normal*	*Low Ebb*
Best of all possible situations, in love	Routine living with no major stresses or highs	High stress, breakdown, deep depression
At my best	Adult functioning	At my worst
In this mode, you will see me being loving, heroic, compassionate. There is little need for work on myself!	In this mode, I am clear, reliable, and committed to the work of addressing, processing, and resolving things.	In this mode you will see my mean streak, self-pity, paranoia. No relationship work is possible here. Personal work is required first.

Mature people go from best to worst and back to the center many times. To accept this as a fact releases us from taking a partner's behavior too personally, from blaming, and even from fear—all ways of letting go of ego. When we are stuck in the low ebb mode—as in the mythic theme of the ship stuck in port—we need to take especially strong action, because standing still may have become more comfortable than the effort it takes to move. This is why risk becomes the hero's style.

Or to use another metaphor, nature requires the breakdown of established structures to accommodate new conditions in the environment. This means that life necessarily includes turbulence and even dissolution, the harbingers of transformation. In fact, natural systems zealously participate in their own self-transcendence. St. John of the Cross speaks in just these terms about his ego: "Swiftly, with nothing spared, I am being entirely dismantled." He does not merely say that but prays for it. Disturbance of the status quo and the dismantling of old forms are signs of healthy evolution. Nature rejoices in the sprouts of spring but is equally excited by autumn, which ensures another and richer spring. Can we see our conflicts in this same, optimistic way?

The process of evolution is wildly self-transcendent.

—KEN WILBER

Working Things Out

The difficult demands of love turn out to be the only ingredients of wholeness and adulthood. This is because we can work cooperatively with our partner to make things better and/or we can build our own self-nurturant powers if a partner fails to come through for us.

Defending our position is the opposite of addressing it. And commitment to a relationship entails addressing, processing, and resolving our personal and mutual issues. If we fear real closeness, we will run from the thought of such a process. We have to feel safe enough to look at what we may have kept hidden in ourselves or avoided addressing in our partner. Of course, most of us have the knack of not heeding what we know will require a difficult or painful response. But such denial can cost us our own sensitivity and vulnerability. And, like any virtue, the courage it

takes to address painful issues is easily accessed by practice. What follows shows how that can happen.

A leaky faucet is not a tragedy to the householder with tools and skill.
Our conflicts can have wonderful results for us if we show mutual respect and use tools that help us cooperate rather than strategies that
show we're right. To work problems out cooperatively is to turn conflict
into commitment. In fact, commitment is articulated in our willingness
to handle obstacles rather than evade them, be stymied by them, or hold
resentments because of them. Working things out is one threshold on
the heroic journey to intimacy: a painful challenge that leads to change.
When we have successfully crossed this threshold, we transform a hur-
dle into a bridge. The energy once tied up in ego competition now fuels
responsible adult behavior. We say: "I can negotiate with you, and we
can grow closer through our struggles. Our love is not about being
lovey-dovey; it is about an adult commitment to dealing directly with
our feelings and concerns."

Most of us have such a hard time being with each other, yet love involves a choice to keep working things out. When we refuse to do that or
do it only reluctantly, we do not really love anymore. We may still feel a
bond of sentiment or history or obligation, but that is not love, nor will it
be enough for happy and effective relating.

What makes relationships so perplexing is that they are not based on
logical, discursive thought but on ambiguous and confusing feelings and
needs that elude the mind and stagger the heart. Love works automatically at times, but mostly it works because we work on it. We can easily
locate what has to be worked on: Whatever does not work requires
work. Since every adult has things to work on, refusal to work is the
equivalent of reluctance to relate as an adult. And if a reasonable amount
of work has been done and no change has resulted, the relationship is
ready to be released so both parties can move on. Some relationships
will never work, and when we waste our energy trying to rejuvenate
them, we simply end up feeling depleted.

Thus, it is not selfish to want to let go of a relationship that does not
make us happy. The purpose of relating is not to endure pain. Although
pain is part of every human life, our challenge as adults is to live through

it and move past it rather than to "hover on the dreadful shore of Styx," as Shakespeare says in *Titus Andronicus*. This is not to say that we should drop a relationship at the first sign of pain. Anyone can feel the difference between endless volumes of pain and occasional chapters of it. The former are unacceptable, except to a victim. The latter are a challenge fit for a hero, one who works through pain and is transformed by it. A motto from the stock market also applies to healthy relationships: volatility in the short run but growth in the long run.

We grow in relationships when we have a program of spiritual practice that teaches us to let go of ego entitlement—of expectations and preconceived notions about what relationships are supposed to be like, what our partner is supposed to give us, or how he or she is supposed to look or behave. In spiritual practice, we also let go of old habits of manipulating and others hiding ourselves and begin to let ourselves be seen (ex-*posed*) as we are. As a result, we can cooperate with another's energy instead of needing to conquer it. We can make agreements to change, the keeping of which is the best sign a relationship will work.

Cooperation—partnership—is the heart of conflict resolution. *We are not working individually for the ascendancy of our own positions. We work together for the health and happiness of the relationship.* As in Eastern martial arts, harmonious movements take the place of adversarial struggle. This nonresistant, nondominant, nonpassive, nonviolent love arises from unconditional disarmament and thus has no place for "I am good, you are bad" or "I am right, you are wrong." If we get caught in such dualism, we project the face of an opponent onto our partner, and both of us have already lost. Free of such dualism, we alternate as teacher/student and friend/friend. But the only way to get there is by being more humbly loving than we have ever been. If both of us are merely fair toward one another, love will never begin, let alone last. Someone has to be generous first.

This may seem like giving in. But strength does not always mean assertiveness. An adult finds the balance between asserting her autonomy and acknowledging her interdependence with others. Consider Margo, for example. She is married to Evan, a loving man but one who construes any no as a rejection. This intimidated her in the first years of their marriage, when she was always conciliatory and walked on eggshells. But as Margo did the work of becoming an adult, she grew stronger. She felt compassion for Evan, with his fear and his automatic defensiveness. Evan's antennae were so sensitive to rejection, because of its force in his past, that he could not help but find it everywhere. She realized that it would help him if she were careful about how she phrased things. Formerly Margo was critical of Evan's sloppiness, using accusatory "you" statements ("You always make a mess and never clean it up") to which he bristled and exploded. Now she uses "I" statements that report her personal reactions to his habits ("I feel hurt when you make a mess in our home because it makes me feel that I don't matter to you"). Evan gets the message without feeling scolded. In such a context, a holding environment, shifts in behavior happen more easily. Processing her own fear in the light of his, she stopped tiptoeing around him. She picked up on his wavelength. Now she can accommodate his fears without having to pander to them or feel diminished by them herself. This happened because Margo is letting go of her ego and letting love in, having noticed that just the right partner came along at just the right time so she could do her work—that is, become a more understanding adult.

Margo and Evan made changes fairly quickly. In a relationship, one person may be ready to deal with an issue as soon as it comes up. Another waits awhile in order to incubate a response. We need to respect each person's unique timing and not take it personally if a partner does not respond as quickly as desired. It is like the speed at which a phone message we leave on an answering machine is returned: It does not reflect how much the recipient of the message respects us. It is entirely about his own timing. One person calls back the minute he gets a message, another waits a day or more. It is about personal style, not a question of insulting or respecting us.

Indeed, a slow response may be a good sign, a sign of slow, deliberate processing. In great drama each event is processed, while in soap operas nothing is processed. Shakespeare's soliloquies process the action that has just occurred. In melodramas, events simply pile on top of one another without closure, resolution, or transformation.

Processing experience means that we bring consciousness to it. Without it, life becomes a series of episodes, one after the next with no movement through them toward new insights and growth. Episodic living is the opposite of cohesive living. If an adult daughter of an alcoholic marries three alcoholics in a row and her worldview is episodic, she sees her failed marriages as a coincidence and laments her bad luck. If she sees her life in context and cohesively, she recognizes her pattern and its connection to her childhood. She then is more likely to explore the organizing principles of her life and look for ways to reconfigure them so that she may have healthier relationships.

To redeem our past experience, we need to see ourselves and our story in context and with continuity. To see our story this way is to see where we need work. And attempting to establish intimacy while personal issues remain to be cleared up is like attempting to construct a seaworthy vessel while at sea. First we have to make an individual commitment to address, process, and resolve our own problems and demons. Some of us have personal issues so deep that we may require many years of working on ourselves before we can relate intimately to someone else.

A commitment to processing also means a commitment to stop making unilateral or peremptory decisions. Instead, each person shares his or her feelings about how the relationship is going, each declares what feels good and not so good, what works and what may need changing, what it feels like to be in a particular situation, and how things can be done differently so that both parties are happier. When something feels good all over—head, heart, gut—it usually means that a need is being truly fulfilled.

Working things out involves two steps: articulating the truth as each person experiences it and acting in accord with it. (Frustration results when we articulate without acting.) Your truth includes your feelings about the issue at hand as well as your personality type, your shadow side, your needs and wishes, your moral standards, your life goals, your aptitudes and gifts, your limitations, your family heritage, your personal history, and the impact of your past experience on your present life. To act in accord with personal truths means making allowances for your limitations; activating your potential to use your gifts and talents; and making choices that reflect your standard, values, and integrity.

Processing leads to resolution when each person feels heard on the level of emotions, receives something he wanted, and makes an agreement that leads to change. If you and your partner cannot do this together, ask for help in therapy or from an objective friend who can mediate. (Caution: Thinking "I can handle it all" may be an excuse for fear of asking for help.) Healthy relationships use therapy to resolve conflicts that stump the partners. Therapy also means regular checkups. We would not think of omitting such consultations for our physical health but we might omit them for our happiness.

One caveat: Some conflicts do not respond to addressing or processing. Only time and grace can heal them. Similarly, heroic journeys often begin with a situation that has no solution. Such difficult situations are meant to deflate the ego's belief that it can solve all life's problems by its own will power and without relying on grace. In all of us there is something that does and something that lets. To become fully human, we need to honor both those inner powers.

> It was an unspoken pleasure that having . . . ruined so much
> and repaired so little, we had endured.
>
> —LILLIAN HELLMAN

The Past in the Present

> Remembered bouquets long since dead . . . left in my mem-
> ory the bygone charm with which I . . . burdened this new
> bouquet.
>
> —HENRI MATISSE

We humans memorialize our past. But eventually our archaic needs intrude, bill in hand, to present their unpaid claims. We deal with our past issues so that they do not come up over and over in our present relationships—or if they do, we notice their appearance and take responsibility for it. Without consciousness of our past, we may appear to be involved in an adult relationship, but underneath we are playing out a scenario from long ago. Memories of the past will arise in direct proportion to the rise of intimacy. This is because both the past and the present held out or hold out the chance to receive what we always yearned for:

attention, acceptance, appreciation, affection, and being allowed and encouraged to be who we are.

How can we tell whether the issue that is troubling us in an adult relationship is a present-day issue or a carryover from the past? By mindful self-examination. If Mother so absorbed and contaminated my experience of women, what chance do I have to see this woman as she really is? When I feel a familiar panic, experience an anger that surprises me, or react with more intensity than fits the circumstance and do not know why, then I may surmise I am not really seeing my partner's face but my mother's. This becomes especially clear when I feel more uncomfortable and hold on to pain longer than fits my situation. Only issues that carry the weight of an unresolved, abusive, or still resented past could account for such overreaction. (And in a sense, it is not truly an overreaction, since the inner child is responding to a trauma from the past that still smolders.)

All of us experience moments of feeling powerless, scared, trapped, compelled, and out of control. We are hearing the voice of the inner child calling for our attention and our adult intercession. The inner child does not know how to make her case directly, so she stammers her message through diffident acts and pitifully awkward feelings. Once we understand this consciously, we automatically become more adult and more compassionate toward ourselves. When consciousness connects our present experiences to its childhood determinants, we gain a sense of expanded meaning in our life experience. This is part of our capacity to self-soothe.

Reasoned, adult behavior at work and childish out-of-control behavior at home with my partner point to the difference between the powers of the present and past to ignite us. When the fires of the past flare up again, we treat issues and conflicts compulsively, and they seem to have an either/or quality, obstructing the opportunity for compromise or negotiation. An ordinary transaction can replicate an early scenario that still carries pain. We are usually blind to its connection to our past. Our rational mind fools us into believing that the transaction is a here-and-now fact, when actually it is also an artifact of the past, evoking grief and needing completion.

Processing grief, which makes us feel isolated, is our toughest task in life, so we try to avoid it by configuring past losses as present inconveniences. As long as we think our uneasiness has to do with a partner in the here and now, we do not have to face an old grief. Traumatic memories—always present but never known—may reside in our bodies and not in our conscious minds. For example, we may have been programmed to feel an obligation to suffer abuse and to believe self-disparaging messages, which, since they were stored in our cells, now come up as automatic reactions that pilot our behavior. For example, we may have been held down in a sexually abusive or suffocating way, and now we automatically tense up when we are hugged or even touched. We may feel the pain of abandonment as adults when we are kept waiting by the person who was supposed to pick us up at the airport. A childhood belief that we cannot do anything right comes up to haunt us at the time of a divorce. We cannot avoid that belief; it is a cellular reflex that cannot be stopped anymore than we can stop our mind from thinking "49" when we see "7x7."

We cannot, of course, avoid or permanently rid ourselves of old beliefs and reactions. But we can call them by name, and like any ghost, they may slink away when we finally shine the light on them. How do we do this? When past issues arise, they come with the sense of being real in the present. It helps to *refile* them in the mental folder of the past: "I feel this way because of something long gone that I have not fully dealt with." Next time, facing past issues will be easier, and gradually the old thoughts and reflexes will yield to the liberating radiance of consciousness.

We live in the present of this and now rather than the past of never again or the future of not yet. Touching, frightening, or humbling recollections linger in our memory a lifetime long. We are never through with the past. The humdrum yesterday yes, but not that morning long ago when someone left us so suddenly, not that afternoon someone stayed with us so loyally, not that evening someone touched us so wrongly, not that night someone wept with us so strongly. The past is not through with us. No, not ever gone the all of then, not yet shall fade the all of this.

Men and Women

> It is fatal to be a man or woman pure and simple; one must be
> woman-manly and man-womanly.
>
> —VIRGINIA WOOLF

Opposites are not disjunctions but two ends of a spectrum. Thus male and female—like mind and body—are not a dichotomy. As a man I contain a spectrum of gender identity that includes the feminine. The opposite is true for every woman. What is more, masculine and feminine qualities complement each other, and to combine complementary energies is to embrace the entire spectrum between them.

Divisions are man-made, like the wall between East and West Berlin, which not one bird or cloud ever respected. The fear associated with scaling it existed in the human mind; the fearlessness involved in demolishing it came when the heart joined in. The sharp dichotomies between men and women or between gay and straight or black and white are, like the wall, contrivances of the scared and scariest part of the human shadow. The whole point of mindful spirituality is to acclaim affiliation and defy division. Then we see differences as mere adornments to similarities, and the fear of differences fades away.

For male-female couples, division along gender lines is particularly fatal to harmonious relating. Yet the fractures between men and women are not owing to their differences but to the fact that they have not worked through their early life enigmas; let go of their egos; or learned to address, process, and resolve their issues. In fact, in Roman mythology, Venus and Mars produce a divine child named Harmony, the result of a union of love and aggression, the two central organizing powers of the human psyche. This suggests that to tolerate Venus/love and Mars/anger in a relationship can lead to harmony.

Yet such tolerance requires work; although we contain both genders, we often fear the power in the opposite sex and desire to possess or be possessed by it. In addition, the ego, which is driven by fear and grasping, can be rigid, attached to stereotypes, defensive, and conditional about love. Spiritual practice can release us from this dysfunctional ego, from being trapped in fear and desire. *There is a reality in me that transcends ego and that I contact when I am free of fear and desire. Fear and desire recede not because I give them up but because they no longer rule me.* Release from them means no longer being driven by obsession or compulsion. Our challenge is to find some of what we desire in others in our own contrasexual energy—a woman's male energy or a man's female energy—and transform in ourselves what we fear in others.

"Husband and wife are in each of our bodies," says the thirteenth-century Taoist teacher, Li Daoqun. In the Jungian vocabulary, a man's contrasexual energy is called the *anima*, while a woman's contrasexual energy is called the *animus*. The male fear of the powerful and ego-dissolving anima can turn to rage and sadism, as shown by a long historical record. The male-dominated medieval and Renaissance worlds condemned nature-wise women as witches, while violation of women by rape and violence of all kinds is a dreadful ingredient of contemporary life. Misogynist men, whose image of maleness includes dominance, come down with a vengeful fury on women and in the process desecrate their own anima. A balance of power characterizes true intimacy, which follows the model of partnership not that of hierarchy.

Maturity means redesigning our models to accommodate the full archetype: True men have warmth, caring, humor, the courage to show their feelings, vulnerability, no fear of touching without being sexual. Real men can show or learn to show all five A's. They are not always in control, not always potent, not always on top. They do not have to be violent or retaliatory. *Being a man is loving as much as this man can. As long as I hold on to being in control, I am not discovering the riches of my manhood.*

The style of addressing, processing, and resolving conflicts may be different for men than for women, so that even couples who have committed to all three may not really agree on what they have committed to. For men addressing may mean stating the problem now, getting straight to the point, getting directly to the bottom line. Similarly, processing may mean solving it now, and resolving it may mean forgetting it and going on. When quick resolution is the main priority, we may discount others' feelings.

For women, on the other hand, addressing may mean talking and talking until we know what we are talking about. This involves going around and around the issue, not as a means of avoidance but as a way of giving it our attention. Processing for women means feeling into both this and past issues. It also means having feelings heard and appreciated. As for resolution, it may easily follow from a sense of being heard and cared about, from being mirrored with love. Thus, problem solving may be the lowest priority for women, mirrored feelings the highest.

Introvert or Extrovert?

Though gender differences certainly exist, it may also be true that characteristics we ascribe to a partner's gender, or to our fears about it, actually reflect the partner's introversion or extroversion. Understanding a prospective or present partner may mean reckoning with the differences between introvert and extrovert. These two inborn psychological typologies are equally healthy. One is no more superior to the other than brown hair is superior to black hair. Indeed, the world needs both to function creatively. But the five A's are given and received differently by extroverts and introverts, as will be seen in the description that follows.

An extrovert is animated by the company of others; an introvert is depleted by it. An extrovert seeks people with whom to socialize; an introvert avoids socializing. An extrovert is in danger of burning out; an introvert is in danger of isolation. An extrovert gives priority to immediate experience; an introvert gives priority to understanding over experience. For an introvert the inner alarm of physical sensation urgently warns: "I have to get out of here." For an extrovert, the inner alarm blares: "I have to be with someone." Both these reactions may feel compulsive to the person experiencing them.

In a relationship, these opposing styles can lead to conflict. I am an extrovert; you are an introvert. I jump in without looking, and you see this as foolish. You look first and pause, and this feels to me like timidity and lack of spontaneity. When I feel bad, I seek people out; when you feel bad, you want to be alone. I believe you are rejecting me, and you believe I am invading your privacy. I want to go; you want to stay. I come home to talk; you come home to get away. I welcome questions and appreciate them as a sign of interest in me; you resent questions and find them intrusive. I reveal myself and my wishes and feelings easily; you see this as superficial or dangerous. You keep things to yourself; I see this as secretive and as a sign that you do not trust me. I need to keep talking to clarify my thoughts. You do not think well on your feet but require long, silent cogitation. In a strange town, I ask directions of someone; you look at the map to find your way.

If I am an introvert, you may be angry at me because I do not want to socialize with friends as much as you do. But if you accept my introversion as a given of my character, you will understand my need for aloneness and not take my absence so personally. In short, type is a fact not a fault.

Introverts may have learned that anger is sometimes the only way to get people away from them. This may make them look grumpy. To an extrovert, an introvert's need to get away may feel like rejection. An introvert may seek projects he knows only he can do, or he may have learned to find some time away through watching TV, going out for a smoke or a drink, sitting at the computer, and so on. When an inner alarm tells the introvert he is "peopled-out," he has to doze off or dissociate. This again may feel like rejection or abandonment to a partner. Even his hours of reading without looking up may be thought of as a form of distancing.

Some people are so deeply and extremely introverted they are better off not being in a relationship. An extrovert who marries an introvert may have to realize that a partner's need to be alone may be stronger than his need to be with the other. An introvert is well trained in self-reliance and less well trained in cooperation, and he may feel guilty about this and about his time alone. An introvert is a minority, a left-hander in a right-handed world, and so he may always be uncomfortable to some degree. Like all minorities, he has a unique set of givens and choices to face if he is to relate well to others.

An introvert is easily misunderstood, and so he will often have to explain himself and his behavior or he will feel like an outsider. When he feels the need to pull back, he will have to ask for time out rather than withdraw unilaterally—which may feel to the other like rejection. An introvert will also most likely have to fight for the right to be himself. When his partner needs him to be other than he is, he will feel pressure to be false in order to be loved. An introvert may even feel so lonely, or so afraid of being lonely, that he learns to act like an extrovert in order to obtain approval: In his true self he is an introvert, but he has learned to be an extrovert in his false self.

Part of the work of becoming healthy is knowing our authentic psychological type and then making choices that are consonant with it. If we are introverted, we need a job that does not require us to work with the public all day. If we cannot think on our feet, we need to ask for time to make a decision or give an opinion. In any case, we acknowledge that as introverts we automatically have to be more assertive than most people, even though assertiveness doesn't come naturally to us. The trick is to find a balance between asserting ourselves and being true to ourselves.

The question arises: If introverts and extroverts require such uniquely tailored responses in daily life, are they also to be loved in diverse ways? These charts may help:

The Five A's	How to Love an Introvert	How to Love an Extrovert
Attention	Show an awareness and loyalty that she will not interpret as scrutiny or intrusion.	Take frequent notice of and an active interest in what she is doing.
Acceptance	Validate her need for distance without taking it as rejection.	Show that you are on her side and at her side.
Affection	Let her give the signal for closeness of any kind.	Be frequently demonstrative— physically and verbally—of your love.
Appreciation	Express gratitude for and recognition of kindness, and a willingness to accommodate you.	Make frequent mention and on special occasions a special mention of your recognition.

| Allowing | Respect her need to be alone until she asks for time together. | Join her and share in her interests in some way as often as possible. |

The Five A's	*How an Introvert Shows Love*	*How an Extrovert Shows Love*
Attention	I notice a lot but do not say much.	I notice and tell you what I see.
Acceptance	I am not critical.	I actively want you to be yourself.
Affection	I will get close only when I feel ready.	I always love to give physical touches.
Appreciation	I always feel appreciation but show it only when to do so is not embarrassing or required.	I show appreciation with words and actions that are meant to evoke a response from you.
Allowing	I grant full freedom to you and your lifestyle.	I offer to include you in what matters to me.

Practices

GAUGING HAPPINESS • If you are unhappy in a relationship, it may not be your partner's fault. It may be because you do not believe you have a right to happiness. Consider these signs of such a belief. Which ones apply to you? Write for three minutes about each of them as you experience them. Then formulate the opposite of each statement and write about how it might apply to you.

- I believe my purpose in life is not to enjoy but to endure.
- Others always come first.
- Loyalty to others comes at the expense of loyalty to myself: I am motivated by indebtedness, history, guilt, pity.
- I continually deny my self-protective instinct.

- I cannot speak up about or change or leave a relationship because that might hurt someone else. I say to myself, "You made your bed, now lie in it."
- Before I claim my own power or fulfill my needs, I must first make others happy.
- As long as I keep my partner happy, my relationship is successful.
- I am willing to let a partner injure my heart.

If my parents or cultural or religious beliefs modeled the style described by these statements, does that mean they still rule my psyche? When do I take over the Oval Office of my own psyche?

ADDRESSING, PROCESSING, RESOLVING • Make a commitment to yourself and to your partner that you will bring up all your concerns rather than covering them up or disregarding them. To address an issue is to make the implicit explicit. This includes what gnaws at you from within or what you keep feeling but fail to mention. All human feelings are legitimate. To accept the validity of one another's feelings is to listen to them with the five A's, without ego defense or argumentativeness. To address an issue is thus a choice to be more loving since it is a respectful commitment to one another's truth.

If you find it difficult to know the full implications and nuances of your feelings, here is an easy and entertaining technique that may help you. Take the one word that best describes what you are feeling and look it up in a thesaurus. Read the list of words under that entry to your partner, commenting after each word whether and how it fits. For instance, you may feel frustrated, but after a visit to Roget's, you realize that includes plaintive or bitter disappointment and perhaps an expectation that was too high!

To process an issue means to explore and work through the implications of an event and the intentions behind the behavior of the principals. This happens both with attention to feelings and in search of a change. Here is a simple three-step technique for processing events: Say what happened as you saw it; express what you felt then and what you feel now; explore what is left to be resolved and followed up. Doing this on a daily basis makes for fewer problems and less stress.

Resolution begins when you make the agreement to change a pattern of behavior so that a dysfunctional cycle can be broken. It is complete when a new and more fulfilling style of relating has become second nature. For adults, there is then no abiding grudge or bringing up of the past. Full resolution is ultimately the automatic result of full addressing and processing. An unwillingness to address, process, and resolve issues may be a sign of despair, the death knell of a relationship.

REPORTING IMPACT • Anything our partner does that gives rise to a feeling in us deserves a report about that feeling and its impact on us. We say, "When you did/said this, I felt this." We say it mindfully—that is, without blame or expectation; it is simply information. No one causes a feeling, but actions and words are the catalysts of feelings. The other partner listens—without offering an immediate solution or becoming defensive—and asks, "What do you fear? What do you believe about me or about this? What do you want from me right now?" Get together with your partner and repeat these questions back and forth for five minutes. When we are committed to working on ourselves, we welcome the questions raised in this book and the information about ourselves that we learn from answering them. Are you beginning to welcome them?

FINDING A CENTER • Successful agreements require responsibility. In a relationship in which one partner is substantially more responsible than the other, it can seem as if the one needs to get the other to change. For instance, one partner may always show up exactly on time and do exactly what he plans or promises to do no matter what the circumstances. The other may be lackadaisical or irresponsible, not following through on commitments and not dependable. The highly responsible partner may blame or try to fix the other with little success. One person errs by excess and the other by defect. The virtue is in the middle, the mindful center—not on either side of the fault line. The goal for one partner is less compulsion and for the other more reliability. If only one does the work and changes, he can still accept his partner and see her with amusement and compassion, no longer with complaint. Being in the center makes us feel so good, we feel less of a need to get others to change. Consider this chart:

An Irresponsible Extreme	The Mindful Center	A Compulsive Extreme
Not enough energy	Stillness	Too much energy
May ask what all the fuss is about	Sees all that happens with gentle amusement and sincere compassion	May blame his partner and feel disrespected when she fails to live up to his definition of responsibility

Are you and your partner opposites in this regard, and if so, how are you handling that? Do you insist that the other change, or can you see and admit when something is a personal issue?

PROTECTING ENERGY • Silently ask yourself the following questions about your life at the moment:

Am I in a relationship with someone who presses down on my lively energy like an incubus, an invisible yet nonetheless weighty presence? (Our lively energy is the energy that wants to light us up from within and light the world through us.) Why do I allow anyone to limit my energy? Is it a habit from early life? Am I with someone who depletes my energy? Am I with someone who delights in my energy and encourages its release? Here are some suggestions that may help reignite the light of your energy if it has failed:

- Let go of control over others. Every unit of energy that we invest in changing others is subtracted doubly from our own lively energy. We may be controlling not so much to prevent bad things from happening as to prevent ourselves from feeling grief, anger, or disappointment.
- Ask for what you want 100 percent of the time. Say yes to yourself twice as often as you say no, but be willing to compromise.
- Choose reconciliation over ongoing feuding. Never retaliate or use violence no matter what the provocation. Correcting others' inappropriate actions requires instruction and compassion not punishment and retaliation.

- Confront or turn away from those who bring you down, put you down, or try to control, abuse, or scare you—no matter how close they are to you.
- Express your creativity; begin a project you have only imagined.
- Be yourself sexually—responsibly, of course. This may include enacting the fantasy or lifestyle you have kept inside too long.
- Cultivate a sense of humor, learning to play and to see the humor in daily events, in others' behavior, and in your reactions.
- Be bold in your self-presentation and decisions.
- Make friends with nature.
- Dance or write poetry or songs about your feelings and the events of your life.
- Find an alternative when faced with an apparently "insurmountable" problem. (Lively energy is joy, and joy happens when we find an alternative to the either . . . or's.)
- Tell the secret you have complicated your life to keep.
- Drop every "Yes, but" that comes to mind as you read this list!

NOT HAVING TO KNOW • The famous painting of Saint George battling the dragon is not always the best metaphor for struggle. Most of our dragons today are subtle and psychic. Some have confusing configurations that have to be contemplated before they can be understood and then confronted. Thus we cannot always confront our issues as soon as they arise. Confusion is a totally legitimate phase of working things out. We may need a period of ambiguity, uncertainty, or lack of clarity before we can see what is going on. When either or both partners are confused, the time is right for mindful sitting with the confusion. This means no attachment to it or attempts to control it or insistence on ending it. It has a life of its own. It is like the time dough needs in darkness so it can rise, and it cannot be rushed. Patience is an ingredient of bread and love. If we respect our timing and our moods, we grow in self-trust. Reverend Sydney Smith offered this delightful suggestion back in the eighteenth century, "In times of depression, take short views of human life—not further than dinner or tea."

Ask one another: Can you stay together flexibly, holding your tension without premature gestures to end it? Can you relate to your tension or confusion rather than be pushed or intimidated by it? Make an oral commitment to address and process only when both of you are equally ready. If you never seem ready at the same time, that is another and prior issue to be addressed, before you are ready.

Consider the following: Sometimes it is necessary to let my feelings happen without acting on them. Sometimes holding is more important to my growth than releasing. This means surrendering control over my feelings and riding them where they may go or stay. This way I respect my own timing and trust myself. In your journal, cite some examples of when you did or didn't surrender to your feelings and respect your own timing.

AUDITING • Power has a built-in shadow side: corruption. Cults, for example, destroy the individual freedom of their members because one person makes the rules and enforces them for all. One reason our democracy works is because of its built-in checks and balances. Relationships also require such a system of auditing, of quality control, to work effectively. Seeking therapy for tune-ups and checkups helps. So does feedback about your relationship from those you trust. The practices in this book also may help, especially if you occasionally share one or more of them with another couple. Experiment as you see fit.

DISTINGUISHING CONFLICT FROM DRAMA • Conflict can be worked out with the tools we have been learning—addressing, processing, and resolving. Drama does not respond to these tools. Rather, it requires a spiritual program and a great deal of personal work. Use the following chart to see where you stand with whatever issue is facing you now. List the styles on the left that most appeal to you, write them out in the form of affirmations, and post them where they can be seen by both of you and by visiting friends.

Healthy Conflict	*Stressful Drama*
The problem is placed on the table between us, and we see it in perspective.	The problem becomes bigger than than both of us; we are possessed by it and lose perspective.
We explore the situation.	We exploit the situation.
We address the issue directly.	We sidestep the issue or cover it up.
We express our feelings candidly, taking responsibility for them as our own, without blaming the other or feeling ashamed.	We use invective to dump our feelings on one another or engage in theatrical/histrionic displays meant to manipulate, intimidate, or distance the other.
We are looking for a way to keep the relationship stable, and we don't use violence.	We explode, act violently, retaliate, or withdraw sullenly.
We remain focused on the present issue.	We use the present issue to bring up an old resentment that contaminates the present process.
We are committed to a bilateral style in processing issues and making decisions.	One of us makes a unilateral or secret decision.
The issue is resolved with an agreement to change something for the better.	The issue remains an open wound with lingering resentment and ongoing stress.
Both of us are looking for a way to make our relationship better.	One of us has to win and see the other lose.
We fight fairly.	We use cutthroat tactics.
We admit mutual responsibility for the problem.	We are convinced the problem is entirely the other's fault.
We are committed to working things out, but we respect the other's timing.	We insist this problem be fixed in accord with our timing, showing no tolerance for a time-out.
We try to deal with the issue one-on-one.	We crowd the stage by bringing someone else or something else in as a distraction (e.g., an affair, drinking).
If necessary, we seek help in therapy or a support group.	We refuse help or attempt to use it to justify our personal position.
We want both of us to grow from this conflict.	We want the other to learn a lesson.

Healthy Conflict (cont.)	*Stressful Drama (cont.)*
We let go of our attachment to the outcome we wanted in favor of a resolution we can both live with.	We each insist on getting our own way.
We are aware of any complexities.	We see only in black and white.
It is acceptable to agree to disagree.	Ambiguity is intolerable.
We notice, mirror, and feel deep compassion for the other's pain.	We are so caught up in our own pain we do not see the other's pain, or we think, "He/she deserves it."
We admit it if our behavior is connected to childhood.	We are adamant that the issue is entirely about the here and now.
We each acknowledge how our shadow might be involved.	We see the other's shadow but not our own.
Our conflict is love-based, and we want to show the five A's.	Our drama is fear-based, and we *have* to save face, protect our ego.
We are centered in mindfulness.	We are distracted by the mindsets of ego.

SPACING THE PROBLEM • Draw a circle for a pie chart. Describe the problem you are facing in writing in the center of it, using the simplest possible terms with no editorializing—for example, "My partner left." This fact taken alone leads to appropriate grief. Consider how the ego interferes by adding fear, attachment to an outcome, the need to control, blame, sense of abandonment, and so forth. These are all additional sources of unnecessary pain. Divide the pie to show the varying size of each of these pain sources, giving a visible indication of how you are being distracted from attending to the pure experience, which is simply that your partner left. Now draw the pie again with only the simple phrase in the center and notice the sense of space that results. This is how mindfulness puts space around our experiences so they can be what they are and nothing else. This, in turn, allows us to feel the pain of a situation—a loss, for instance—without the added pain of all the centrifugal forces our mind has generated.

ACTING WITH MORAL INTEGRITY • Conflict in relationships is more than a psychological issue. It is also a moral one. The following Buddhist moral precepts directly apply to the building of healthy relationships: I commit myself to give, preserve, and save life; to be generous;

to be sexually responsible; to tell and love the truth; to create reconcilia-tion, forgiveness, and friendship; to detach myself from fear and grasp-ing; to love unconditionally. Mindfulness in a relationship is a path with heart because it requires our attention to one another without judgment, control, expectation, and all the other heartless invasions of ego. Shake-speare (by this point in our journey together surely acknowledged as a bodhisattva of wisdom) in *Measure for Measure* shows us the path: "Go to your bosom, knock there, and ask your heart what it doth know."

Copy these precepts into your journal and give an example of how you practice each precept or fail to practice it. Make amends for the fail-ures wherever possible through specific behaviors and/or verbal apolo-gies. Ask yourself: To what extent does your relationship help make you more morally conscious? To what extent does it allow you and your partner to revisit and repair your failures? How committed are you to not retaliate in the face of perceived injustice?

BEING MORE ADULT • What do I seek in relationships when I am needy for childhood fulfillments? What do I seek when I have adult needs? Answer these questions by locating where you are on the follow-ing chart:

A needy child says	*A healthy adult says*
End my loneliness.	Be my companion while both of us respect each other's need to be alone at times.
Make me feel good.	I take responsibility for my own feelings and don't expect or need to feel good all the time.
Give in to me.	Negotiate with me.
Never betray me, lie to me, or disappoint me.	I accept you as fallible and seek to address, process, and resolve issues with you.
Help me not have to fear. I depend on you.	Help me learn to love. We depend on each other.
Totally fulfill my needs.	Moderately fulfill my needs.
Help me repeat old, painful scenarios from childhood and former relationships.	I have mourned the past, learned from it, and now want something better.
Indulge my ego.	Confront and free my ego.

This list adds up to:	*This list adds up to:*
I demand 100 percent of my need fulfillment from you.	I hope to get about 25 percent of my need fulfillment from you.
The child says: I am looking for stability outside myself.	*The adult says: I am looking for a setting that honors and enriches the stability I have inside.*

Ask yourself these questions and journal your responses: Which partners in my life have appealed to my adult self? Whom do I think of when I am at my best? Which partners appealed to my needy child self? Whose face comes up when I am at my lowest ebb? You might also ask: Which of my hobbies or pastimes are nurturing me as an adult and which are coddling my inner child's neediness?

If you are having trouble locating the adult voice, the mirroring parent voice, tell your story to your friends. You will hear your adult voice in their response. Is this because they are more adult than you? No, they are simply not deafened by the adult-distorting decibels of your drama.

HONESTLY SEEING • Probably the only issues that we treat matter-of-factly, without melodrama or strong reaction, are the ones with no connection to our past. Admit to yourself that there is an element in most of your charged issues that harkens back to your past. List in your journal some ways you may be keeping the past alive so that it sabotages the present. "Emily Dickinson wrote: "The shapes we buried dwell about / Familiar, in the rooms."

When we find ourselves reacting sharply to someone's behavior or words, we may be acting appropriately or we may be overreacting. When this happens, it is helpful to "S.E.E."—that is, to ask ourselves, "Is it my shadow? Ego? Early-life issues?"

Shadow: The shadow is the part of us that we disown, repress, and deny while we project it onto others. It may be our shadow speaking when we notice another doing something that we would do, but we cannot admit that we would. We despise seeing in the other what is unconscious in ourselves. Our work is to befriend our shadow by acknowledging our own projections and reclaiming them as ours.

Ego: As we have already seen, the ego is neurotic and inappropriate when it is driven by fear of not being accepted or by arrogance, retaliation, or entitlement. We have a bruised ego when we say: "How dare you do this to *me*?" "I'll get you for this!" "Don't you realize who *I* am?"

Early-life issues: We may be reacting to early unfinished business if we find ourselves thinking: Y*ou are replicating what was done to me in childhood. I see you recreating a scenario from the past that is highly charged for me. I am reacting in the present to a stimulus from the past.* "It feels like a remembrance," Keats remarked, speaking of the ease of writing certain lines of poetry. How much of what we feel is just like that? Transactions that seem to be taking place in the here and now are usually throwbacks to the past in all three of these ways. Take a recent experience with someone who distressed you and to whom you reacted strongly. S.E.E. it in the ways outlined in this practice and then admit to the person who disturbed you what you have discovered about your true motivation. Ask yourself: Does he upset me because I am projecting my shadow onto him and seeing the worst of myself in him? Am I reacting this way because my entitled ego is outraged? Am I having all these feelings because something from my early life is being resurrected? The same S.E.E. technique is useful for exploring any of our attitudes, beliefs, reactions, biases, or causes for upset. Make an ongoing commitment to S.E.E. the three suspects within and to bring them out into the open.

Sometimes we act upset, and it is not the shadow or ego or even early material. *Upset* sometimes means grieved. We are sad because something has not gone our way or something or someone has hurt or disappointed us. Grief is a reaction we often fail to recognize, admit, or feel. We prefer to use anger to cover it up. For instance, we may be upset because our partner does not speak up about her feelings toward us, so we are always guessing at her reactions. We may react angrily when our bedrock reaction may be grief that she cannot be sincere and open with us. The most frequently disguised feeling in relationships is grief, so it is useful to look there first for our authentic inner reactions to painful stimuli. Trade griefs with your partner. Take turns completing this sentence: "I am sad when you _____." You may want to add: "And I hide my sadness by _____."

INTROVERT OR EXTROVERT? • Look at the introvert-extrovert chart on page 140 and find your usual style of behavior and that of your partner. Ask her to do the same for herself and you. Do the versions match? Discuss any divergent impressions.

Respond to these questions in your journal: Do I accept myself as I am and my partner as who he/she is? I can answer yes if I am not trying to change myself or her. Do I accept that both introversion and extroversion are completely legitimate? I can answer yes if I do not complain about my partner's style or feel ashamed of my own. Can I also acknowledge that I may be so far at the end of the spectrum of introversion or extroversion that I have a limited ability to relate to someone on the opposite side?

HEALING AND HELP • Success in any relationship is not the absence of conflict but the ability to be in conflict mindfully, for example, without attachment to the intrusive mindsets of ego: fear, desire, control, judgment, or illusion. Mindfulness awakes our inner-healer archetype. Experiment with healing one another by taking turns in this way: lay hands on one another's heads in silence while placing a strongly conscious intention to bring healing to your partner. Consciously affirm that you do this as a conduit of the higher Self or however you configure a power greater than the human ego.

Since the work it takes to have a healthy relationship is too much for one or two people, in addition to the gods and saints we call upon for support, we can also recall our ancestors. Summon to mind those family members or friends in childhood who had relationships you respected and be aware they are with you in spirit as guides. Plutarch wrote:

> According to Hesiod, the souls delivered from birth are at rest and absolved. They become guardian spirits of humankind.... Like old athletes, they do not lose interest in us but show goodwill and sympathetic zeal to us still engaged in life, setting forth with us and shouting encouragement as they see us draw near and at last attain our hoped-for goal.

6

Fears Rush In—
and Dangers, Too

I was afraid because I was naked and I hid myself.
                    —Adam in the Garden of Eden, *Gen.* 3:10

The worst thing about fear is what it does to you when you
try to hide it.
                                        —Nicholas Christopher

Close relationships arouse fear. We fear intimacy because we fear
what may happen if we show the five A's and allow ourselves to
get truly close to a partner. Intimacy fears are normal in an uncertain
world like ours. Fears are even useful as long as we are not driven or
stopped by them. *Though fear may follow me, it never has to lead me.* We
fear the perilous givens of relating: betrayal, hurt, love, confrontation of
egos, self-disclosure, abandonment, and engulfment. The last two of
these are the central fears in relationships.

Engulfment or Abandonment

To fear engulfment means to fear that if someone gets too close to us
physically or emotionally, we will feel smothered or lose our freedom.
This is the equivalent of too much attention or affection and not enough

acceptance and allowing. If we feel engulfment, we say, "Let me be." To fear abandonment means to fear that if someone leaves us, we may be so bereft that we will not survive emotionally. This is the equivalent of a loss of attention, appreciation, or affection. If we fear abandonment, we say, "Stay with me." In either case, we feel fear when power seems to be "out there" and not in ourselves. We then feel trapped and controlled, at the mercy of others.

A healthy person may feel both abandonment and engulfment fears, though one or the other tends to predominate in any one person or relationship. We may feel these fears without ever calling them by name or knowing their origin. Moreover, since they are physically rather than intellectually remembered and maintained, they are often immune to ordinary will power; they appear to be automatic reactions to authentic stimuli. For instance, a hug may feel threatening to a person with a strong fear of engulfment. *Am I the warden of a body in which every cell holds a prisoner pacing with rage for crimes he did not commit?*

We continually alternate between our need for closeness and our fear of closeness. In infancy and early childhood, we may have felt our identity endangered if one or both of our parents smothered us with attention, appreciation, or affection. As a result, we felt the fear of losing our identity and learned to set rigid boundaries. We rejected the hugs, said no to the demands, and hid from the attention. Thus we built a wall that keeps out the dangerous love but also, sadly, almost any love. The more severe the rejection, the more rigorous the withdrawal. Understanding this makes withdrawal, in others or by us, a trigger for compassion.

A fear of engulfment may be the result of a parent's having tried to use us inappropriately to fulfill a need. This could have taken the form of abuse, whether physical, sexual, or emotional. In later life, the victim of childhood abuse may be afraid to see need coming at him, even appropriately, from another adult. A fear of abandonment, on the other hand, may be traceable to something entirely innocent. For example, a child may have felt abandoned when his mother was hospitalized for a while. Explanations to a child usually do not reach the forum in which the fears are lodged: the primitive, cellular feeling-sense of events that configures absence as rejection.

If closeness was associated with danger in the past, it may remain so as a post-traumatic stress reaction. The fear of closeness and engulfment is subtle and long-lived; we are only released from it when we work through it and practice overriding it again and again. We do this when we allow the other person to direct our love rather than controlling how much or in what way we show it. To let go of control that way is terrifying to someone who fears closeness.

What scares us ultimately may not be closeness itself but the feelings it evokes. For someone with a fear of engulfment, closeness may set in motion an old, familiar cycle in which closeness led to abandonment or abuse. Now we believe, cellularly though not necessarily intellectually, that if someone gets close, he will abandon or abuse us.

We men have been taught to concentrate on being brave and strong. But the fear that gets in the way of our being strong doesn't matter as much as the fear that gets in the way of loving, because love is the most precious strength a man can have. May we care about becoming loving more than anything else in life.

Learning from Our Fears

Fear wished not to evade as love wished to pursue.

—FRANCIS THOMPSON

The worm likes the apple only when it is ripe. Likewise, fear usually rears its ugly head exactly when we are ripe for a change. The fact that fear pops up when we are ready to address, process, and resolve it makes it a friendly stowaway. If the program described in this section works for us, we are ready to transcend our fear. If it does not, we are receiving a signal to step back and work on ourselves in other ways, gaining more inner resources first and then dealing with our fear when we are ready. If the program doesn't work for you, it's not a reason to feel shame or failure, only to reconsider your timing. The work on fear can benefit us spiritually as well as psychologically because we feel compassion toward ourselves when we realize that the "deep inability to love" we suspect in ourselves is not really an insurmountable obstacle or selfishness or badness, but a habit we learned and can work through. We can take a similar approach to the fear that what we have will be taken from us, which may have become a governing principle of our life, leading us to hold on too tightly to what we have. We may find that stinginess has the poignant terror of loss behind it. Compassion for the tight hands on the purse and a gentle loosening of them is more appropriate than censure and slapping them.

> *Fear follows us all our lives; that is our human condition.*
> *Fear sometimes catches up with us; that is our occasional*
>   *predicament.*
> *Fear never has to stop us; that is the purpose of our work.*

When we do the work, we find that fewer childhood forces are working on us and more adult choices are available. We also notice more flexibility in our handling of changes and transitions. And we no longer insist on perfection in our world, our partners, or ourselves. Approximations become acceptable, and preferences take the place of demands. Questioning of and arguments with reality turn to acknowledgment and consent. We take things that happen to us or people's reactions toward us as information rather than as unalterable verdicts. We can reframe our dramatic experiences: "He abandoned me" becomes "He left." "She engulfs me" becomes "She crowds me sometimes." "I was betrayed" becomes "I was fooled." "I feel empty inside" becomes "I am finding more space inside."

> It is only in the state of complete abandonment and loneliness that we experience the helpful powers of our own natures. . . . *Child* means evolving toward independence. This requires detachment from origins. So abandonment is a necessary condition.
>
> —C. G. JUNG

Jealousy

Milton calls jealousy "the injured lover's hell." But we can turn it into something a little better—a purgatory, say—when we work with it as grief. Jealousy is a combination of three feelings: hurt, anger, and fear. We are hurt and angered by a perceived betrayal. We are scared by the possibility of losing a source of nurturance and of never being able thereafter to find another—the paranoid belief that makes jealousy so poignant. Jealousy stands at the threshold of grief, which our ego does not let us cross. Instead of weeping in sadness and fear, our arrogant, affronted, possessive ego enters the fray and we lash out and blame, engaging in abuse instead of healthy anger as we declare our indignation about the perceived betrayal.

Ego-driven jealousy exposes our possessiveness, our dependency, our resentment of another's freedom, our refusal to be vulnerable. Deep down, we know we are not really democratic, not really free of the old style of hierarchical ownership in relationships, not really ready to admit our fear of facing the sometimes harsh conditions of the relationship: abandonment, engulfment, betrayal, and so on. Our ego demands that our partner save us: "Stop doing what I do not want to grieve for." It is a perfectly normal reaction at first. But as we address, process, and resolve our true feelings, we see where our work is. We acknowledge our pain, find someone to mirror it, and stay with it until it is resolved. Our partner may not be able to help with this. But therapy, friends, and support systems can assist us in getting past our ego to face our vulnerability, the dearest gift of human love.

Jealousy challenges our power to stay open and centered, without blame or withdrawal, in the midst of rejection. To go through it rather than simply bolster our ego shows us a path to maturity and liberation. After all, experiences like jealousy are the ones that make us learn to let go so we can grow. At first, we may hate the one who makes us let go. But as our feelings are resolved, we become thankful that we found out so much about our partner and ourselves. Jealousy shows us that no matter how indomitable we may imagine ourselves to be, we are still fragile and childlike underneath. Jealousy can thus deflate our ego, a giant spiritual step.

A final note on jealousy: Some men gawk at other women in the presence of their partners. This may cause the partner unnecessary and understandable pain or jealousy. The turned head feels like a dismissal or abandonment. A man *can* exercise custody over his roving eye while in the company of his wife or partner. The excuse "I can't help it" is not acceptable from an adult. We have the right to look to our heart's content at those we find attractive, but when a partner is present, the better part of love and caring is eyes front.

Infidelity

The conventional paradigm has been "If you play by the rules, then you deserve a faithful spouse and a stable relationship." Such a promise engenders a sense of entitlement. Someone who was always faithful will have an especially hard time dealing with abandonment or infidelity. Her ego feels affronted, with the possible result of a long-lived and frustrating bitterness against the offending partner: "I thought I would be taken care of forever, not cast aside for someone else (younger)." The deepest pain in infidelity may hit us when we recognize: "He does have the five A's to give, but he is giving them to someone else. I received them from him at first and then saw them vanish. I waited for those A's to reappear in him, and when they did, he was in someone else's arms."

Infidelity is a state-of-the-union address, forcing us to see the truth about our relationship. Triangles form in the psyche when a dyad is in trouble, when we do not want to let go of the original partner but instead only make the unlivable livable. The third angle may take the form of an adult lover, a crisis, an addiction, and so on. Can we confront the dyadic issue without creating another angle?

Infidelity is always a couple's issue, not an individual issue. One partner is not the victim, nor is the other the persecutor. The affair is not the disturbance but a symptom of disturbance. The "other man" does not cause distance but is being used to achieve distance. Infidelity seems to point to what our offending partner lacks but actually may reveal what we are afraid to show—for example, vulnerability, tenderness, playfulness, generosity, free abandon in sex. A frustrated partner finds someone else to colonize the empty space rather than address it or grieve its emptiness directly.

Acquiring a new lover may be the only way to leave a relationship for someone who feels she lacks the strength to leave on her own, or it may be a way of seeking satisfaction in areas of need that seem unfulfillable in the primary relationship. Like Walter in chapter 3, I may seek the gratification of my need for a holding environment with my wife and my needs for excitement in an affair. I may gratify my dependency needs in marriage and my domination needs in an affair. I may find mirroring of a feeling or a potential in a new partner that my present partner does not offer. The new partner may also evoke the positive shadow side of me: a hidden positive potential that may have lain fallow and unacknowledged before.

While infidelity may be a bold and extreme measure to make the relationship tolerable when it seems to have become unendurable and intimacy seems impossible, those avoiding intimacy with the original partner will most likely keep avoiding it with a new partner. What is more, the secrecy and time constraints of an affair make intimacy ultimately impossible in that relationship, too. So ultimately, two lovers are less than one. No one is offering his or her entire self anywhere in the triangle.

Infidelity also brings up abandonment terrors in the cuckolded partner. This explains the sense of powerlessness and pain that may be so excruciating to the one left behind. Powerlessness in this case means the inability to get someone to give us the five A's, and it is our clue to unresolved childhood issues. It is useful at such a time to work in therapy on the issues and grief that have pursued us all our life and are now presenting their bill. We feel infidelity as a metaphor for what happened long ago or has continued to happen—loss or absence of the five A's. Once we see that our anguish is not literally about this partner and her choice to abandon us, we are on the trail of our long-standing psychological material that has awaited our attention and calls for work on ourselves. Thus, betrayal by a partner can become the springboard to real growth in ourselves.

In a breakup or infidelity crisis, when one partner does something big, like leaving with someone else, the other may react with something equally big, like also taking up with a new partner. It is healthier for us when a big deal leads to a big look at ourselves, not to a big reaction or a big reprisal. Retaliation feels good to our ego, but *the reflex to retaliate is a sign that the real grief is being put to sleep*. In addition, a new relationship cannot begin in a healthy way when we are using it to distract ourselves from our need to grieve. A truly healthy person will not enter a relationship with us when he sees that it entails being used that way.

In the style of neediness, I go from my first partner to a second with the first as a backup, then to a third partner with the first and second as backups. In the healthy adult style, I go from one to none, and while alone, I work in therapy, addressing, processing, and resolving issues in myself with a plan to make changes. It is an immensely rich time for personal knowledge and healing. Endings that lead to self-exploration are painful but profitable to one who is committed to personal evolution. And, most wonderful of all, brokenhearted leads to openhearted. Can I keep it that way after it mends?

Often when our partner is unfaithful, we wonder: "How can he go to someone new so fast? He has been with me for years, and now I am nothing and the she of two months is everything!" But it is not so difficult to understand: His romantic feelings for you may have only been a projection onto you of his wish for an ideal partner. He has now simply projected them onto someone else. The new attachment is not about you or her. He is simply moving something of his own, his projection, as a light bulb can be moved from a lamp in the kitchen to one in the bedroom. And what she can offer may not match the inflated promise of his projection. Sadly, this is something he may not find out until he has given up many other valuable things—like you, your life together, and your children.

It is also typical for the cuckolded partner to hear: "I am in love with this new person and no longer in love with you." Could it be that *in love*, in this context, simply means an attachment that feels good, that has a bodily resonance of excitement and sexual desire, that provides a sense of certitude that he has finally found the perfect complement to himself? "I'm not in love with you anymore" may mean, "I'm still attached to you, but it no longer feels good."

For her part, the partner who is left behind may say, "I should be able to go along with him having another partner," even though her body says, "I can't stand it." This is sixties-era training. The "free love" part of the sixties was not in our best interest as self-nurturant adults. Go with your body's information, recalling that a relationship is about honesty and happiness not about enduring pain.

As for the third person in the triangle—"the other man/woman"—he or she can cause great pain to the betrayed partner. A deeply spiritual practice is to decide and resolve—right now?—never to play that role in the future. Let someone already in a relationship bring closure to that relationship—not merely promises of closure—before you will relate intimately with him. This is a commitment to act respectfully and lovingly to other vulnerable humans: I will not inflict pain on anyone else. That is spirituality in practice.

Finally, it's important to point out that fidelity is more than just monogamy. Fidelity also means a commitment to work problems out. This includes not reacting to one infidelity with finality and separation but by exploring the implications of what happened and working it out, with amends given and received. When the affair ends, fidelity can begin again, and partners can go on together with forgiveness and new energy for a better life together. This takes egolessness, which has become easier for readers of this book, who are doing the practices that lead to it.

Dealing with Disappointment

Expectations can add a lively energy to our enterprises and relationships. They can help us find our leading edge rather than letting us be satisfied with the mediocre. Psychological health does not mean having no expectations; it means not being possessed by them. This makes room for lively expectancy. Such expectancy is followed by agreements that fulfill it or acceptance of disappointment as a legitimate condition of existence, to be greeted without protest or blame. The alternative is ego-entitlement with its brazen mindsets of wish and demand.

Our inner life is complex and multifaceted, like a vast and varied landscape requiring diverse experiences to cultivate it. At times, we are challenged to walk and run, at other times to stay and sit. Disappointment is as crucial to our inner life as reliability, the same way that cold is as necessary to the life of a lilac bush as is the sun. When Buddha taught that the first noble truth is the unsatisfactoriness of life, he was not being a doomsayer, but pointing to a necessary ingredient of our common humanity. Beings like us could never stay in bloom in a tropical world of uninterrupted satisfactions. We need all seasons for a fully realized human experience. Only in a world with shadows can our inner life flourish. The challenge is ruthless fealty to the seasons of life and change. This includes losses, abandonments, and endings chosen or imposed. While receiving the five A's is gratifying, disappointment may also be a grace, "the fastest chariot to enlightenment," as the Tibetan saying goes.

So many frayed strands of disappointment, some barely noticeable, dangle from our hearts in the complex tapestry of a lifetime. We may experience a great and crushing disappointment about our partner or our relationship at one time or another, or many little ones along the way. Disappointment is a kind of loss, the loss of what we had hoped something was or could be. At bottom is the loss of an illusion to which we were clinging or on which we relied. The only thing that can be lost, after all, is illusion.

Disappointment can lead to despair, the illusion that there is no alternative. But to experience disappointment consciously is to embrace it, learn from it, and go on loving, to accept that all humans are a combination of contradictions. Anyone can please and displease, come through and fail, satisfy and disappoint. No one pleases all the time, yet we do not give up on others.

Projections about another person's perfection or trustworthiness collapse as we grow up and arrive at realism. When Dorothy saw that the Wizard of Oz was a bungling—though well-meaning—old man, she felt deep disappointment, but that was the turning point on her journey of learning to trust herself. The little dog that pulled the curtain back showed her that the only dependable wizardry would be her own, not someone else's. (It is usually the instinctive, animal part of us that makes the discovery.) As Dorothy learned, there were no coattails to hang on to, no shortcuts to the summit, no godfather to do things for her. Disappointment was a necessary step on her path to adulthood—that is, to taking care of herself while still supporting and being supported by others.

We can learn from Dorothy that seeing someone's "clay feet" can teach us even more than "sitting at his feet." Disappointment is "dis-illusion-ment," or freedom from illusion, projection, and expectation. All that is left is mindfulness. *To someone who disappointed me, I can say, "Thank you for freeing me from yet another of my illusions."*

When Dorothy sees there is no wizard, she learns it is not here to be had: What I was certain was here is not here. I will have to do it all myself. This is precisely what we all learn at the end of a relationship. Disappointment was what it took for Dorothy to face the given of existence: I alone take full responsibility for myself. Others—the three friends and the good witch (earthly and spiritual companions)—could assist her, but only Dorothy could click her heels together and access her power.

Disappointment empowers us when it helps us learn to locate and trust ourselves while still relating to a partner. But it can also disempower us when it leads only to regret about how foolish we were to love our partner or when it leads us to blame her for failing us. Such a sense of betrayal puts us in the role of the victim. Regret as a reaction to disappointment further disempowers us: "If only I had not gotten into this to begin with" or "If only I had done it all differently, maybe he would not have betrayed me." Regret becomes shame, and shame prevents us from experiencing the full career of our disappointment: realizing it, grieving it, growing because of it. As this book has pointed out again and again, growth is required for any human experience to be truly complete.

So when we feel disappointment, we need to work on our grief. But other people can help us, too. If someone understands our disappointment—or any other pain we feel—and shows empathy, it revives and comforts us. Receiving attention and acceptance from such a person is more powerful than gratification. Here is an example of how empathy can help process an interpersonal disappointment:

HE: I know I disappointed you when I did not stand up for you at the party last night. It has been bothering me all day. I keep seeing the hurt look on your face, and I feel sorry for not being there for you. I have felt that way in my life with other people, and I know how lonely it feels. I'm here for you now and want to make up for it.

SHE: Thank you. I feel safe with you because this is a relationship in which my needs and feelings can come out. I see how they are met with attention, acceptance, appreciation, affection, and allowing me to be myself as I am in the moment. I trust that I can revive with you my archaic needs and wishes without demanding that you fulfill them perfectly. You make it possible for me to try again and to moderate my needs according to what adults can give other adults. I feel such awe and hopefulness that this is possible for me with you, and I offer it to you, too.

Yes, that is how you can sound when you do the work, a work that is only complete when it has that spiritual dimension of compassion.

Katrina's story exemplifies not only disappointment but also a way out of it: Katrina, born in Eastern Europe, has lived in this country for sixty years. She was married to Robert for forty-five years and recently stayed by him through his long bout with Alzheimer's. Now, at sixty-five, Katrina feels cheated and angry. She never felt loved by Robert, who had numerous affairs and unilaterally decided to altogether stop having sex with her when she was forty because he said he no longer found her attractive. She realizes now he meant for her only to be the mother of his children and keep house for him. Her cultural beliefs prepared her for this sort of life, in which women were forbidden to go beyond the house-keeper/mother model or to expect love and respect, let alone equality. Thus, Katrina is a grieving widow but not for her dead husband. She is mourning her own lost life and all she missed out on over the years. She is actually experiencing post-traumatic stress syndrome in the sense that she is finally feeling what she stopped herself from feeling years ago. Now that Robert is gone and she has no specific task, she has nothing to distract her from the reality of her empty and purloined life.

The deal Katrina made in marriage did not include being loved but only being taken care of by a breadwinner. Her religion, which supported the arrangement, gave her comfort but also kept her tied to the model of servitude. Now Katrina has nothing but her memories and feelings, and they frighten her. But if she can feel those feelings, love herself, and forgive her past, she can go on with the rest of her life without bitterness. The work of mourning the past makes that possible since it involves feeling fully and letting go fully, too. Perhaps Katrina can then pursue new goals that finally reflect her deepest needs and wishes. She can reinvent herself rather than simply manage her old age until she dies, as so many of her friends are doing. Katrina was indeed cheated, but she will still be able to reap a profit if she can invest in herself at last.

> The most empowering relationships are those in which each partner lifts the other to a higher possession of their own being.
>
> —TEILHARD DE CHARDIN

Practices

DEALING WITH ABANDONMENT AND ENGULFMENT •
Find yourself on the following chart:

Fear of Abandonment ("The Pursuer")	*Fear of Engulfment* ("The Distancer")
Cannot easily pull back when a partner needs space	Cannot easily make a commitment when a partner needs assurance
Clings or cannot seem to get enough contact	Distances or cannot seem to get enough space
Is overly attentive, overly accepting, overly allowing	Takes a partner's attentions for granted or feels smothered by them
Willingly shares feelings and information	Maintains secrets or a secret life and may become angry at being asked questions
Takes more care of a partner than of himself/herself	Feels entitled to be taken care of without reciprocation
Feels he/she can never give enough	Construes giving and receiving as smothering or obligating
Goes along with a partner's agenda or timing	Insists on being in control and making the decisions
Has poor boundaries and tolerates abuse, unhappiness, or infidelity	Maintains rigid boundaries and has no tolerance for abuse, disloyalty, or deficiency

Fear of Abandonment (cont.)	*Fear of Engulfment (cont.)*
Is addicted to the partner and keeps giving more	Seduces the other and then withholds
Yearns for continual affection and affectionate displays	Is embarrassed or angered by assurance
Is encouraged by a partner's exuberance	Is threatened or annoyed by a partner's exuberance
May settle for sex as proof of love or use it to purchase feelings of security	May use frequent sex as a substitute for closeness or withhold sex to manipulate
May give up appropriate sexual boundaries to please the other being defenseless against predation	May use sexual distance or lack of interest as a way of maintaining independence, a defense against vulnerability
Needs a partner to be a constant companion ("Stay with me")	Needs a partner to stay put while he/she comes and goes ("Let me be")
Seeks connection and closeness	Seeks connection but not closeness
Feels at a loss without the presence of the partner	Is made anxious by extended togetherness
Rationalizes—i.e., makes excuses	Intellectualizes, replaces feelings with logic
Shows fear, hides anger	Shows anger, hides fear
Walks on eggshells, always compromising	Acts hostile, creates uproar, or picks fights to establish distance
Feels distress about comings/goings	Feels distress about giving/receiving
Lets needs become neediness	Turns needs into expectations
Looks like the one reaching out, which seems like love but may really be fear	Looks like the cold one, which seems unloving but may really be fear
May be the one more likely to leave!	May be the one who notices abandonment fears arising when left!*

* Behind the fear of engulfment is the fear of rejection.

The left column may indicate the codependent and borderline styles, the right column the narcissist style.

USING THE "TRIPLE-A APPROACH" TO FEAR • Admit, Allow, Act As If. *ADMIT* you fear abandonment or engulfment or both when appropriate. To admit your fears is to avow and disclose them to yourself and others. This means naming your fears without blaming anyone. Remember that if you feel loved when or because someone stays with you, then abandonment will affect you more seriously because it will have the extra weight of taking away a required love that is uniquely meaningful to you. Admit this to yourself and your partner if it is true.

ALLOW the fears, feeling them fully and not judging them by calling them bad. Become intimate with your feelings, allowing yourself to feel them fully as your own. This does not mean becoming identified with any specific feeling, nor does it mean denying any; it means allowing every one of them to emerge and then to let it go after it has had its full career. This intimacy with our own feelings legitimates them and us and gives us freedom.

To allow fear is to feel it all the way, to tremble, sweat, and shake if that is what it takes. It is also enlisting the adult part of you to hold and cradle the scared child part of you. You can fall apart *while* maintaining yourself. This means allowing the fear without taking it out on someone else or letting it ransack your self-esteem or drive you to an addiction. Fear is part of you, and as such it can be granted the five A's. Then it reveals itself as having wisdom and purpose. This is how the paradox of the practice gets resolved and letting go becomes possible. *Only if we tolerate the discomfort of fear can we master it.*

When we begin to feel fear or melancholy, we may wonder why and to try to rid ourselves of it. But it may be an example of synchronicity, a meaningful coincidence of a feeling state and a new transition being ushered into our consciousness. In that sense, the disturbing feeling may be like an owl that has suddenly perched in our oak tree and seems to be staying for a while. It has come because it has noticed many pests in our garden, and it will consider them prey. The owl, which seems to us a dark presence, is thus actually our ally. A clutching and uninvited feeling may be just like that. The mindful style is to let it perch and do what it does. Gradually we notice the graces that result.

According to Buddhist teaching, we attain satisfaction not by indulgence of desires but by renunciation of clinging. Thus, this spiritual discipline directly targets our abandonment fears. Practice it in mindful meditation by cradling the clinging child in you without any attempt to judge, fix, or change it and maintaining the embrace. This is not giving up on yourself.

Likewise, make a plan to be more sensitive to the many ways you have of abandoning others emotionally. Find ways to stay with them in their hurts—to maintain the embrace—especially the hurts you may have caused. Cradling of self or others means creating a holding environment, the optimal setting for growth to occur. In fact, finding a holding environment that honors and nurtures our needs is the goal of personal evolution. Likewise, the goal of universal evolution is the whole world, in its every nook and moment, might become that holding environment. Trungpa Rinpoche suggests, "Hold the sadness and pain of samsara [*suffering*] in your heart and at the same time the power and vision of the great Eastern sun."

Here are affirmations that may help: *I let myself feel this fear. I handle it now by holding it and letting it pass. I am holding both my fear and my power in one embrace. As I hold this way, I feel more compassion for others. May my assisting forces (angels, bodhisattvas, etc.) be with me as I face my fear, live through it, and let it go. May all those I love and all those I find difficult face their fears and be free of them. I join in the loving intent of the universe. The universe cradles me already and always.*

After cradling, use the Tibetan Buddhist practice of receiving white light by visualizing it and saying, "May light now enter at the crown of my head and flow through my body to the soles of my feet." It is a short step from this to Virginia Woolf's "Moment by moment things are losing their hardness; even my body now lets the light through." Words that bring a more personal feeling to the practice might be "May the caring being who absolves all inadequacies fill me with light from the crown of my head to the soles of my feet." Be sure to use this practice only *after* cradling lest it become an escape from our experience rather than a completion of it. This combination of the psychological and the spiritual also serves to acknowledge the role of grace in healing, the gift of light unconjured by effort, of fire unstruck by flint.

ACT AS IF you have no fear. If you fear abandonment, risk allowing the other to go away for one minute more than you can stand. Cling one minute less than you feel you need to. If you fear engulfment, allow the other to get one inch closer than you can stand. Stay away one minute less than you feel you need to. By acting in these ways, you are playing with your pain, a healing device too often neglected by those of us who take things too seriously.

Each of the A's in the triple-A practice encourages individual change. But as you look more deeply, you will find that each of them can also engender intimacy between you and your partner. Ask your partner to consider the following suggestions: When you admit being afraid, your partner can allow it, receiving the information openly and respectfully—that is, without blame or protest or an attempt to fix or stop you. This means *active listening,* to hear the gut feeling and not immediately respond with words of comfort. No one can talk the gut out of its own reality; we can only honor its reality. Then, when you begin to act so that things change, your partner can respect your timing and not try to hurry or delay the process. A partner who can join you in these ways is genuinely ready for intimacy. Indeed, when you express the fear, your partner can hold the space in which that can happen safely. *"Holding the space" means that your partner stays with you in your feeling, while showing the five A's.*

WELCOMING CLOSENESS   •   We don't fear physical closeness because we fear proximity itself. Most of us earnestly want physical contact with those who love us. *Rather we fear what we will feel when we get too close. The real fear, then, is of ourselves.* This fear is not something to rebuke ourselves for. It is our deepest vulnerability, the very quality that makes us most lovable. How ironic that we hide what makes us most appealing, or is this the work of the inner ego trickster who has invented yet another airtight stratagem to protect us from human nearness?

Consider these questions in your journal: How do I avoid closeness with those I love? (Ask them for help in answering this question.) How does my style resemble that of my parents and the ways they related to me or one another during my childhood? Can I say this to my partner: "If you give me space, you see my love because I relax and give it on my own time and in my own way. Otherwise, the best you get is my acting dutifully and not from my heart"?

BEING ALONE • To leave our family home and enter another home on our wedding day deprives the psyche of the solitude it needs for its full development. Beings as complex as ourselves need retreats from others to explore the depths of our character and our destiny. We need regular periods of solitude to replenish ourselves, to locate new sources of creativity and self-knowledge, and to discover possibilities in our souls that are invisible when we are with others. This is how we find our central evolutionary opportunity whether we are introverts or extroverts. Journal an answer to the following question, and then discuss it with your partner: Does our relationship include, permit, and encourage time alone?

Therapy is completed when a child can play alone.
—D. W. WINNICOTT

MONEY MATTERS IN RELATIONSHIPS • After repeated abandonment experiences, a child learns to give up on emotional goods and replace them with attachment to material things. After all, toys do not let us down. Are we still doing this as adults? Do we use things to distract and console ourselves when we have despaired of human nurturance?

In a healthy childhood, a baby is cradled and comforted by a trusted adult so he can experience feelings fully. Later this child will not seek distractions and consolations in material things or in addictions but in the attention and comfort that come from the five A's. We never lose the desire/need to be held when we cry. We never outgrow our need for human touch. We only learn to hide the needs we have despaired of fulfilling. Imagine what desperate and futile anguish lies buried in their hiding place.

A parent may have tried to show us love by giving us things or doing things instead of comforting or cradling us. Later, in an adult relationship, we may think that is all love is and may manipulate people into giving things to us and doing things for us to prove their love. This does not make us feel loved, however, because our need for it is insatiable and unfulfillable, like any childhood need that is mistakenly brought to an adult relationship for fulfillment.

Money is used in an exchange, a form of giving and receiving—precisely what intimacy is about. Thus money can easily symbolize love. As we become healthy, money becomes nothing more than a tool for living and giving. It is no longer a symbol of the emotional goods we missed out on. Like a fishing rod, it is something we use to acquire what we want, and then we share the catch joyfully and generously.

Respond in your journal to the question of whether you have difficulty with buying or selling, donating or spending, borrowing or lending, owing or being owed, earning or saving, paying or paying back, losing or wasting, hiring or renting, sharing or being shared with, treating or being treated? Do you expect a partner to do things for you or give you things as a sign of love? Do you operate from a belief in scarcity or abundance? Check in with your partner on all of this. Examining how you handle money may give you information on how you handle intimacy. For example, trying to get something for free may mean, in a relationship, that you're likely to expect a commitment from a partner without making one yourself.

The narcissistic ego thrives on external status. It is easy prey for Madison Avenue, Detroit, Hollywood, Paris, and Milan. Thus, we may use possessions in a vain attempt to garner what we were supposed to get from parents, partners, and ourselves: the five A's. Cars are for transportation, but shiny models with fancy features promise that their owners will stand out as trendy and appealing. Clothing is for warmth and protection, but being scrupulously up-to-date on fashion draws attention and gives the impression of wealth and class.

These functional items take on inflated meanings, but authentic meaningfulness comes from the soul, the ego-transcending power of the spiritual Self. Living mindfully does not mean that we repudiate beauti-

ful material things; it means that we do not fall victim to the game behind them. We see through the tinsel to the really important markers of
status in life: virtue, integrity, generosity, unconditional love. Those are
the qualities that make all we possess a lucent joy and a medium for
generosity.

Consider your possessions and ask yourself what end they serve. Recall how you made the decisions to buy what you have—car, house,
clothes, and so on. Compare the care you put into buying with the care
you take in choosing which charities to donate to. Discuss this with your
partner. What is the virtue that is waiting to be practiced?

Finally, it is normal never to be completely integrated in three areas:
sex, money, and food. *Can I find compassion in myself for my disheveled
history with these three?*

I give you my love more precise than money.

—WALT WHITMAN

HANDLING THREAT AND JEALOUSY IN YOUR PARTNER • Your
partner may feel threatened by the friendship you have with someone
else. Within the context of an intimate bond with someone, the statement "I am free to pursue relationships" becomes "I am free to pursue
relationships, but I have to design them carefully and appropriately in
relation to the reactions of my partner."

Ask your partner to rate her fear on a scale of one to ten, with ten
being the most severe. If she rates the fear at five or higher, it will be in the
best interests of the relationship to stop doing what scares her. You
would do this out of free choice based on compassion and respect for
her feelings. If she rates the fear at less than five, then continue what you
are doing and keep checking in. At the same time, your partner can address the issue for herself in therapy or in dialogue with you or her
friends.

STEWARDS OF CLOSENESS • No one is making sure your relationship will survive or your closeness will deepen. Can you agree to be the
team with that purpose?

In childhood, adults watch over us. In our adulthood, we oversee our own activities. It is up to us to pilot our relationships if they are to remain on course. For instance, one partner goes back to school and the other spends a great deal of time on his job. In this instance, the partners may drift apart and intimacy may be in jeopardy. There is a simple technique that may help them become sponsors and overseers who watch out for and maintain closeness. The technique is to ask this question anytime we embark upon a project: "How can we do this in such a way that we become closer?" Usually, the answer includes two elements: showing the five A's and mutually sharing in the project in some way.

For instance, one partner wants to go back to college and the other is willing to work hard to help pay for it. Both are involved in the project and the sacrifices of each can be acknowledged. Acknowledgment is a form of appreciation. Attention happens when the working partner inquires about and attends school activities and the student takes a genuine interest in what goes on at work. Affection happens with the pat on the back or the hug as she is off to school or he is off to work. Acceptance and allowing happen when he says yes to the plan without resentment and she says yes to his need for time off occasionally, especially time together. Finally, we hear often of the fear of commitment to others but we do not notice that we may neglect commitment to ourselves. We stress our bodies with heavy schedules of obligation at home and work. A useful extension of the practice outlined above is to ask: "How can I take on this task in such a way that I still take care of myself." This is not selfishness but self-nurturance.

7

Letting Go of Ego

Are you willing to be sponged out, erased, canceled, made nothing? If not, you will never really change.

—D. H. LAWRENCE

If the partners in a relationship are mainly concerned with proving themselves right, then ego rules the relationship. If they are concerned with how to make the relationship work, then cooperative love rules. Ego, which means "I," is the main obstacle to intimacy, which implies "we." In reality, there is no solid, separate self. We are all interconnected and contingent upon one another.

Ego is the conventional word for the center of our conscious rational life. The ego is functional when it helps us fulfill our goals in life. It is this healthy ego that lets us be fair and alert witnesses without the interference of meddling mindsets. It is our healthy ego that assesses opportunity or danger and acts accordingly. It is our healthy ego that makes the choices necessary to live in accord with our deepest needs, values, and wishes. Most admirably, the healthy ego accepts human paradoxes: the same person can be both good and bad, close and distant, loyal and betraying, fair and unfair, courteous and curt, need-fulfilling and needy. The healthy ego is the part of us that has come to terms with all the givens of human behavior, however unappealing, and still is able to love.

Felicitously, a healthy ego *evokes* the five A's from others. When we have the courage to share who we are in unique and free-spirited ways, we are likely to receive attention. When we accept ourselves, are proud of who we are and, at the same time, admit our mistakes, we are likely to be accepted. When we show generosity, compassion, and integrity, we are likely to be appreciated. When we offer affectionate touch and consideration, we are likely to receive affection in return. And when we act assertively, with clear boundaries and respect for others' rights, it is likely that others will allow us the freedom to be ourselves.

Our ego (the center of our conscious rational life) is functional when it helps us reach our goals. It is dysfunctional—or neurotic—when it distracts us from our goals or sabotages our attempts to reach them. Behind every neurosis is a cunning fear that has never been addressed or resolved. Indeed, *neurotic* means useless repetition of an archaic and unnecessary way of protecting ourselves from such a fear. Some of us display the healthy adult ego at work and the needy child's neurotic ego at home. Take the double lifestyle of Edna Sue: She is greeted with respect and love by her staff at the bank this morning as she arrives punctually to assume her daily duties as chief loan officer. Today she will, as usual, grant and refuse loans on intelligent, unsentimental grounds; foreclose on mortgages while still feeling compassion; and supervise her staff with limit setting and reasonable allowances for errors. But at lunchtime, Edna Sue will—unbeknownst to anyone at the bank—frantically rush home, driven by her out-of-control fear of abandonment and her addictive clinging, to beg her boyfriend, Earl Joe, not to leave her as he threatened he would. During this past month, Earl Joe, a cocaine addict, has stolen her food money, broken her wrist, and insisted she force her teenage son to go and live with her ex-husband. But none of this matters because there is a split between the functional Edna Sue at work and the dysfunctional Edna Sue at home. At work she insists on the best or nothing. In relationships she would rather have less and less than nothing. In the first case, she acts within the boundaries of her functional ego; in the second, she acts from her neurotic ego and sets no boundaries.

Jung proposes that in addition to an ego, our psyche also includes (and is included by) a Self, "the God archetype" within, the analogue of the buddha mind. The Self is the center and circumference of the psyche and has both unconscious and conscious components. It is an "objective psyche," unlimited and undefined by individual personality. In fact, it is the same in everyone, consisting of unconditional love, eternal wisdom, and the power to heal ourselves and others—as well as the shadow of each of these. In short, the Self identifies our wholeness; the ego identifies our uniqueness.

Our destiny is to bring more and more consciousness to what has remained unconscious, "to kindle a light in the darkness of mere being," as Jung says. We do this by doing our psychological work, which is to bring ego into the service of the Self and to design our every thought, word, and deed so that it will manifest the love, wisdom, and healing that abides unconditionally within us. Our spiritual work is simply to allow this process and to be receptive to the graces always available to us to fulfill it. Graces take the form of any boons and challenges that come along to help us activate our potential for love and befriend our shadow. Relationship is certainly just such a spiritual grace. Having done our psychological and spiritual work, we can then articulate in our mortal lives the immortal gifts of the Self.

Relationships provide the most powerful tools for the work. With every passing day a relationship ruthlessly erases our self-centeredness and demolishes our hubris. In a relationship, we keep discovering the price of authentic love and that it can turn out to be blissful to let go of ego. This is because in a relationship we finally notice that we give the five A's more easily when our ego steps out of the way and takes our fears with it. The timorous ego unnecessarily fears just what the stalwart ego has always longed for. That strong ego is joyously liberated when it no longer has to promote and uphold its power but can let go and trust itself to life unfolding in its own way. The paradox is that less ego means more ability to handle what happens.

The neurotic, inflated ego fears the Self because it believes that in alliance with the Self it will lose its distinctiveness. But actually the Self acts *through* our distinctiveness. It finds its incarnation in every individual ego and thus fulfills our evolutionary destiny. When the Dalai Lama says he forgives the Chinese for their poor treatment of Tibet and will not retaliate, he is not speaking as an individual. Rather the higher Self, the buddha mind, is speaking through his unique, distinctive personality. Human intellect and will cannot account for such largesse. It takes the graces of egolessness and enlightenment. Tenzin Gyatso, a man who is fulfilling the evolutionary role of the Dalai Lama, is making a contribution to the evolution of the world. That is what happens to us when we pledge our ego powers to the gentle dominion of the Self. We do not lose; the world gains.

Martin Luther distinguished two kinds of love. He said that in human love we seek a love-worthy object. In divine love, God, by grace, creates a love-worthy object. We can find an archetypal human truth in this distinction. In conditional, ego-centered love, we show love only to someone who meets our specifications. In unconditional love, we create loveability by freely giving the five A's. In this generous form of human grace-giving, there is no set of criteria to be met by the love object. In other words, love's range is infinite and anyone can be loved. The five A's are thus not only the ways love is made; they can actually be love-*making*. This is yet another way to see how mindful love leads to universal compassion.

> My love, you win again and again;
> But let's play this game of chess.
> I will not be trying to win,
> Only to surrender everything to you
> All to you, my love, even my body and soul.
>
> —Wen Ito

Anatomy of the Arrogant Ego

The arrogant sphinx killed herself when she was bested by Oedipus, who figured out her riddle. Circe, on the other hand, met Ulysses and saw that he was superior to her, but that only drew him more intensely to her attention. She offered herself as his sexual companion, even promising to share her divinity with him. In doing so, she humbly chose life over death and even offered Ulysses access to a larger life. She showed that relationship thrives spiritually and erotically when ego steps aside.

Ego appears in statements like "I'm right," "My way is the right way; I'm perfect," "There is no need for me to change." We fear changing because it may mean admitting we were wrong or grieving a loss (of something that we valued in ourselves or of a sense of safety). It boils down to the fear of closeness: "If I soften and open myself to others, they will get too close." "You can't tell me anything" is the same as "You can't get close enough to affect me." We may act our fear of closeness out as stubbornness, a refusal to cooperate, an inflexible need to win or to be right, an inability to admit we were wrong, or an inability to apologize.

The arrogant ego fights intimate love because we keep trying not to lose face. This F.A.C.E. of the inflated ego is Fear, Attachment, Control, and Entitlement—the most vicious enemies of intimacy. The self-centeredness of entitlement keeps us from giving anyone our attention and appreciation. We cannot give someone our acceptance and allowing when control takes precedence over equality or when we get too attached to our own version of reality. We cannot easily show authentic affection when we are driven by fear.

We fear (usually unconsciously) not finding approval or not getting our way. We are attached to our version of how life and others should be and we may become stubborn. We demand control over others and over how things turn out. We believe we are entitled to be loved and honored by everyone and to exact reprisals if we are offended.

The ego is not a stable identity. It is an assumed identity, based on injury or love that we respond to with fear, attachment, control, or entitlement. Since any of these reactions happen so habitually we imagine it *is* who we are. We confuse rejoinder with agency. Instead, our ways of behaving can be observed in the mindful space of bare attention. *That space* is who we are, not the strategies that attempt to fill it. Thus, in mindfulness we can use pain or love in a new way: to bring our ego into focus. That shift of attention to the man behind the curtain is how we finally snap out of our mesmerized stare at the wizard of ego.

We need a F.A.C.E.-lift so that fear can become excitement. Then we may act *with* fear but not *because* of it, and we are no longer afraid to show our fear or our vulnerability, which is the vulnerability that is a

given of existence not the vulnerability of a victim. Such healthy vulnerability is more likely to emerge when our own sense of inadequacy and
shame about it vanishes and when we trust that in showing it we run no
risk of humiliation.

Unconditional love is love without the conditions—the F.A.C.E.—of
ego. Such love is free of fear. When we love unconditionally, attachment
turns into healthy, committed, intelligent bonding. We establish and
maintain ties but do not become possessive, nor do we let ourselves be
possessed. Instead of trying to control a partner we respect his boundaries and gain his respect. Entitlement gives way to a self-nurturant assertiveness that gracefully bows to the fact that we do not always get what
we want. This admirable quality not only brings us the respect of others
but self-respect, too.

Tibetan Buddhist scholar Robert Thurman says the best time to observe the ego is during episodes of "injured innocence." (Another time is
during road rage.) When we express feelings of entitlement to fairness or
to exemption from any condition of existence, that is evidence of ego energy in us. We know this kind of energy is not healthy because it makes
us feel stressed, hurt, compulsive, frustrated, and intimidated.

What is the difference between ego entitlement and a legitimate sense
of one's rights? Entitlement is an expectation, an attachment, a demand—the familiar ego manifestations and mindsets that cause suffering
and are the opposite of mindfulness. If such an expectation is not met,
we feel justified in retaliating. Retaliation is not justice. It is mean-
spirited comfort to an indignant ego and despair of human change and
of the power of grace. In contrast, we ask for our rights legitimately when
we do it directly and nonviolently, fighting fairly but not inflicting
reprisals if we are denied. Instead we go to a higher authority, such as a
court, and work for our rights within appropriate channels. If the law itself is unfair, we engage in nonviolent resistance but always with love for
all concerned, thereby combining mindfulness and moral integrity.

One caution: The ego was never meant to be annihilated, only dismantled and rebuilt to make it more constructive. Then and only then
does intimacy become possible. Here are a few constructive responses
for when we feel our ego being aroused:

When I feel	*I choose instead to*
Fear	Love
Attached	Let go
Controlling	Grant freedom
Entitled	See myself as equal

Every one of the ingredients of the neurotic ego is a source of pain: It hurts to be so afraid that we are always on guard and yet always wounded. It's painful to have to hold our reins tightly. It is stressful to constantly try to control others. It hurts to face the conditions of existence without the promise of an exemption from them. It would be tragic to die having successfully saved face in all our relationships. Yet no matter how bad something about us may be, it also has a positive dimension. There is a kernel of goodness, an untapped potential in each element of the neurotic ego:

Fear	Prudent caution and intelligent assessment of danger
Attachment	Perseverance and commitment to stay through hard times
Control	Ability to get things done and be efficient at addressing, processing, and resolving
Entitlement	Healthy self-esteem and standing up for one's rights but with a willingness to accept the given that sometimes things are unfair

To trust ourselves does not mean we can be sure we will face life without fear, attachment, control, or entitlement. To trust ourselves means that we have surrendered to being just exactly who we are in each moment *and* that a mindful awareness will kick in to show us an alternative to our ego habits. This is the spiritual paradox of accepting ourselves as we are while simultaneously becoming more than we ever were. It is a forsaking of any attachment to a polarity so that our only refuge is the center, where synthesis awaits us.

Anatomy of the Impoverished Ego

In contrast to the inflated, arrogant ego style is the second style of dysfunctional, neurotic ego. The deflated, impoverished ego style is a fear-based, submissive or victim style that prevents nonhierarchical intimacy. The following attitudes characterize the impoverished ego:

- Victim. "I do not control my life. I am a victim of people and circumstances. Everything that happens to me is someone else's doing (or fault). I am powerless to change anything." Behind this attitude lies the fear of being held accountable as an adult. Self-pity and belief in oneself as a victim can also be forms of despair, falling prey to the illusion that there is no alternative to one's painful predicament.
- Follower. "Everyone knows what to do but me. I have to follow others. Tell me what to do and believe, and I will do it and believe it." Behind this attitude lies the fear of taking charge of one's life or of making a mistake.
- Self-blamer. "I am always wrong or bad. I blame myself for everything bad that happens. I am ashamed of myself and guilt-ridden." Behind this attitude lies the fear of responsibility.
- Unworthy. "I deserve nothing, not abundance, not love, not respect." Behind this attitude lies the fear of receiving.
- Unimportant. "No one cares about me. I do not matter. I make no difference." Behind this attitude lies the fear of being loved, the fear of the five A's (which can be seen as lying behind every self-diminishment).

Fortunately, each of these elements of the impoverished ego contains an alchemical kernel of value, as shown in the right column below.

Victim	Ability to find resources and evoke compassionate love
Follower	Ability to cooperate and recognize one's limitations
Self-blamer	Ability to assess one's own deficiencies
Unworthy	Ability to relate with humility
Unimportant	Ability to discriminate and grant precedence appropriately

To transform the impoverished ego requires the building of self-esteem, assertiveness, and cooperative skills. The challenge is always how to stand assertively and still stay connected. It is the psychological work of becoming an adult and a necessary precursor to intimacy.

The arrogant ego and the impoverished ego are actually two sides of one coin. Indeed, the neurotic ego has been called the "King Baby." Like a king the arrogant ego believes it has a divine right (entitlement) to be in full control, to be loved and respected by everyone, and to have first or center place in everything. Like a baby the impoverished ego looks helpless, and yet it has the power to mobilize people around its needs. After all, a baby is the center of attention. A baby controls others' behavior. A baby is entitled to special treatment. Moral (and psychological) adulthood means deposing the royal ego and letting the infantile ego grow up. Self-inflation and self-deflation are the neurotic edges of ego. The healthy ego, like virtue, is in the center between them.

The inflated ego with its status and success at control is less likely than the healthy ego to elicit the five A's from others. The deflated ego is too wounded and insecure to ask for them. Both find it hard to show them or receive them. Since giving and receiving the five A's are the basis for intimacy, what chance does the untransformed ego have for love?

TRANSFORMING THE IMPOVERISHED EGO

The victim changes by acknowledging his own power. The follower changes by making independent decisions. The self-blamer changes by taking responsibility. The unworthy person and the "unimportant" person both change by learning to appreciate themselves and to accept appreciation from others.

Changing involves acting as if the opposite of our thoughts and posturings were true. With practice, gradually our attitudes alter to fit the new behavior. Plan ways to do this work if you are a victim, follower, or self-blamer, or if you feel unworthy or unimportant. To reverse the victim position, take responsibility for your choices and look for ways to make the best of what you did not choose but cannot change. To step out of the follower role, take the initiative in speaking up in any circumstance or relationship that is presently disturbing you. To cease blaming yourself, acknowledge accountability for your behavior while also having an appreciation of how you acted in accord with the light you had at the time.

The choice of acting as if we had value and adult ability is both psychological and spiritual because it places the ego on the same axis as the Self and fulfills our destiny to align the display of our life with a divine design; the limited grants hospitality to the limitless. More and more conscious wholeness is thereby expressed in our daily life. The result is a radiance of love, wisdom, and healing to everyone. This is why a healthful personal choice is a moral choice and personal work results in planetary gain.

The Riches of Ego and How to Find Them

The impoverished ego feigns humility. The inflated ego feigns self-respect, pride, honor. But the healthy ego shows authentic self-respect and, by granting the five A's to others, unconditional love.

To love unconditionally calls for mindfulness: We let go of expectation, fear, grasping, shame, blame, retaliation, and the need to victimize or be victimized, the demands of the inflated—and frightened—ego that militate against intimacy. Most of us were taught to build the layers of ego not to let go of them, so this task kicks against the goad. In addition we cannot accomplish it by psychological work alone. *The neurotic ego has no motivation to give itself up. It takes grace, a force beyond ego, for such a move.* What's needed is not just a psychological change but spiritual transformation through love, wisdom, and healing power, the qualities of the Self.

Ordinarily we disregard, discredit, or disavow our essential Self. While ego is existential, tied to the moment's predicaments, caught up in drama and addiction, our Self/essence is unaffected by existential circumstances or personal attachments. Thus the Self feels like emptiness, and we fear that. If we stay with the emptiness in the Self, however, we come through the hole to wholeness. The emptiness becomes the portal to a wider richness that we were missing out on. Freedom from ego's drama is freedom to contact our own soul, a soul mate unparalleled.

If the mindsets of ego serve a neurotic purpose, providing distractions and consolations against the onslaught of reality and change, mindfulness is a pause, a deliberate resting between the distractions and consolations. Only mindfulness puts an end to obsession and compulsion, and without such barriers love flourishes. *If our capacity to love is still intact, everything happened at the right time and place.*

Saying Yes to the Things We Cannot Change

To free ourselves from our neurotic ego is ultimately to accept the conditions of existence and to see ourselves not as victims or opponents of the givens of reality, but as adults who face up to them honestly. These givens include the following: things change and end; life is not always fair; we pay for growth with suffering; things do not always go according to plan; people are not always loyal or loving. Accepting the conditions of existence means first of all admitting our vulnerability to them. To let go of the entitlement to an exemption is thus to be ready for love.

When we realize that the givens of life no matter how ferocious, are not penalties but ingredients of depth, lovability, and character, we can let go of the belief that we are immune (or need to be). "That can't happen to me" or "How dare they do that to me!" change to "Anything human can happen to me, and I will do my best to handle it." The strength to handle challenges, in fact, is directly proportional to how much we let go of entitlement.

Once we cease our dispute with circumstances and simply face them and deal with them, we feel serenity, changing what can be changed and accepting what cannot be changed. By doing so, we build a strong foundation for self-respect, a healthy alternative to universal entitlement. This means, among other things, establishing and maintaining personal boundaries so that others do not take advantage of us. Thus, self-respect is strength not weakness, but it gives us power for something, not over anything. It overcomes our fear of scarcity and deprivation. We feel love and freedom springing up abundantly within.

Jung suggests we say an unconditional yes to the givens of existence without protest or blame. In so doing we find the best of religion and depth psychology. For instance, we learn the following:

- *Everything changes and ends—yet can be renewed.* This knowledge is our entry into the archetype of resurrection.
- *Suffering is part of growth—yet we keep finding ways to bring good from evil.* This opens the archetype of redemption.
- *Things do not always go according to plan—yet we can find the equanimity to say yes to what is and thanks for what has been.* This opens the archetype of synchronicity and of a divine plan that makes our destiny larger than we ever imagined.
- *Life is not always fair—yet we can be fair and even generous.* This gives us a sense of justice and strengthens our commitment to fight for it, in keeping with the archetypes of karma and of atonement and forgiveness.
- *People are not loving and loyal all the time—yet we do not have to retaliate but can act with love and loyalty while never giving up on others.* This opens the archetype of unconditional love.

Thus the givens—the locus of our deepest fears—turn out to be the requisite of personal evolution and compassion. The givens are like the law, severe but not cruel. The unconditional yes is simply mindfulness, fidelity to reality without succumbing to seditious and tempting mindsets. Accepting each is a stage in our unfolding. Dealing with each instead of quarreling with it equips us for the heroic journey we are called to. As we grow, we let go of our ego's claim to exemptions from our universal heritage. Suffering results when we take a fiercely combative position toward the conditions of existence. Ego is suffering. A predicament is a path to liberation.

The dynamic of thesis, antithesis, and synthesis helps us understand the process. The thesis is the conditions themselves and our dislike of them. The antithesis is our unconditional yes. The synthesis is our transformation, using the givens as the ingredients for our growth.

We sometimes think we are alone, and that makes the givens terrifying and disempowering. When we ask why things change, why the innocent suffer, why people hurt us, we feel despair and bitterness. But when we say yes to the givens, we notice they are not about doom but about reality and its abundant potential. They connect us to the rest of humanity. They ground us in what is, in mindfulness, not in the wishes or expectations of ego. The call to say the unconditional yes shows that spirituality is not about transcendence of the world but deeper involvement in it.

An acceptant poise in the midst of life's conditions takes us through any crisis with equanimity. That poise is mindfulness. To say yes to life's mortal conditions is automatically to say yes to each of its immortal, archetypal possibilities—this means identifying with buddha mind in the midst of our difficulties and confusion. In this sense, greeting life with an unconditional yes is a way of finding eternity within time.

How do we say yes? By showing the five A's mindfully. As witnesses of what is, we give our *attention* to the changes and endings, the failed plans, the unfairness, the suffering, the occasional disloyalty in our life story. We *accept* all that as part of the mix of a human life. We *appreciate* it all as somehow valuable to our development. We look with *affection* on what is and what has been. We *allow* events and people to be themselves.

Combining the five A's with mindfulness in this way builds confidence in ourselves because it shows us we can handle reality without distractions from it and without embroideries around it. It contributes to our power to be intimate because it is a way of being present in a truly attentive, accepting, appreciative, and allowing way. It makes us more realistic because we acknowledge a world that exists beyond our wishes and manipulations. It teaches us how to love the moment, which is all we have, and to love in the moment with all we are.

A yes to the conditions of existence thus mends our existential alienation and provides the best launching pad for intimacy. The ego is not dragged kicking and screaming to the feet of Self but leaps for joy into its waiting arms. The ego is relieved to know there is an alternative to the pain it has known in fear, attachment, control, and entitlement. As Rilke writes to his own ego: "How I would love to see you under siege . . . for as many years as it may take."

Finally, we may notice that we have two paths opening to us: on the one hand, as some schools of Buddhism suggest, we can find happiness and full enlightenment in this life. Yet Jung proposes that suffering and shadow are inescapable no matter how healthy we become. The challenge is to hold these opposites with merriment.

Practices

GOING BEYOND EITHER/OR • Our ego is so uncomfortable with uncertainty that it insists on seeing things in terms of black and white, win or lose. When we simply hold in our hearts and minds the opposites that face us, when we let them coexist in us without choosing one over the other, we befriend the ambiguity of our predicament. This is a form of mindful trusting. To be caught in the polarities devised by the arrogant ego is to live in fear. Egolessness, by contrast, means letting an all-inclusive love come through.

For example, when we let go of control, the either/or of "I have to be in charge, or everything will fall apart" changes to "I let the chips fall where they may." This liberates us by changing our fear of spontaneity to a welcoming of fear *and* of whatever may happen beyond our control. Make a chart in your journal with the either/ors in your life on the left and ways they can become both/ands on the right. Show this to your partner or best friend and discuss ways to put the both/ands into practice. Ask her or him for support in this venture since it will probably be scary for you.

Perhaps every regret we have about the past is directly traceable to either/or thinking and choices. We may feel shame as part of regret. The work is to acknowledge our shame and regret and forgive ourselves. Imagine how much of your lively energy is crushed by old regrets. Will you give yourself your turn at happiness by doing the work it takes to get past all that? Write examples of regrets from your past in your journal and discuss how you will get past them. Ask for support from others where necessary.

BECOMING NONVIOLENT • Assertiveness, like any perfect act, "leaves no wake," as the Zen saying tells us. Ego, by contrast, leaves a grudge behind and creates a feud. In the Sermon on the Mount—the

Christian recipe for the dissolution of ego—Jesus addresses this question directly when he says: "If someone compels you to go one mile with him, go with him two." A healthy person simply learns to speak up when injustice occurs and attempts to rectify it, focusing on the objective fact (injustice), not on a personal interpretation of it (affront). The sense of affront betrays the presence of a neurotic ego investment. In fact, the word *affront*—like the word *turf*—has no meaning for anyone who has a functional, adult ego! Such a person fends off insults nonviolently, reckoning them as information about the aggressive anger of the other person, whose frustration might even engender compassion. Make a commitment to forgo the style of retaliation and to look for ways to create reconciliation. Make this commitment silently first within yourself and then aloud to your partner.

The indignant ego is sly. It may seek indirect reprisals for being hurt or disappointed. You might actually find yourself hoping that your partner will experience misfortune in life. If you catch yourself hoping for this kind of indirect retribution, admit to it and ask for forgiveness. Such heartfelt humility can free you from seeking this subtle form of retaliation. Though this admission might be embarrassing for you, egoless love blooms from just such self-disclosures.

TRANSFORMING THE NEED TO BE RIGHT • The need to be right comes from our fear of loss of approval. "If I'm wrong," we think, "I lose my identity and thus my approvability." Our need to be right may take the form of an inability to accept criticism, which we usually equate with insult. It may also take the form of always having to explain that we were completely warranted in a decision or action whenever we are called to account. It may include inordinate insistence that others apologize. These reactions are automatic for most of us—in other words, not conscious. To be an adult means expending the effort to become conscious of how much ego underlies our behavior, thoughts, and motivation. "My way is the right way" can be transformed into "I negotiate so that both of us win. I look for what is true and build on it." Opening ourselves to others' winning also leads to and creates safety in the very closeness we feared.

TRANSFORMING SELF-JUSTIFICATION • Affirm: *I allow others their opinions of me with no attempt to correct their impressions or make myself look good. This includes naming the reality of events without blame.* ("She left me" replaces "She was wrong and unfair to leave me.")

As we transform our ego in this way, we no longer answer a snide remark with sarcasm. Instead, we attend to the pain and defensiveness behind mean comments and feel compassion for their source. Sarcastic comebacks, even in jest, are a way of sneaking out unexpressed anger, another example of the retaliation model. A healthy adult tries to follow the reconciliation model, having become highly sensitive to her own infliction of pain and to the pain behind the infliction of it by others. Such a person lets go of the need for approval and makes fewer attempts to gain it. She evaluates herself from within, where the Self is, not from outside, where other scared egos are. If you use sarcasm, ridicule, teasing, pinching, tickling, or barbed kidding at times, make a commitment to cease using these passive-aggressive weapons against your partner or anyone. Make this commitment first to yourself silently and then aloud to your partner.

FREEING OURSELVES FROM EGO ENTITLEMENT • Answer the questions in this section silently. Do you believe "I am entitled to have things go my way; to be told the truth; to be loved, cared about, and appreciated by everyone; to have promises made to me and then kept; and to be given special treatment or special consideration in everything I do"? Behind these beliefs are the rationalizations "Promises should be kept," "I am special," "It can't happen to me," and "How dare they!" Such beliefs may mask the fear of deprivation: "I won't get enough," "I won't get what's rightfully mine," "I won't survive as an individual person if I have to be like everyone else." To think this way is to ignore a condition of existence: Things are not always fair or equal.

Entitlement can take the form of expectations, overreaction to being taken advantage of, a sense of being owed something, or a belief that we are being cheated. The best example of this feature of ego is the reaction we might have when we are cut off in traffic. Does the feeling of "How dare he do that to me?" turn into a frenetic and vengeful chase?

Does it stick in your craw for the rest of the day? Vengefulness and indignation are clues to the presence of an arrogant, narcissistic—and ultimately very scared—ego. But behind the angry sense of humiliation is sadness that we have not been treated with love and respect—the things we believe we are entitled to from everyone. What we really mean to say when someone cuts us off in traffic is "How dare you not treat me with respect! How dare you not love me!" Secretly, the ego believes it has always had a right to that. Make a commitment to ask for love directly each time you notice yourself falling into one of the ego reactions described in this chapter.

DROPPING PRETENSE • Self-centeredness can be transformed to healthy self-appreciation and self-love, including a healthy desire to let everything we do or say reveal us authentically. We may feel "If they really knew me, they would not like me." Actually, this feeling is based not on what they find out about us but how. People dislike us for what they uncover not about us but about what we hide. Indeed, they like and respect us for our disarming admissions about our limits and inadequacies. Knowing this gives us yet another chance to articulate our truth, to drop a pretense. The healthy adult moves from pose to poise. He wants to be ex-posed so that he can act freely with no further need to invent or protect a self-created image. Do you have it in you to be ruthless in your journey to freedom from ego?

The reason we fear self-disclosure is directly related to one of the five A's: We fear not being accepted if we show anything about ourselves that others might consider unsavory or inadequate. We may have decided early on that to keep those A's coming means hiding what raises eyebrows and showing what brings a smile of approbation.

Does the preceding paragraph describe you? In your journal, write about some examples from childhood and the recent past. Silently make a commitment to drop pretenses with your partner, asking yourself on a scale of one to ten how comfortable this prospect feels. This will give you information about your level of trust in the relationship. Share the information with your partner.

LETTING GO OF POUTING • If you notice yourself pouting like a child when you do not get your way, try this triple-A program to undo ego entitlement:

- Acknowledge the pouting to the person you are doing it in front of.
- Ask for what you want in a direct and non-demanding way.
- Accept the answer "Yes" with gratitude and "No" with cheerfulness.

ASKING FOR AN EGO AUDIT • Throughout this book, I have recommended looking for feedback from others about our behavior and attitudes. As adults we consider everyone our teacher and no one our competitor. Thus, to act defensively means losing out on useful input. To defend how we are is to stay as we are, and it ruins our chances at personal development and intimacy. Instead, listen to feedback in such a way as to find a useful truth in it. Nothing is so disarming as receptivity. Receiving feedback willingly soon reveals itself as a way of receiving more love. Make a commitment to ask for and open yourself to the feedback of others regarding your ego reactions. Do this silently within yourself and then aloud to your partner.

LETTING GO OF BLAME • We may use blame and criticism to cover up needs that we have not expressed or that have not been met. Our essential needs await fulfillment behind all the ego layers: fear, attachment, control, complaint, and defenses. To state our needs rather than to blame others for not fulfilling them leads to the very openness and vulnerability that makes for authentic intimacy. Apply this knowledge by understanding the impulse to blame as a signal of some unmet need and stating the need instead of blaming. Change "You were wrong to do this" to "I need your attention, acceptance, appreciation, affection, or allowing."

When you find yourself thinking critically about a partner or friend ("You should stop smoking"), try changing the criticism to an affirmative, even prayerful, and kindhearted wish ("May you find the strength to stop smoking"). Use this same technique when you are self-critical: "May I access the strength I know is in me to let go of this habit." When listening to the news and seeing a criminal or someone you find repugnant, practice saying within yourself, "May he find Buddha's way. May he become a great saint." *This is what is meant by not giving up on anyone, the royal road to freedom from the retaliatory instinct of ego.* We allow the consequences of others' acts to catch up with them—or not. We do not impose the judgment ourselves or even pronounce it. We are not executioners or jurors, only fair and alert witnesses. We are not glad "they got theirs." We only hope they can wake up.

GOING BEYOND OUR VICES • In Buddhism, the "six poisons" of pride, envy, desire, greed, ignorance, and aggression are the ego vices that keep us stuck in samsara, the world of continuous rebirth. We can liberate ourselves from them by making choices that emanate from the brighter side of the ego. Thus, pride gives way to humility. Envy gives way to joy at others' good fortune. Desire for more gives way to satisfaction with what we have. Greed gives way to generosity. Ignorance gives way to the will and commitment to inform ourselves. Aggression gives way to nonviolent compassion. This is how the poisoned ego realm becomes a space wherein we can awaken. Draw up a chart. In the left-hand column, list the six poisons and the symptoms you show when you are poisoned by them. In the right-hand column, list the ways you will behave and feel when you are purged of them.

CONFESSING • Mindful, loving justice in a relationship is not retributive but restorative. It moves us from alienation to reunion in an atmosphere of mended failures. It fosters healthy vulnerability and diminishment of ego, which reduces hurtful behavior in the future.

Spiritual adulthood includes a frequent examination of conscience and a need to make amends when appropriate. The alternative—that evil is only out there in others—grants us a sinister permission to retaliate and punish.

We build trust when we admit we are not perfect. Partners can practice an occasional confession to one another by following these steps:

> 1. Acknowledge to yourself that you may have failed in mirroring your partner by showing a willful deficit in attention, acceptance, appreciation, affection, or allowing freedom of individuality. Have

you refused to address, process, or resolve issues? Have you placed selfish concerns over those of the relationship, shown disrespect, lied, betrayed, disregarded tender feelings, been critical, not shown appreciation, let your anger erupt into abuse, disappointed your partner, broken an agreement, denied responsibility for your actions or choices, gossiped, not respected privacy, taken advantage, manipulated or controlled, been greedy, retaliated, and so forth? Devising your list requires a careful examination of conscience, a willingness to see your own inadequacies, and a desire to work on them. Do the remaining steps together with your partner.

2. Admit your deficiencies in words. Admitting wrongdoing touchingly combines pride and humility. The toxic dimension of something you are ashamed of does not reside in the horror about what you have done but in the isolated way in which you hold it. Keeping it a secret does more harm to you than having done it. The tragedy is that the more hidden your pain, the more you lose your chance for comfort and release. As Shakespeare says: "Give sorrow words, the grief that does not speak whispers the o'erfraught heart and bids it break."

3. Show feelings of sadness and regret.

4. Make amends to your partner. (Self-destructive penitence—for example, Oedipus blinding himself—is really retaliation turned on oneself, another trick of ego.)

5. Resolve not to repeat the behavior. This may include making a plan to police yourself or asking for feedback throughout the coming week.

6. Appreciate and thank each other for this opportunity.

These six steps disarm the offended other and elicit forgiveness, the natural and automatic human response to penitence. As Shakespeare says in *The Tempest*, "They being penitent, the sole drift of my purpose doth extend not a frown further."

A short version of the six steps is this triple-A approach: admit, apologize, amend. We need a simple model like this one when—at Thanksgiving dinner, for instance—our children bring up something from their past that shows one of our shortcomings as parents. Our ego wants to defend or forget, but our love for them helps us let go of our pride. When we love, we feel sorrow and say we are sorry when we see someone in pain because of something we did, no matter how well intended. The impact of our actions on others is all that matters when we love. *The stirring purpose of this and of all our work is to let a loving response come out first rather than an ego reaction.*

Some of us were raised with religious practices that included confession to a priest who gave us penance for our sins. In this approach we take responsibility for making amends to those we may have hurt. Such penance is not a form of retaliation against ourselves but rather an adult way of redeeming ourselves and becoming free of guilt. Twelve-step programs use a similar approach to recovery. Humility is the foundation of all transformation. And relationships are spiritual powerhouses because they humble us again and again; eventually we *choose* that humility—and then a virtue has arisen in us.

Finally, when someone hurts us, we may feel victimized. "You did this to me" is the experience of isolation, emphasizing our polarities. However, when you discover that you have that same tendency or sometimes act in the same way, the experience becomes one of connection. "I am like that too" does not excuse abuse but it helps us find a path to compassionate communication and reconciliation.

INCREASING COMPASSION • Grandiosity and entitlement ("big ego") may be panic-driven attempts to shore up a crumbling sense of self and to stave off the threat of annihilation. ("The ego is the true seat of anxiety," according to Freud.) The next time you see someone acting arrogantly, realize what pain and fear he carries under that mask of omnipotence and have compassion toward him. Compassion builds in us when we also realize that the inflated ego often has its roots in uneven or ineffective childhood nurturance. A person who was humiliated, insulted, belittled, criticized sarcastically, and so on may do these same things to others later, a poignant and pathetic way of showing to the world how—and how deeply—he was wounded. Cultivate a compassionate response toward those people in your life who seem most ego-driven. They may need love the most. (The five A's are themselves a practice for letting go of ego and for being supportive and compassionate.) The victory of love makes the sports of ego no longer so appealing. Make a commitment to become conscious of moments in which the ego of another person is inflamed. Instead of letting your ego follow suit, respond with tender and disarming love. This is how we change the reflex to compete and create distance into a choice to care and be close.

LETTING GO OF EGO SO WE CAN LOVE • The habits of ego— fear, grasping, censure, control, attachment to outcome, preference, complaint, biases, defenses—are *interferences*. They contravene mirroring, while protecting and endorsing ego. Respond to these questions in your journal after a meditation session: Is my meditation practice helping me go beyond my ego's interferences? Does it teach me that I have it in me to witness my own and other people's feelings and behavior without the dramatic overlays of my neurotic ego getting in the way?

Follow up with these affirmations: *I notice how and when I act from ego, and I apologize. I am choosing to act in ways that are free of ego. I let go of the inclination to fear, hold on, complain, control, censure, and so forth. I ask those around me to point out any words or deeds indicating that ego may be arising in me.* This is the path of ruthless fealty to truth. It is also a way to free ourselves from suffering and to stop causing suffering in others.

BECOMING PRESENT • Mindfulness means presence without the habits listed on the left side of the following chart. These dramatic artifacts, devised by the ego, defend us against authentic intimacy, the full brunt of our here-and-now predicament, and a full understanding of ourselves and our partner. They allow us to avoid being really present to ourselves and others. Indeed, they are forms of violence; the habits listed on the right side of the chart—like mindfulness itself—are forms of nonviolence.

The terror that strikes us in a crisis comes from the powerlessness we feel in the face of it. (Joseph Campbell defines hell as being "stuck in ego.") We escape being devastated by crises only if we have delivered ourselves from the causes of collapse: the habits listed on the left side of the chart. We do this by forming the alternative habits, listed on the right side of the chart, which are the keys to equanimity and living with felicity and through adversity. Mindfulness is thus a sane response not a dramatic re-action to the stresses of life and the crises that arise in a relationship. Note how the habits listed on the left, the textures of the neurotic ego, both de-flate our power to face reality and inflate the power of reality over us.

Interferences of Neurotic Ego	*Healthy Possibilities in Mindfulness*
Fear and defensiveness	Caution
Greed	Wanting only what is necessary and sharing with others
Subjective interpretation	Open-mindedness
Judgment, bias	Fair assessment
Censorship	Openness
Blame	Fair assessment
Attachment to an outcome	Perseverance toward goals
Control	Cooperation
Retaliation/retribution	Asking for amends and forgiving others
Demand	Request
Expectation	Agreement
Analysis	Contemplation
Comparison or evaluation based on a model of perfection	Acceptance of what is as it is
These are the elaborations of the dysfunctional ego standing alone.	*These are the collaborations of the healthy ego in relationship with others.*

Use the chart to take an inventory of how you see your partner or the issue that is facing you at the moment. *Notice that most problems or pain in a relationship are caused by an attitude or belief that originates from a habit on the left side of the chart.* The neurotic ego listings are learned through conditioning. Unconditional love, like mindfulness, is free of these interferences. This is how mindfulness is directly related to mature love. It is freedom from the conditions of ego.

PRACTICING LOJONG • Our ego diminishes and everyone becomes our valued friend when we follow the *lojong* teachings of Tibetan Buddhism, designed in the twelfth century by Geshe Langri Tangpa to summarize Buddhist concepts. The central point of these teachings is contained in this statement: "Whenever others . . . revile and treat me in other unjust ways, may I accept this defeat myself, and offer the victory to others." By cultivating compassion and by overcoming the illusion of an independent self, we can love in such a humble way. The implications of this exalted teaching for intimate relating become clear once we realize that love is other-concerned, that it has no hierarchy, and that it does not insist on individual autonomy or cherish self-vindication.

Here is a summary of the *lojong* teachings. Read each statement aloud, with meditative pauses, every day:

> May I consider all beings precious.
>
> May I always respect others as superior while maintaining self-esteem.
>
> May I face my inner darkness and turn it to good.
>
> May I be moved with compassion for the pain behind the spite others may show me.
>
> When I am hurt by others, may I forgo retaliation while always fighting injustice.
>
> May I reckon those who betray me as sacred teachers.
>
> May I offer joy to all beings and secretly take on their suffering.
>
> May all beings and I be free from ego concerns of loss and gain.

BUILDING A HEALTHY EGO • Our healthy self-esteem can increase when we look at ourselves mindfully, granting ourselves the five A's. We do this by affirming ourselves just as we are:

do this by affirming ourselves just as we are:

> I look at myself and my life without fear of what I may see or what I may find I have to work on. I look at myself without censure, blame, or shame but with a sense of accountability for any ways I have hurt others, and I make amends. I accept myself as I am without an attachment to fixing, changing, or controlling my natural inclinations and attributes. I let go of any attachment to the outcome of what is happening in my life right now or what will happen in my life in the future. I allow myself to live in accord with my deepest needs and wishes. I love myself as I am and take care of myself. I pay attention to my body and what it tells me about myself and the joys and stresses of my circumstances. I am free of fear and craving. I share with others the gifts I receive. May all beings have happiness because of my work, my gifts, and my practice.

TAKING IT PERSONALLY • Consider each of the five conditions of existence listed on page 185, adding any of your own, and write out examples of each from your own life. Then say yes to each of them in this way: "Yes, this happened, and I grant it attention, acceptance, appreciation, and affection, and I allow it to be what it was/is. I am thankful for how I have grown from this experience. I am compassionate toward those who are going through it today. May all beings find happiness in life as it is."

Next, write this or say it aloud: "It takes a long time to get it; all these conditions apply to me. There will be no exemption, no special deal. I am totally vulnerable to all the conditions of existence all the time no matter where I go or how good I am. Really getting this deconditions me from illusion and entitlement. To say yes to the conditions of existence liberates me. I face them rather than F.A.C.E. them!"

> When I see I am nothing, that is wisdom. When I see I am everything, that is love. My life is a movement between these two.
>
> —NISARGADATTA MAHARAJ

8
When Relationships End

We become whole through relationships and through letting go of relationships.

—Sigmund Freud

There seems to be no better way to learn what a relationship is really about than to see how it ends and how we are in the ending. All relationships end—some with separation, some with divorce, some with death. This means that in entering a relationship we implicitly accept that the other will leave us or we will leave him. Grieving is therefore included in what we sign on for. But grief is built into all of life because of life's painful events, changes, transitions, and losses.

The grief at the end of a relationship comes from no longer getting one's needs met, especially the five A's. We think we only feel it at the very end, but we have probably felt it during the relationship, too. At the end and afterward, we remember the grief we felt during the relationship not only the grief we felt at the end. Perhaps we did not notice it before because we were raising children, having dinner, having sex, going to movies, sharing cocktails, hanging curtains. Ironically, the worse the relationship was, the worse our grief will be. This is because when we end a very difficult relationship, we are not only letting go of a partner but of all the hope and work we invested in trying to keep alive something that had expired long before. We thought wrongly—and sadly—that those five A's were in her somewhere and all we had to do was keep trying to evoke them and someday we would see them emerge. Now we finally have to admit that such a someday will never come.

But we feel the pain most severely when we uselessly fight against a necessary ending. Holding on is the painful element of letting go. What do we let go of? What we thought the relationship was and found out it was not, what we tried to make it into and could not, what we hoped it would become and saw that it did not, what we believed was there and was not there at all. The most painful element of grief may be this last realization that what we expected was not there to be had. How familiar and especially tormenting that may be if we had the same experience in childhood.

Emily Dickinson wrote: "A loss of something ever felt I, / The first that I could recollect, bereft I was." I grow up when I admit that neediness, loneliness, and longing persist in me in my adult life. There is always that child inside wanting more. He is the one who makes me buy those chocolate chip cookies when I stopped at the store intending to buy only cabbage.

That is why the steps of grief work about childhood losses (see the Appendix) apply to the end of relationships also. If we have stronger feelings after a relationship than we ever experienced while it was going on, it is a sign that our grief resembles and is reviving past losses. We are grieving more than just this ending. Many endings were stacked inside us awaiting their chance for the attention of tears.

During a painful ending or in the midst of a crisis of infidelity or betrayal, our spiritual practice and all our psychological work may not restore us to serenity. Our obsessive thoughts prevent us from meditating for long, while psychological insights prove to be only palliatives. This does not reflect a deficiency in our program or practice, neither of which work best when adrenaline is flowing. If we cannot appreciate Mozart and the *Mona Lisa* at this time, either, it does not mean art is useless. All bets are off when someone has hurt us. In such utter bereftness the ego confronts its true face: frustrated, scared, caught in a painful attachment, powerless to alter what others may be doing to us. The hero arriving at such a threshold can only say, "This must be the place!"

The risky move is also the only reasonable option for us: to let go completely. This requires enormous discipline because the ego wants to assert itself and regain its power. We now see why breaking up is part of the struggle phase of the heroic journey. Yet our work during a breakup is also immensely simple: to witness the events and players rather than to be players. We let the chips fall where they may and use the pieces we are left with as the building blocks for whatever comes next.

Finally, leaving may not be about wanting to get out of the relationship. It may be a way of getting some space or breaking out of the doldrums rather than a comment on a partner's suitability. Many a relationship has ended when all that was needed was some time out.

Note that in this chapter the practices are integrated into the text.

Ending with Grace and Moving On

> On the first day, I sobbed and wept so uncontrollably, I could not go to work. On the second day, I felt so depressed and cried so much I could not go to work. On the third day, I wept and then worked half a day. Now I'm working overtime.

> At first, I wailed, "She abandoned me!" Then I lamented, "She left me!" Today I said, "She no longer lives at this address."

If you are wondering about whether to leave a relationship or not, it is crucial to discuss your concerns with your partner. Then it is wise for the two of you to see a competent therapist to address, process, and resolve your concerns together. As a start, it may be useful to ask yourself the following questions and notice if the majority of your answers are yes or no. Respond to these questions individually and then you might compare your answers.

- Do you and your partner show one another love, respect, and support by giving and receiving the five A's?
- Do you enjoy and feel safe in one another's company?
- Do you regularly make time for one another?

- Is this relationship fully in keeping with your own deepest needs, values, and wishes?
- Is your sex life together satisfactory?
- Are you remaining faithful to one another?
- Do you trust your partner?
- Are you and your partner willing to work on conflicts together?
- Are you keeping agreements with one another?
- Regarding past hurts, do you now live in an atmosphere of mended failures rather than of stubbornly held resentments?
- Does your partnership match what you always wanted for yourself in an intimate relationship?
- Are you together by choice rather than because of history, family, social convention, financial security, religious influence, the absence of an immediate alternative, or the inconvenience in or fear of separating?
- When you describe how you first met or how you first knew you were in love, is it with detail, enthusiasm, and a sense that it was fortunate?
- Does your inner trio—heart, head, gut—assent to continuing the relationship?

When a relationship ends by separation or divorce, there are some practical suggestions that may be helpful. First, we need a space in which to grieve alone and let go. To avoid this by jumping into a new relationship contradicts the course of nature. Grief work gives us an impetus for growth by helping us advance to a higher level of consciousness. The person I find immediately upon ending a relationship is likely to be at the same level of maturity as my ex-partner. The person I find when I have been alone for a while—and have had a chance to reflect, process, and grow from my experience—is more likely to be at a higher level of maturity. *I commit myself to mourn and learn, taking all the time I need and not letting a new relationship distract me from my work.*

As you grieve you are not available to others. Your children miss their absent parent, and thus they turn into mourners, too. In turn, expect their grief to compound yours, because you are mirroring them. This is a normal element of grief within a family, especially since the family unit is lost.

The ending of a relationship does not have to be hateful and ego-competitive. A commitment to compassion can configure the process of ending as *hospicing* not as slaying. Partners—or at least one of them—can let go of the relationship with lovingkindness, a spiritual practice. *May we/I hospice the ending of our relationship.*

Sleep disorders are to be expected at this time. You may also fall into your customary patterns of self-destruction—for example, anorexia, addiction to a substance, or suicidal thoughts. Grief involves an ending, something our bodies may associate with a wish to die that has laid buried within us since childhood.

Therapy is crucial during this period; it can assist us in addressing, processing, and resolving issues/planning change. Since we are never mourning only the current issue, therapy will also help us work on buried issues from the past. Ask yourself: "Is this why losses happen? Is the universe giving me a chance at rising from my ancient tomb?"

Grief is a cold turkey. Alcohol and drugs only distract us from it. "I felt so bad, I took a tranquilizer." The opening clause of that sentence bespeaks grief. The second clause bespeaks the avoidance of grief. *I commit myself to getting through this without harmful or distracting substances.*

At the end of a relationship, we wonder about our lovability. "He didn't really love me (I now realize)," therefore "I'm unlovable" (I blame myself)" or "He cannot love anybody" (I blame him)." But how about "I'm lovable; he can love; and he doesn't love me." Adults embrace this last, realistic view. *Anyone can love. No one is unlovable. Not everyone will love me.*

It is common to feel compelled to tell your story to anyone who will listen. This is a normal phase of grief work. Repeating the traumatic details helps you absorb the shock and stress of what occurred. Someday, however, while telling the story of how right you were and how bad she was, you will bore yourself. That is the instinctive signal that the storytelling no longer serves a useful purpose. Then you will stop. With luck, you have enough friends that they are not all worn out from hearing the story again and again by the time you get to that liberating moment!

Someday the other person and the relationship and all that has happened will simply be information. That will signal that the grief has run its course and that you have moved on. It takes patience to get there, but you can build patience with practice. Then someone will offhandedly say, "You were both unhappy together and it had stopped working for you, and now that you are apart, you have a chance at happiness," and the simple honesty of that statement will land inside you with the thud of truth.

Stress obstructs clear thinking. It is wise to declare a moratorium during this time on important financial and legal decisions, relocating, child custody, and so on. It is common during breakups to fantasize about moving away—from the pain. If only it could be that easy! Embarking on any new venture without therapy or feedback from friends at a time like this is dangerous. *A good rule may be to have to want something for thirty consecutive days before you decide to proceed with it.* This applies especially to getting back together.

The desire for vengeance against the partner who hurt you will probably arise. This is the ego's way of avoiding grief by substituting interaction for inner action—that is, personal work. Allow any feeling or thought, but refrain from acting on it. In the words of an old saying, any bird can fly over your head, but it is up to you whether it builds a nest in your hair.

This is from the letter of a close and admirable friend of mine during the time of his difficult divorce: "I feel I have become a kinder person, not wanting to hurt others. I do have cruel thoughts about how to deal with her, but I don't act on them. She has no peace within herself, and someday she may wake up and change, but that is not my business." This is the sound of an opening heart and a crumbling ego.

You may fear that you will never find anyone else; no one will ever want you. This sort of paranoid delusion is to be dismissed as such, but it also serves the grief work. It prevents you from looking for someone else before you are ready to see who you are.

You may be unable to get the other person or the betrayal out of your mind. The ego prefers to choose one side of a polarity and ignore the other, which helps explain the origin and longevity of obsessive thoughts in which we can focus on only one option. You are not in the control tower. Rather you are challenged to become the landing strip. Simply allow any feelings and thoughts that may safely land or crash on you. They are normal and usually fade with time.

It is a mistake to recontact a former partner too soon. In this instance, it helps to have an ego that is too proud to beg for contact! When is the time right for reconnecting in a friendly way? Probably when you have stopped obsessing and no longer want or need to change him or get even with him. *The time for recontact is when you no longer need contact but are ready to normalize relations. That happens when the charge is gone.* (Normalizing relations is especially important when you have children's issues to negotiate.)

Grief cannot be willed away. It is best not to attempt to let it go but to let it happen. Allow it—that is, yourself—to take all the time needed, no matter what friends say about how long it is supposed to take to "get over it."

Beware of false hopes that arise when a partner who leaves seems to be on the fence about resuming the relationship. This may not be a sign that she wants to reunite. Ambivalence is normal in any breakup. There are usually many back-and-forth gestures between the statement of an ending and the actual ending. Let time tell you whether there is reasonable hope.

A person who has been left may feel like a little boy with hat in hand, waiting for the other to be kind or to relent and take him back. This is a normal way to feel and can lead to a healthy vulnerability for the future. The psyche has many ways of learning to let go of its hardness and let in the light. At the same time, the little, begging boy helps you learn that you have expected too much from other people. Here is a love poem by the Sixth Dalai Lama: "O, I demanded so much of you / In this short lifetime. / Maybe we will find one another again / In the beginning of the next."

"Your wound is beyond healing," said the prophet Jeremiah (30:12). Every grief has an element of inconsolability. There will always be something unresolved, ineradicable in a major loss. Such inconsolability is familiar from childhood. It is what fuels the longing for the perfect partner. Unfortunately, it often becomes synonymous with a sense of unlovability, so we cannot let in 100 percent of the love that comes our way in adult life.

The scars left by grief can be ugly for years or can heal reasonably well. The outcome depends on the skill of our grief work, just as scars on our body show the varying levels of the skill of the doctors who treated us over the years.

If your relationship ended when your partner found someone new, how would you feel about writing a letter to the intruder? It would simply state what you have been feeling and going through as a result of the betrayal: not eating, not sleeping, crying all the time, and so forth. The motive of this impact letter is not to change anything. It is simply to let the intruder know what happened to you as a result of her willingness to enter a relationship with someone who was not yet finished with his own partner. Do not attempt this unless you expect no answer and have no wish to hurt anyone. An alternative is to write it and not mail it.

Resist the wish to tell your partner one last thing or give him one necessary piece of information that is actually an argument meant to manipulate him into whatever response you desire. Tell it to the moon instead, and the goddess there will see that he finds out just what he needs to know:

> A full moon poised above the sea
> Makes the face of heaven radiant
> And brings to hearts that are apart
> The poignant pensiveness of night.
> I blow out my candle but it is just as bright here;
> I put on a coat but it is just as cold.
> So I can only read my message to the moon
> As I lay me down and long for dreams of you.
> —CHANG CHUI-LING

Read the following paragraphs slowly and then sit meditatively. They summarize the spiritual process we have been learning and apply it to endings and other kinds of crisis.

The neurotic pastimes of the ego—fear, attachment, blame, complaint, expectation, judgment, preference, attachment to outcomes, the need to fix things, control, attraction, aversion, and preference—create intrusion. The practice of mindfulness can liberate me from such limiting shelters and help me face my experience fearlessly just as it is. If my world crumbles, then the resulting groundlessness is a liberating invitation to reinvent my life. In fact, without the customary ground on which to run away from it, I can befriend my suffering unconditionally. Mindfulness is like seeing something for the first time—without the distracting intrusions of ego—and hence another name for it is *beginner's mind*. It offers me a way of working with reality rather than against it.

The point of the practice is not to calm our inner storm or manage it but to sit quietly in its eye and thereby to mirror and receive its energy. My frantic attempts to fix a painful collapse are a way of running from that possibility. My predicament is myself, no matter how negative or scary it may be. All my avoidances of it are escapes from the full impact of my life as it is now and the teaching it is meant to impart to me. The wisdom is in not escaping at all. Mindfulness is not about becoming composed but about composing ourselves fully in our here and now, truly mirroring our immediate reality.

Meaninglessness occasionally greets me in the course of life. When I allow it, move into it, let myself be with it, and stay through it, I feel lighter, enlightened. To allow is not to wallow. I wallow when I become a victim of my thoughts. I allow a felt sense of its darkness to arise in my body, free of thought, full of space. This is body mindfulness. I now practice a nonverbal attention to my body parts gradually—from sole to crown—while releasing any tension stored in them.

Whatever my current negative thought or feeling, it is bearable when it is granted the hospitality of mindful awareness. Then I have pure experiences, with Zen-like immediacy—for example, to see one lilac without a wish for more or to taste an apple without a fear of not having enough:

I am thankful that I cannot outsmart the ways of the universe.
May I honor my confusions as my path.
May everything that happens expose my self-deceptions and
my attempts at hiding out.
May my body become my witness and my teacher.
May my current predicament and all my practice bring happi-
ness to every earthly being.
May my former partner become an enlightened buddha.

When Somebody Leaves You

Selene is a psychiatrist in her mid-forties with what has so far been a
well-nigh insuperable fear of engulfment. She has been in therapy off
and on for years and avidly reads books like this one. Nonetheless, her
fear gains ascendancy in direct proportion to the building of a relationship. Her distancing from her partner, Jesse, has made life painful for
both of them. Jesse, an engineer in his early thirties, fears abandonment
as strongly as Selene fears engulfment. He would not read a book like
this. During their relationship, the more Selene demanded space, the
more Jesse clung to her. And the more he clung, the more space she demanded.

After five years together, Jesse told Selene he had been involved with
someone else for a while and was leaving Selene. Their relationship had
not worked for either of them in a long time. Neither one had been a
source of nurturance to the other, and neither could share feelings with
the other. Selene had actually wanted a break, but now she suddenly
wanted the relationship more than ever. Jesse's name became a thousand
times more dear to her once it became associated with abandonment.
Her fear of engulfment became an intolerance of abandonment.

Selene has been in therapy now for five months, and here are some selections from the journal she is keeping. Some concern Jesse and some
are addressed to him, but none have been sent to him because Selene
knows these writings are really about her:

Jesse is no longer only Jesse but also the movie star of my inner
drama. He is the latest man I came to, starving and desperate, for a

nurturance he proved over and over that he could not give me. My powerful feelings of loyalty to this bond and my reactions to the loss of it cannot be accounted for by the literal Jesse. My actual relationship with Jesse was hurtful, and I know it was for the best that it was broken off. As long as I take him literally and not as a metaphor, I do not face my work. Could it be that once anyone is gone, he becomes simply a metaphor and no longer the literal person?

Jesse is the actor who can play Hamlet while others have only succeeded at playing Jack to my Jill. My story has an "abandonment by father" theme. Uncannily, Jesse has abandoned me for someone else. My intuitive inner wisdom must have known of this possibility from the very first kiss and brought me a partner with the precise flavor of my lost dad. When the literal Jesse leaves, the symbolic Jesse steps forward in my dreams and in my heart. I fail to realize the difference! I imagine there is only one Jesse for me. But there is an archaically elaborated Jesse inside me as well as the ordinary Jesse outside. The outside Jesse cannot account for this amount of pain. This loss is the loss of the illusion of him as the one in whom I finally found the love I was seeking all my life. In reality, though, I am only losing the chance to continue using him as the mannequin who can wear the garments of my unfulfilled wishes— this is the essence of my lifelong loneliness.

You and this grief allowed me to open, but you cannot meet the need you helped me to identify. You can open me but do not fill me. This is not your fault. It is about me.

Bereftness and longing have been in me all my life. I thought this partner could help me heal it. My work is to heal it myself and eventually find someone to join me in that enterprise. Now that this partner is gone, I generate the illusion that all would be well if only he were here. This is probably because he stumbled upon the sealed door in my psyche, and now I associate him with fulfillment since the relationship with him was a significant one. Actually, he was not the important person but the important trigger. Now he is the important image of the triggering.

How can I so easily forget that I was not safe from loneliness even with him? I enlisted him to defend me against my own feelings and to rescue me from ever falling into the ancient void of my childhood. Now, of course, he appears automatically in my mind whenever I feel desolate and alone. When I feel scared, I invest him with heroic powers rather than deputize myself to be the hero of my own story. I have to dismiss him and face the battle alone as an adult.

The Jesse I lost is everyone I ever loved and lost. I was never really loving only him. My net was cast much more broadly. I wanted all the love I ever missed. He offered the chance of that. He made all my hope and need to be loved seem fulfillable at last. When it was clear that he could not deliver, I projected the rest onto him, rooting him even more firmly in my life. "The hopes and fears of all the years are met in thee tonight!" (I just heard this line from the Christmas carol in my head. Now I see that I have known this concept since early in my childhood.)

I received a letter from the literal Jesse and had powerful feelings of hope and panic. I know I need time away as I heal from the wound of his leaving. Yet I miss him and want contact. I imagine I am missing only the physical Jesse, whom I am better off without. Actually, I am missing Dad and all the men who have left me—the emissary and personification of whom is the man who sent this letter. If I write back, I am taking this feeling literally, as if my feelings were about the physical Jesse. If I write to him in my journal and do not send him a letter, I am working profitably with the inner Jesse, my social worker in the struggle for self-location. I was a missing person until Jesse brought me home to myself. I came home when he left home.

I know I was inadequate for him, too. I promised him anything to get him back when he first left. But I can't fool myself. I would not have been any better as a partner once the smoke cleared and our old routine recommenced.

How I deny all the previously unacceptable facts about him! I keep fooling myself by thinking he was perfect and I messed up the best thing I ever had. I embellish and inflate his virtues (perhaps as he inflates my vices). My grief begins with a denial that protects me from the full onslaught of the powerful loss. My denial suspends my ability to assess accurately. I then magnify, distort, and embellish the value of what I have lost. That is what keeps me wanting him back so desperately.

I am craving to the max what satisfies the least. Can I accept such contradiction, irrational neediness as an OK part of me? I am OK as long as I don't act on my neediness by calling him for a fix. What makes me entertain that option? I am desperate for closeness. I am an addict, seeking what I need from someone who cannot give it to me. It is not that no one can, only that he cannot. I have to stay with myself now in this utterly ragged state. Witnessing the fragile waif within me may help me gain compassion for a self I have abandoned so many times. Could such compassion be an empowering way to get through this?

I recall the times I would hold you lovingly and listen to you and cuddle your little foibles. What I did for you is what I myself needed and longed for. *I showed you how I wanted to be loved by loving you in that way.* I did not notice that you did not return the favor. The part of me that wants you back is the scared, needy child who really needs a hearing and holding from me. The part of me that knows it is time to let go is the adult. The loving and powerful part of me lets you go and me go on.

My defenses are down, and I hear from others that I look more appealing. A fertile time for me: I can break old self-defeating and intimacy-sabotaging habits. How long before I slip back into the old patterns of fear?

Conversations in my head about things somehow working out between us in the future are part of the bargaining phase of grief. They also seem to help me get some semblance of my power back.

Jesse, how can you see me in this pain and not stop it? All you have to do is come back. I know I want the relationship back only to bring an end to my grief and not to recover something really valuable. I feel the sadness of the relationship itself and imagine I am feeling only the sadness of its ending.

I feel abandoned now that you are gone. But I was emotionally abandoned by you all through the relationship and never saw it that way. Even now, instead of admitting that fact, I am idealizing the past with you. Not that you are to blame; this is all about me and the fierceness with which I hold on to illusions. You are perfect as you are, Jesse.

I see through my magical belief in words: Letters or words to you to manipulate a response won't be answered or work now. It is as if I am calling someone whose line is busy as he talks to someone else. I can no longer fool myself. I know my need to contact you is not purely to see you and hear your voice but rather to convince and manipulate you. My ego wants to win, and that is why I have to stay away. If I got you back in order to win, it would empower my defeated ego.

I would never have stepped out of this terrible relationship. You and your new partner intervened where I could not. You are ending what I was prolonging. I lament that you are gone and simultaneously that we let it go on that long.

Do I crave the old relationship with no future that had to go or the possible new relationship with a future that cannot begin until I let go of the old? Selene, don't blow this chance to be free!

I feel like a child lamenting that my longtime friend is now playing with someone new and not me. This loss hits me right at the little-rejected-kid level of my psyche. My old unfulfilled need for nurturance accounts for the fierceness with which I am holding on at the end.

Sex was the best catalyst for my self-delusion. Sex is not a reliable indicator of a good relationship because it can be great even when we are utterly mismatched—as in our case. None of this is your fault, Jesse.

Jesse was not providing what I needed in a partner. But if I had let go of all my hope, I would have despaired, so I held on. Even now, he has all the divinity and aura of love's longing and stands as an idol no matter how sure my mind is that he is only a plaster saint. When these two images finally separate, my bid to be loved will come back to its source in me, and he will be reduced in size and only be "someone I once knew." Doing the work and maintaining no contact is the best path to a liberating iconoclasm.

Instead of holding out for fulfillment, will I settle for a repetition of an old cycle? I can make this mistake again. A new face makes someone seem to be a new person, but it may only be the same projection—it's like I'm casting a new actor in the same old role. Perhaps what I long for is, after all, an unopened potential for self-nurturance. My longing is not to find my fortune in someone else, but rather to find clues to where I will find my own buried treasure.

I have to watch this relationship go the same way I watch the roses fade: with neither blame nor grief. I will give a gift to the world in thanks for all I am learning.

PART THREE

Returning the Blessing

Once we accept that even between the closest human beings infinite distances continue to exist, we can live wonderfully side by side. As long as we succeed in loving the distance between one another, each of us can see each other as whole against the sky.

—RAINER MARIA RILKE

9

Our Commitment and How It Deepens

✠

B y coming home, the heroine of a heroic journey shows she has attained a higher consciousness about herself and the world. Coming home in this case is a metaphor for realizing that all we need is within us and within the hearts of those around us. Feeling the need for a relationship is thus a homing instinct, one consistent with the intent of the universe.

In the culminating phase of a relationship, our love is not limited to one person but reaches out to the entire world. We can attain universal compassion through the experience of loving one person. How? By commitment: giving and receiving the five A's, working problems out, and keeping agreements. Doing all this within our immediate partnership softens us to the point where we can do it with others. Success in this relationship makes us believe it is possible everywhere. The obstacles in our life become bridges.

But what exactly happens in us to open us to the world? In a committed relationship we finally let go of our ego's formidable insistence on being right, on getting our way, on competing and winning. We may still have arguments, but they do not last as long, they end in resolution, and they involve less replay of the past. We take the content of the argument as information rather than as grist for the mill of resentment. Instead of demanding that our expectations be met, we seek agreements. Now we fight but do not stop loving. We can take each other's ego more lightly. We cease to use power *over* one another but instead find ways to use power *for* the common goals of the relationship.

We begin to notice a humorous insubstantiality—like the no-self of Buddhism—in the posturings we devise in the face of conflicts. We cannot substantiate the claim that our positions are quite so nonnegotiable once compassion and wisdom bathe them fully. We look with mild amusement at what once seemed so enormous, and we let go of our seriousness, finally having recognized it as a form of pain. Now pain opens in a new way and leads to compassion and change, not blame and shame.

Once we realize that we are capable of anything that humans do, we are not so threatened by the hurtful behavior of others, and compassion flourishes. As Trungpa Rinpoche said, "The bodhisattva is never surprised." An intimate adult commitment is based on informed consent: "I know the architecture of your ego and the unlit corners of your shadow, and I commit myself to you with my eyes wide open. The territoriality and competitiveness of ego are loosening in me. Before, I wanted to possess you to gratify my ego. Now I dispossess myself of ego to strengthen our relationship." The compelling force of romance gives way to the impelling choice of real engagement. This is the time for marriage.

Partners now accept each other as perfect—but only the way an old shirt is perfect. Real love looks different in each phase of a relationship. Although an oak looks different in spring, summer, fall, and winter, it is always an oak. We give the five A's romantically in the romance phase, dramatically in the conflict phase, and serenely and reliably in the commitment phase (when we also bring them to the world). *The practices suggested in this book are not meant just to make my relationship better but to make all relationships better.*

Our relationship journey thus mirrors our journey to creative human fulfillment. Our intrapersonal goals become interpersonal and then transpersonal. The phases of relationships take us from an ego ideal through an ego and its shadow to a self that then transcends ego and embraces the universe. This is the same sequence that can happen within us (not only between us). We can discover the all-embracing circle of psychology and spirituality in the realm of relating. As Emily Dickinson said, "My business is circumference."

The psychological problems we have in a relationship are the shadow side of our spiritual potential. There is no clear division between the psychological and the spiritual, only a distinction. The accompanying chart shows the nexus between the personal and spiritual sides of our psyches and between our personal and transpersonal partnerships, too.

Psychological Problem: *The Symptom*	*Spiritual Potential:* *What Is Ready to Happen*
Fear of abandonment	Facing the wilderness within
Fear of engulfment	Surrendering to a higher power
Narcissism and self-centeredness	Opening to contact with the spiritual Self
Refusal to do psychological work or spiritual practice	Opening to one's calling
Retaliatory reactions	Self-forgiveness
Arrogant ego	Readiness for humility
Addiction	Search for spirit and readiness to receive it
Jealousy	Readiness for the sufficiency of grace
Infidelity	Search for the anima/animus
Rigid boundaries	Protection of the inner world
Loose boundaries	Openness to grace and unity

We can become so caught up in our own story, with all its past and present conflicts, that we lose perspective. Then we fail to realize what Shakespeare says in *Coriolanus,* "There is a world elsewhere." When something beyond our past and our relationships absorbs and animates us, we open to new potentials in the world and in ourselves. We let go of the past to create the future. Together we engage in a social cause, family concerns, service, career, religion, or other world-changing enterprises. No transformation is entirely personal because goodness cannot help but diffuse itself. Our partnership expands to include the whole world, and we contribute to planetary evolution. The original goal of leaving home to start a home of one's own expands to become the more general goal of making the world a home for all people. When we make a commitment to a partner by giving the five A's, we also become carriers and providers of these five aspects of love to the world.

The Virtues of Intimate Love

"I TRUST A LIVELY ENERGY IN AND BETWEEN US"

There is an inborn, organismic wisdom in our bodies. This wisdom knows and accesses our potential. It is homeostatic in that any imbalance that arises in our psyche-body immediately engages an inner resource to correct itself. David Palmer, the founder of chiropractic, called this wisdom the "innate intelligence" of the body. By this he meant an instinct in every cell that promotes balance, healing, and regeneration. He later referred to a "universal intelligence" in the cosmos. Finally, he realized that this intelligence and our bodily wisdom are one and the same. This is equivalent to saying that our bodily wisdom is infinite and infinitely accessible, that our core and the core of the world are the same, as is the core of the divine.

If we keep this in mind, we will realize our needs, because the five A's are not inadequacies; rather, they are our life force. To trust ourselves is to believe that our needs and feelings are precisely the invincible power that makes it possible to withstand the full force of reality, to handle the conditions of existence and to respond accordingly. If I run from reality or disguise or deform it, my lively energy is lost in the shuffle. That is ultimately the meaning of low self-esteem, of perceiving myself as a victim, and of childish neediness.

Lively energy has a unique shape in each of us. For instance, if I never had a period of time alone (without a parent or partner in my life), I may never have found my personal liveliness. (Liveliness means allowing feelings, and trust grows when I show and receive feelings.) I may never have felt my deeper feelings and become comfortable with them. I may believe that I can only find—or maintain—my own lively energy in the context of a relationship. This sense of need may be a signal of how I have lost touch with myself. Another way of saying this might be "I have avoided allowing my true self to emerge by always making sure that I have someone in my life. I use relationships to find out who I am, which means I never find out who I am."

Lively energy makes us trust ourselves more and more. A person with self-trust knows that a healthy relationship is not based on absolute trust in anyone else. No one is trustworthy all the time. Adult relationships are based on acceptance of that given of human fallibility, not on rigid trust but on flexible, unconditional love that allows us to get angry about betrayal but then leaves us enough heart to forgive it when a partner apologizes, makes amends, and truly changes.

When we find the five A's in someone, we trust him or her and feel supported. We trust ourselves when we can give ourselves these same five A's. To trust someone is to let in his love and handle his failings, and to do both fearlessly. To do this is an exacting adult task: *I trust myself to receive your love and loyalty when you are loving and loyal. I trust myself to confront and handle your betrayals, not letting you get away with them but not going away from you because of them unless you refuse to stop them.* To trust our lively energy is no longer to need others to protect us from our feelings and the impact of our experience: "Be nice to me and never hurt me so that I will never have to feel bad." Do I want an adult-to-adult relationship, or do I want a safe harbor from the stormy vicissitudes of intimacy?

> Where's that palace whereinto foul things
> Sometimes intrude not?
> —SHAKESPEARE, *Othello*

"I GIVE AND RECEIVE THE FIVE A'S"

Giving and receiving in intimacy reflect a healthy dual process that we see in most areas of human life. For instance, our body survives by both letting oxygen in and letting carbon dioxide out. Cells are porous in order to let in nutrients and excrete waste. We communicate by both speaking and listening. Spiritually we receive grace and give love. Even reading this book means taking in words and ideas and putting them into practice in the world!

What we give and receive in an intimate relationship exactly matches both our earliest needs and our adult spiritual practice: the five A's. We give to the other and receive from her the very same love we instinctively required in childhood. The difference is that now we see it as an enriching gift, desired instead of required. It helps us increase our self-esteem now, just as it was necessary for establishing a self-concept in early life.

How exactly do we give and receive? The first way is a simple/difficult technique: Ask for what you want and listen to your partner. Asking for what you want combines the most crucial elements of intimacy. It gives the other the gift of knowing you, your needs, and your vulnerability. It also means receiving the other's free response. Both are risky, and therefore both make you more mature. You learn to let go of your insistence on a yes, to be vulnerable to a no, and to accept a no without feeling the need to punish.

To listen intimately to a partner asking for what he wants is to pick up on the feeling and need beneath the request. It is to appreciate where the request came from. It is to feel compassion for any pain that may lurk in the request. It is to give the other credit for risking rejection or misunderstanding. We hear with our ears; we listen with our intuition and our heart. Giving and receiving entail the ability to accommodate the full spectrum of a partner's fears and foibles and to distinguish between needs we can and cannot expect to see fulfilled.

A second way intimate adults give and receive is through mutually chosen sex and playfulness: You make love when both of you want it, not when one of you pushes the other into it. You can be intimate without having to be sexual. You know how to have fun together. You play without hurting each other, without engaging in sarcasm or ridicule, without laughing at each other's shortcomings.

Finally, we give and receive by granting equality, freedom from hierarchy, to our partner and ourselves. Only the healthy ego, and not another person, is meant to preside over your life. In true intimacy, partners have an equal voice in decision making. One partner does not insist on dominating the other.

Granted, some couples choose to experiment with submission/dominance in sex. This can be a form of play (since it involves roles) and can be a healthy choice when it is mutual. But if it has a compulsive or violent dimension, it may be a reenactment of abuse from childhood. What is the difference between a submissive erotic style and low self-esteem or no boundaries? Submission/dominance is an erotic game chosen intentionally and consensually. It is not a rut partners fall into by default or when one partner's demands take precedence over the other's needs. It is willing not unwilling, conscious not unconscious. It is joyful instead of fearsome. It transforms rather than deforms love and respect, expanding rather than shrinking the boundaries of self-discovery. Healthy submission/dominance is not a way of gaining power over someone, but a way of playing out inclinations that are in all of us but may never have found legitimate expression. As long as it is not abusive, it can enhance the relationship and teach the partners about themselves, their egos, their limits, and undiscovered parts of their identities.

"I SHOW ANGER WITH A LOVING INTENT"

Closeness evokes both affection and aggression, love and hate. This ambivalence, which is normal, can tear us apart like horses pulling us in opposite directions, or we can accept it as a given of human relating. In committed intimacy, I can be angry at you and still love you. I can let you get mad at me without having to get mad at you. Real relating includes being with *and* standing against one another: "You can be angry at me and oppose me, and all the while I know you still love me. I can do the same with you. Anger does not have us; we have anger. Discrete instances of anger cannot muddle or obstruct the flow of our ongoing love."

The fully actualized self can acknowledge and experience the entire range of human feelings. To say we are incapable of rage, for instance, is to deny our inclination toward aggression that helps us fight injustice in the world. We impoverish ourselves and others when we fear or inhibit our human powers. If we cannot feel all the polarities of human emotion safely and fully, how can we experience the equanimity that is so necessary to self-fulfillment?

Closely connected to anger, the desire to retaliate is ingrained in us. This is not a sign of moral degeneracy but a natural, automatic survival reaction to threat and abuse. Our work, which both goes against our natural inclination and advances our natural evolution, is to accept this as a given of human nature while choosing not to act it out. This does not mean not acting at all but rather finding a way of expressing anger without hurting others. Such nonviolent resistance flows from higher consciousness rather than instinct, and it makes the world a more mindful and loving place.

Some of us have, consciously or unconsciously, sworn an oath of loyalty to the god of revenge. Hate is strong anger felt by the neurotic ego that has become stuck in the desire to retaliate. People who hate and retaliate have a tentative and tattered sense of self. Indeed, hate may serve some functions when our inner self is damaged: providing a sense of coherence when we feel fragmented, proving to ourselves that we exist, giving us a sense of control. But these are ultimately all strategies of agony and hopefully elicit compassion in us when we see someone else caught up in them.

When we are adult, we can hold and experience apparently contradictory feelings or conditions. For instance, we can be committed to someone *and* maintain personal boundaries, have a conflict with someone *and* be working on it, feel anger *and* be loving. We can feel abandoned *while* we remain committed to showing love. In fact, we can go on loving in any predicament, a touching example of how our psychological work can set a spiritual standard. To see others as good or bad is to split the world into those who evoke love and those who evoke hate. Internally, our love will feel like longing and our hate will hide our fear. When we become comfortable with anger we form an arc of connection that makes us feel we are whole and that others are, too. What propels and sustains us in intimacy is love that is comfortable with other feelings. Then anger is a normal and occasional reaction that never cancels love. Nothing can.

Compare the big and generously expressed anger in nature to the constricted anger of a disgruntled neighbor. Nature's great lightning bolt is so unlike the neighbor's minced words and grumbling, downcast face. As adults we have to fearlessly and trenchantly demonstrate our anger because it is a loud and serious cry for help in mending the relationship. Thus, only a caring person shows true anger, which opens to love when it is received with the five A's. This is how it coexists with intimacy and helps it grow.

"I MAINTAIN MY OWN BOUNDARIES WHILE I REMAIN CLOSE TO YOU"

In the Eastern view, the idea that we each have a separate identity is illusory, the result of a flaw in consciousness. But the spiritual truth of this perspective does not eliminate our psychological need for boundaries that safeguard us against predations and assaults from others. Ultimately, we are pure space, but "whilst this muddy vesture of decay doth grossly close us in," as Shakespeare says, it is convenient to operate as if we had an identity and it needed defending. While our spiritual destiny is to acknowledge oneness, our psychological task is to let go of our belief in oneness. For though there is no solid, separate, independent self, each of us has an inviolate, inalienable core of personal responsibility and rights. That core is our healthy ego, a provisional but legitimate feature of who we are.

Boundaries protect our commitment and ourselves. A person without boundaries makes her commitment to the maintenance of the partnership, not to its workability. With clear boundaries, on the other hand, we see when a relationship is not working and enlist our partner in working on it with us. If he agrees and joins us, we are encouraged. If he declines, we hear that message and act on it by asking more emphatically—or if the no is unalterable and unacceptable, by moving on.

"I VALUE YOU FOR MORE THAN THE FIVE A'S"

To maintain a relationship during periods when your needs are not being met means valuing your partner for himself, whether or not you are receiving the five A's continually. It means that it is all right with you, and vice versa, that one of you is weak or needy or not available at times. Yet if it happens too often—if your partner is an addict, say—you have an issue to address: Am I a partner or a caretaker? Each partner in a loving bond takes responsibility to find the help he needs so that he can fulfill his partnership role of granting the five A's.

While it is useful to speak honestly to a partner who is an addict, it is useless to keep nagging him to quit. The best approach seems to be to state the truth and offer support in his following a program of recovery. If he refuses, the rule is to show not tell. An addict who refuses help is basically killing himself, and the appropriate response is mourning. To say "I am beginning the grieving process for you" is to show your truth, not tell him his. It is a ruthlessly adult response to the facts at hand. "If I am addicted to alcohol, I cannot fulfill my part of our contract; I cannot provide even moderate nurturance of or focus on you. If I refuse help, even after you confront me, I am choosing to go farther and farther from you." This suggests you might take the next step you can—for example, get involved in Al-Anon.

There is a fine line between the immature choice to stay with someone who does not fulfill our needs and the mature choice to tolerate the situation temporarily. A healthy person acknowledges the difference between occasional/circumstantial and ongoing/certain. We are not respecting ourselves when we put up with a general pattern of negativity or hardly any need fulfillment or happiness. But we are respecting our commitment when we tolerate occasional periods of deficiency. In fact, since adult growth includes mourning losses and changes, there will always be periods when one or both partners will be sad or angry or depressed or afraid and thereby unable to focus wholeheartedly on the other. To acknowledge that sometimes a person comes through for us and sometimes he does not, to respect his distresses and the damaged areas in his psyche, is a form of tolerance that makes for spiritual compassion: "I make an allowance for this because I know or can guess how you must feel."

Commitment

Essential means intrinsic and abiding. *Existential,* for the purposes of this discussion, means here and now, experiential. An essential bond is a given of intimate adult relating—physical maybe, psychological and spiritual usually. Like all energy, it cannot be created or destroyed. It comes fully into evidence only in the conflict stage of a relationship. The bond in the romance stage consists of excitement, neediness, and attachment to an ideal. The bond that develops in conflict and in working through conflict is a lasting one, no longer dependent on whether you are getting along or are still together. Like the bond of religion, it can even survive our leaving it. An essential bond in a relationship goes on after divorce. It is the unconditional love that can be dismantled but never demolished.

We manifest this essential bond of love by making an existential commitment, a day-to-day choice to address, process, and resolve issues and to keep the agreements that arise from them. When a new, more appealing person comes along, we take that as information not as permission to leave. We have made a commitment to stay with a partner as long as she and we are both engaged in the relationship effectively or both working on the relationship to make it effective.

Dogged determination is not commitment. Marriage is not commitment. Living together is not commitment. A healthy person loves unreservedly but does not make an unreserved commitment. A healthy person can decide the extent and length of his commitment. If it were not this way, commitment would mean submission, no boundaries, no sense of self-worth, and no sense of self.

An adult makes a commitment to a person with whom things are working or workable. She withdraws this commitment when things are no longer workable. Unlike a commitment, a vow is a promise to remain attached to a relationship whether or not it works, whether or not it is workable. Since the purpose of a relationship is human happiness not conservation of an institution—such as marriage—commitment is reasonable and vows are dangerous. A commitment is to workability. A vow is to time ("'til death us do part"). Moreover, vows can be subtle attempts to exempt ourselves from the painful givens of human relating: the other may betray, hurt, or leave. As adults we realize that vows and plans are really nothing more than wishes. They are certainly not the laws by which relationships operate. Religious scholar Mircea Eliade writes of the hero: "The law of life lives in him with his unreserved consent."

Intimacy has become complete when an essential bond is energized by an existential commitment. This entails a series of kept agreements and handled obstacles, the core of an adult commitment. Adults can go on loving a partner unconditionally but do not stay in a relationship with him if the relationship has become unworkable. They think: "I love you no matter what, but I cannot live with you." Here our distinction between the essential bond and the existential commitment is crucial: The

bond of love goes on unimpeded by events, but the day-to-day commitment is entirely conditioned by them. *An adult combines unconditional
love with conditional commitment.* This equates to the sane embrace instead of the addictive clutch. A parent has unconditional love for and
makes an unconditional commitment to a child. An adult has unconditional love for and makes a conditional commitment to a partner. Unconditional love is a spiritual victory since it really means unconditioned
by ego fear, attachment, control, or entitlement—the essence of mindfulness. We show unconditional love for what is unconditioned, the basic
goodness in others, the buddha mind. We show conditional love for
what is conditioned, the multiform personality of ego.

To say "I can love you and leave you" is as healthy as to say "I can fear
something and do it." In codependence, the less we get the five A's, the
more of them we give. We hope the giving will lead the other to give us
more love. Since we do not feel loved enough, we believe we must not be
giving enough. We keep giving more, but since we do not feel loved
enough, we believe we must not be giving enough. We are attempting to
get by giving instead of by sharing in an equal exchange. The result is
guilt.

On a humorous but sobering note, I must confess that the virtuous elements of intimacy outlined in the preceding sections describe what, in
object relations theory, is supposed to be in place for individual development before age three!

Soul Mates

> I can understand another soul only by transforming my own,
> as one person transforms his hand by placing it in another's.
> —PAUL ELUARD

The inflated ego gives only partial knowledge of who we are. Clinging
to our ego is like living under an assumed name, one that conceals our
wholeness, our potential to give and receive unconditional love: pure attention, acceptance, appreciation, affection, and allowing.

Individuals come along to give us these five A's. We imagine that John
or Mary is our other half, and we abandon our connection and commit-

ment to our own other half: the archetypal animus/anima, male and fe-male energies in all of us. It is as if we had an archetypal Robin Hood, a personification of kindheartedness and heroism, within ourselves. We, however, automatically picture him as John. We let the literal external per-son take the place of the internal metaphorical personification of our pow-ers. Instead of imitating him, as we did as children playing together after a Robin Hood movie, we revere him. We thereby diminish our own spir-itual stature and potential. We break the engagement with our full Self for a marriage with someone else, when actually we need both unions. We confuse our intrapersonal work with our interpersonal needs. Only the inner Robin Hood in the Sherwood Forest of our psyche has the authen-tic lively energy that will never die or disappear—the energy powerful enough to join the inner Maid Marion in the cooperative venture of adult love. *A woman's soul mate is not the man who takes over a woman's func-tions but one who mirrors them with pleased encouragement.*

The image of this seductive person or that former partner will visit us in a dream or sustain us in a crisis or wake us up at three in the morning when we are at our lowest ebb. She or he has a hold on us by virtue of an image: It looks as if she offers the fulfillment that is actually available only from the feminine Self. It looks as if he offers the fulfillment that is actu-ally available only from the masculine Self. We think: "I'd feel better or safer if only he were here now." Actually, we feel needy and bereft be-cause he is here in our place. The void we are feeling in that moment is the absence of our full self. *The personal void opens when I am not here for myself but am wishing for and believing in the messianic power of someone else, present or absent.* The void is void of me.

Here is the part that makes this process so paradoxical, enigmatic, and perplexing for us: Our numinous archetypal anima/animus usually cannot be contacted without an articulation through some specific per-son. This follows from our nature as incarnated beings who become who we are through mirroring by others. In our infancy our parents gave us the five A's, and that is how we learned to love ourselves. Their hearts expressed an appreciation of our lovableness and thus enabled us to feel it in our own hearts. We found, and have always found, our inner source of nurturance through our external source of nurturance.

But when we make a literal identification between a parent or partner and one of our own inner powers, we are confusing an archetypal universal image with a personal image, the channel with the source, the raft with the shore, the actor with the hero, the saint with the god, this man with our animus, this woman with our anima. This is how the parent or partner assumes such gigantic stature in our psyche. He becomes, rather than points to, our higher Self. Letting go of attachment to people and things at the ego or literal level is a way to open ourselves to the buddha mind behind all appearances. As Rilke says: "Things live fully only in departure." Indeed, Aeneas recognized his goddess-mother only when he said good-bye to her as his mortal helper.

Yet our inner partner—our soul mate, our true higher power—cannot make his or her presence known to us except through the love we find in individuals. Someone has to show and tell us. Only then can we find ourselves, love ourselves, and marry our inner complementary parts, our male and female energies. It is a mysterious and marvelous fact that it takes someone else to lead us to ourselves. No wonder we confuse our innermost longing for spiritual partnership with a tangible partnership and a specific person. We mistake this feather for the eagle it is meant to lead us to.

Adults accept the fact that fulfillments are temporary, even momentary. They are satisfied with moments of the five A's perfectly given, happiness perfectly felt, or unconditional love perfectly received. Once we are adults, we see these moments as sustaining and sufficient. When we finally accept the impermanence that characterizes human existence, we stop looking, stop asking, stop manipulating in an attempt to achieve permanence or perfection. Instead we are immensely thankful for the moments. Still, no one can blame us for not getting relationships right in one lifetime. Our psyches were constructed with logic-defying and complicated mirth! It takes courageous depth and humor to get the point of it all and to follow the long, winding road to wholeness.

The challenge of mindfulness is to abandon our fascination with the magic-lantern show put on by our egos and marvel instead at the inner pageant of images that continually arise unbidden from the depths of our own psyches. These images appear in dreams and in imagination, often bringing a message or healing. Any image that holds our attention or has archetypal dimensions may be a gift of the Self. Our soul is images and is our soul mate.

Practices

STAYING IN TOUCH AND INTACT • Ask your partner in your journal or directly: Can I feel challenged instead of threatened by your reactions to me? Can I see you angry and not be enraged by it? Can I see you depressed and not become morose? Can I see you feel anything and not be so scared of your feelings that I cannot respond with the five A's?

Read the following paragraph to yourself and then to your partner:

> I ask you to honor my tender core, which is not to be worn on a sleeve for all to see but is an object of diligent search, revealed only to those willing to uncover it. The work that takes is the five A's: attention, acceptance, appreciation, affection, and allowing me to be myself, to have the right to access my deepest needs, values, and wishes. I can be like a daisy, indiscriminately revealing its all to would-be lovers who then pull it to pieces. Or I can be like the peony that hides its core from view but shares it generously with the conscientious bee that dares to linger in its depth and locate its sweetness. Yet too much safety is a barrier, not a boundary, around the sweetness of life and the risks that make it exciting. The danger in constructing boundaries is in our becoming too defensive. Do not a few falls and hurts help us grow and make us more daring?

CONFRONTING MY FEAR OF GIVING OR RECEIVING • Below are two paragraphs, one describing the fear of giving, the other the fear of receiving. Which one applies to you? If you identify with either paragraph, read it aloud to your partner. Make a commitment to act as if you were less and less afraid. Ask your partner to help you in this process.

> *How afraid I am to give:* I could lose that way. If I give, you may want more, and I'll have nothing left. I can tell you about me but not show my feelings; I always hold something back. I close my

eyes when we make love lest you seize my frightened soul. I can listen to your words and advise swiftly, never chancing a meeting with those dangerous strangers: your feelings, your hurts, your needs, your eyes. I want to live on top of our love, parceling out what I can most safely spare from this, my very guarded, frugal, frightened heart.

How afraid am I to receive: I avoid eye contact, for you might look too deeply. I don't like to be surprised or given a gift. That means receiving what you choose to give, and that scares me because it means I am not in control. So I remain picky and hard to please. And if you give me something, I have to be sure to give you something of equal value in return. I tense when you hug me; it is safer to sexualize any touch. I cannot be a sex partner *and* a friend. I can never reveal my needs to you, only my drives. I feel crowded by your supportive embrace. I keep myself self-sufficient. I never allow myself to need your help; I have to be the one who takes care of you, never putting myself at the mercy of your love. My capacity for self-reliance is thus a protective device. I fear depending on you since dependency entails closeness. Rigid, constricted, shut down, ego-armed, I cannot let in appreciation or constructive criticism. I insist you be perfect before I commit to you, and I remain attracted to younger, "perfect" types. You may have noticed that after dinner, I jump to clean up. Without the business of eating to occupy me, I might have to sit there, seeing you and being seen. We might just look at each other too long, too closely. I can also be preoccupied with sports, my computer, the TV. I go out for a cigarette as a last resort. And by the way, I insist that you give me all your love and attention no matter what.

BEING MINDFUL ABOUT GIVING AND RECEIVING • Mindful appreciation of your fears of giving or receiving means taking them as information, without blaming others or feeling shame about yourself. Mindfulness is granting the five A's to the realities and limitations of your life and personality: attend to them, appreciate them, allow them, feel affection for them, and accept them as they are. Sit quietly while paying attention to your breathing. One by one, grant each of the five A's to your fears of giving or receiving.

SHARING AT WORK • The five A's can lead to cooperation and good feeling among people working together. They are especially powerful when given by management to staff, as long as they are expressed sincerely and not as strategies to increase productivity—even though they may ultimately have that result. Give attention to coworkers' feelings and concerns, accept their gifts and limitations, appreciate their accomplishments and difficulties, show personal affection, and allow them their full range of responsibility while expressing your trust and encouragement. Find ways to put these suggestions into practice at your job or church or any other setting outside your home.

CAREGIVING OR CARETAKING? • Being compassionate does not mean becoming a caretaker. Compassion is respectful of the potential for self-activating power in others. Ask yourself, interiorly or in your journal, where you stand on this chart. Take the entries in the left column as your program of compassion.

Caregiving	*Caretaking*
Supports the other person to do it for himself: fosters skill-building	Does it all for the other: fosters dependency
Arises from a motivation to empower the other	Arises from a belief that the other is powerless
Seeks to make a contribution and then let go	Seeks to stay involved in the other's life
Facilitates the other in becoming a more effective adult	Takes over adult responsibilities and may infantilize the other
Teaches a skill for future use	Performs a skill and may continue to do so in the future
Is tailored to the other's willingness to be helped	May be imposed whether it is sought or not
Maintains personal boundaries regarding how and when help is to be given: wisely conditional	Is willing to forsake personal boundaries to satisfy the other's needs: wildly unconditional

Is sincerely responsive to the needs of the other person	May have as a primary agenda the satisfying of one's own needs
Is a form of respect	May be a form of control

DISTINGUISHING ANGER FROM ABUSE • Both mindful anger and hurtful abuse are visceral and involve raised voices, gesticulations, red faces, and intense eye contact. Yet there is a difference, as the accompanying chart will show. Use this chart as a checklist to examine your way of showing anger. Do you relate to your anger mindfully, or do you become possessed by it? Look at the chart on your own and then with your partner. Give one another feedback on where you each fit on it. Make a commitment to become so familiar with this chart that you recall it when you become angry, pausing long enough to remind yourself to practice mindful anger and not abuse. Practice pausing before many ordinary daily activities as a way of preparing. To pause between a stimulus from outside and your own reaction makes for saner, freer, and more responsible choices. Immediate, unconscious reactions often arise from fear and ignorance and cause pain to ourselves and others. The irony of rage is that it seems to be a sluice of release but is ultimately a log jam.

True Anger	*Abuse: The Shadow of Anger*
Authentic self-expression: the hero's way	Theatrical display: the villain's way
Is always mindful	Is ego-driven and caught in mindsets
Expresses a feeling	Becomes a tantrum
May be expressed with a red face, excited gestures, and a raised voice	May be expressed with a red face, menacing gestures, expletives, and a screaming voice
Is a form of assertiveness that shows respect	Is aggressive, an attack
Shows tough love that enriches or repairs the relationship	Explodes in rough and damaging mistreatment that endangers the relationship
Arises from displeasure at an injustice	Arises from the sense of an affront to a bruised, indignant ego
Focuses on the injustice as intolerable but reparable	Focuses on the other person as bad

True Anger (cont.)	*Abuse (cont.)*
Informs the other, creates rapt attention, draws a mindful response	Is meant to threaten the other and drives him or her away
Is meant to communicate, to report an impact	Is meant to silence, intimidate, put down, bully, or dump
Desires a response from the other but does not require one	Insists the other acknowledge how right or justified one is
Asks for change but allows the other to change or not	Masks or expresses a controlling demand that the other change
Asks for accountability and amends	Blames the other* and takes revenge
Is about this present issue and is expressed freshly from incident to incident	Is often a build-up of past unresolved issues and displaced rage, gathering intensity from incident to incident
Has some perspective, can distinguish between minor and major issues	Is trapped in the heat of the moment and explodes vehemently no matter how minor the issue
Relates to the feeling	Is possessed by the feeling
Coexists with other feelings	Occludes other feelings
Takes responsibility for one's own distress	Diverts the blame for one's distress onto the other
Is nonviolent, in control, and always remains within safe limits (manages temper)	Is violent, out of control, derisive, punitive, hostile, and retaliatory (loses temper)
Releases lively energy and leads to repose	Derails lively energy and creates continuing stress
Is brief and lets go with a sense of closure (a flare)	Is held on to as lingering resentment, hate, grudge, or bitterness (a smoldering fire)
Includes grief and acknowledges this	Includes grief but masks it with feigned invulnerability or denial
Believes the other is a catalyst of anger Treats the other as a peer	Believes the other is a cause of anger Treats the other as a target
Originates in and fosters a healthy ego	Originates in and perpetuates an arrogant ego

*Blaming (from the Latin word for *blaspheme*) differs from assessing accountability: In blame, there is censure with an intent to shame and humiliate. The intent is to show that someone is wrong. In assessing accountability the intent is to right a wrong and restore a balance. In mindful, adult living, no one is to blame and everyone is accountable.

True Anger (cont.)	*Abuse (cont.)*
Aims at a deeper and more effective bond: an angry person moves *toward* the other	Wants to get the rage out no matter who gets hurt: an abuser moves *against* the other
Coexists with and empowers love: fearless	Cancels love in favor of fear: fear-based
These are all forms of addressing, processing, and resolving.	*These are all forms of avoiding one's own grief and distress.*

STANDING UP TO ABUSE • No relationship should take away even one of our human rights. A true relationship is cost-free. A relationship in which one partner continually seeks the approval of the other is a child-parent dyad, not an adult-adult dyad. In an adult relationship, however, we can drop our poses, our attempts to look good and earn love. We are loved as we are.

Furthermore, when we live as adults, anyone can hate us, but no one can harm us. We refuse to become victims of abuse; instead we speak up: "You seem to hate me, and I'm sorry for the pain in that for both of us. However, when you come at me in a violent way, I have to stop you. I cannot let you hurt or abuse me; I can only let you tell me what you feel." (Violence includes invective and insult, not just physical assault.) When faced with an abusive situation, I recommend the following three-step approach: (1) stand your ground by showing your pain and stating your limits; (2) stay with your partner if he is open and responsive; (3) get away from him if he refuses to calm down.

These steps simultaneously build intimacy because they contain the most crucial elements of it: To show your pain while standing your ground is vulnerability, not that of a victim but that of a strong person. To state your limits is to maintain boundaries and to be self-disclosing. To stay with the other does not mean to stay put for abuse. It means to engage in addressing, processing, and resolving. To stay through an experience with a tortured person means staying connected to him without letting him torture you. To stay is a practice of mindfulness that involves devotion to the reality of love. When someone who hates you sees that you suffer but do not abandon him, he may trust you and eventually open his hating fist. Staying is not a strategy for making others

change, however. We stay because of our commitment to putting mindfulness before censure and compassion before ego. We return love for
hate, seeking communion not retribution. If we achieve closeness with
the other, we are happy. If it takes time, we stay with it. If it fails, we let go.

BECOMING DIRECT • Passive aggression (that is, expressing anger
indirectly) has no place in an adult relationships. Scan your style of relating on the accompanying chart and ask whether you engage in indirect behavior. If you do, admit this to yourself and to someone you trust,
someone who will join you in devising a plan to change and make
amends.

Expressing Anger Directly	*Expressing Anger Indirectly*
Openly disagreeing or saying what bothers you, expressing your displeasure at what is going on or what happened	Not following through on agreements or messages
Addressing, processing, and resolving your feelings	Teasing/being late
	Sulking, silent treatment, pouting, absence
	Criticism/getting your digs in
	Withholding sex or using infidelity as a weapon
	Contrariness
	Practical jokes or tricks
	Ridicule or sarcasm
	Secretly harming
	Withholding the five A's

Express resentments and appreciations directly to one another without giving feedback. Behind most resentments lies an implicit demand.
Identify yours. Behind most feelings of appreciation lies an implicit wish
for more of the same. Admit that. Guilt is often resentment turned inward. Is there resentment behind your guilt?

WORKING ALONE • If you are alone or want to be alone with your
anger, try walking in a circle, outdoors preferably, saying "No!" over and

over. Or walk in the rhythm of the short sentence that describes why you are angry, for example, "You don't listen to me!" Stamp your foot firmly with the word you want to emphasize, then change the emphasis by stamping your foot when saying different words in the sentence.

COMBINING LOVE AND ANGER • Love can coexist with anger when we include the five A's in our expression of anger. For instance, to show anger with attentiveness to someone's reaction to it means modulating it so the other can receive it safely. In doing so, we are also appreciating and accepting her limits. It is a form of affection, and it allows the other to open to what we feel. Indeed, all feelings become safer when expressed in the context of the five A's, which are forms of emotional support. Ask your partner these questions and suggest he ask them of you:

> I have a right to feel anger. Can you accept me as a person who may be angry?
>
> I have a right to express anger openly. Can you allow that?
>
> When I am angry, I am trying to communicate to you about something that is bothering me. Can you pay attention to what I am angry about?
>
> I go on loving you when I am angry. Can you still love me while I am angry at you?

When we express feelings, it activates love in those who love us. All feelings are legitimate and are meant to lead to addressing, processing, and resolving in mindful ways. Do my feelings arouse compassion and attentiveness in you, or do they activate your ego so that you ridicule me, show contempt for me, or run from me? If so, how can I be present in those moments in such a way that I feel safe to stay and work things out respectfully?

ACCEPTING ONE ANOTHER • There is a Zen saying: "This being the case, how shall I proceed?" This adult question implies an acceptance of reality as it is or of a partner as she is—that is, mindfully. Alternatives would be "This being the case, how should you proceed," or "I can complain," or "I expect you to change it," or "I will retaliate." It is a turning point toward commitment when one partner accepts the other as she is—for example, as a procrastinator—and instead of complaining, looks into himself and asks, "How shall I proceed? Do I wait for her to change, or do I find a way to take care of myself and attend to my concerns using my own resources?" This is not a way of distancing ourselves from her but of taking responsibility for our behavior and predicament. It grants us power because it puts us in touch with our inner authority. Try applying the Zen saying in your relationship.

AFFIRMING YOURSELF • Return to any sentences in this book that you have underlined or copied into your journal. They may have impressed you because they are your own truths. Turn each of them into an affirmation by restating it in the first person, present tense, positively, and as something already true of you. For instance, the sentence "An adult commitment is a thoroughly truthful and adult enterprise of ongoing love" can become "I commit myself to being truthful in my loving." The sentence "Fear should be granted the five A's since it is part of you; then it reveals itself as having wisdom and purpose" becomes "I find wisdom and purpose in my fears as I pay attention to them, accept them, appreciate them, allow them, and treat my scared self with affection."

EXPLORING PRESENT AND PAST • Respond in your journal to these questions and then turn what you write into a letter to your partner: Do you feel an essential bond between yourself and your partner, and do you follow it up with a daily existential commitment? What forms does this commitment take? Ask these same questions about each of your parents and how they treated you as a child. Is your present behavior in your adult relationship a response to your original experience with your parents? Are you trying to redo or undo the past? What keeps you from addressing, processing, and resolving all this in therapy rather than enacting it in your relationship?

The only thing that saves us from reenacting is a plan to change. Making and carrying out such a plan may seem well-nigh impossible, but that is what practice is for. Both spiritual health and psychological health require only practice not perfection. Few of us feel whole except at moments. Likewise, few climbers reach the summit of Everest, but that does not mean no one can reach it. The Everest in the psyche is love, and the ego is perfectly suited to reaching it. All it takes is dying and rising.

LOVINGKINDNESS • Lovingkindness is a Buddhist practice (also called *metta*) based on the premise that we all want the same thing, happiness, and that our kinship with all beings makes us want to love them— that is, to will their happiness and wish them well. Here is a simple format for this practice: Sit quietly and imagine yourself filled with one of the "four immeasurables": compassion, love, joy, and equanimity. Call each of them to yourself, then send them to a widening circle of people until you have included the whole world in your loving wishes: "May I be joyful. May those I love be joyful," and so on. Begin with those who love you, then add those who are your benefactors, then those you love, then friends, and then acquaintances. Go on to the people you don't know well but meet in daily life such as bank tellers and checkout people. Next, add people who do not like you, those you dislike, difficult people, hostile people, enemies (first personal and then political), including figures from history. Finally, beam the love to the whole world— north, south, east, and west.

Notice any resistance as you move down the list. Do not attempt to root out the resistance. Simply form a stronger intention to love, and the resistance will weaken. Something may change in you as you wish love and joy to people you don't know or to enemies. This practice shows the limits to our love and helps us surpass them. It also teaches us to take refuge not in fame or fortune but in heart.

The affirmations also can be configured this way: May I respond with compassion to _____ . May _____ [person's name] have happiness and the causes of happiness. May those who _____ be free from harm. (Lighting a candle or incense while doing this adds a ritualistic dimension that amplifies and focuses the healing energy.) Repeat the affirmations to yourself throughout each day as you encounter people. Leaving the dentist, say, "May he and all helpers bring healing to themselves and others." We affirm not only for people we know and people like them but for those they will reach, too.

When you do this practice habitually, it will kick in when you meet someone who causes you pain, and you may hear this in your head/heart: "I am thankful for this teacher. May he find the light." Affirmations such as this do not mean we necessarily approve of others' behavior, only that we appreciate the potential in the experience for growth. This is another way of never giving up on anyone.

The compassion affirmations free us from the ego's desire to retaliate. The love affirmations free us to love more. Wishing joy to others brings joy to us, and wishing them and ourselves equanimity responds to the conditions of existence for us all. We begin to act based on our practice. We are engaged with others in the world as people committed to a practice. This is spiritual integrity. The organizing principles of the world are the conditions of existence and synchronicity. As we say yes to the givens of life and open ourselves to the messages in synchronicity, that spiritual integrity becomes spiritual wholeness.

Mastering this practice takes time. It is not done in one sitting. Proceed slowly and honor your own timing. It may take a while to get to the level of compassion where we can make an affirmation sincerely. It will require us to transform our relationships and ourselves, but daily attention to the practice will pay off.

Here I would like to add a personal note. Long before knowing of this practice, I joined a tour to Egypt. Our group spent two hours in meditation in the pharaoh's chamber of the Great Pyramid. Lying there, I spontaneously decided to call to mind the images of all the people in my life. I imagined this to be a way of making them present in a place they might never get to in the flesh. One by one, I pictured each family member, friend, acquaintance, and so on. This was the only gift I could give them in that moment, and I felt more loving toward all of them at the end of the meditation. I did not yet know of the metta practice, so I failed to include all humankind—but I do at this moment belatedly.

By the power of the practices in this book,
may I greet the all-illuminating dawn
of love and abundance
and may I care compassionately for those who are still lost
in the ever-darkening sunset of fear and desire.

Epilogue

A tone of some world far from us
Where music and moonlight and feeling are one
—SHELLEY

I WOULD LIKE TO CONCLUDE by reaffirming the core themes of our journey together—the ideas and tools I hope you will return to when the dance of relationship becomes awkward or halting. The five A's are attention, acceptance, appreciation, affection, and allowing. We are on a heroic journey that began with our needing them from our parents, then continued with our seeking them in adult partners, and ends with our giving them to the world as a spiritual enterprise.

Good enough parenting in our childhood favorably affects our adult relationships. Childhood may negatively affect our adult relationships if it left us with feelings of loss or neglect—but those can be grieved and let go of. The holes childhood left in us can even become portals to character and compassion.

We can meet our adult challenges by addressing, processing, and resolving our issues. We can meet our spiritual challenges through the practice of mindfulness and lovingkindness.

We make both psychological and spiritual advances best when we are ready to lose face, the F.A.C.E. of the inflated ego—fear, attachment, control, and entitlement. This happens through a combination of our efforts and a gift of grace. When we let go of F.A.C.E., we gain the knack of loving our partner and our world. These are affirmations of loving partners who dedicate themselves not only to one another but to all of us:

- We believe in the abundant possibility in each of us to bring love into the world. We want to reconcile with those who hurt us and help our friends reconcile with one another. We are hurt if they are feuding. We always look for ways to mend breaks in relationships.
- We care about a good outcome not about who receives credit for it. We care about the effectiveness of our cooperation not the kudos we might garner individually. Our power is not individual, it is relative. We prefer leadership over dominance. If others share this preference, then our status depends on our ability to resolve conflict, to see a new vision, or serve others creatively.
- We do not abandon others. If they seem inadequate, unintelligent, or insensitive, we only have more room in our hearts for them. We notice more tolerance within ourselves and more incentive to offer our time and service to protect them rather than malign them. We relate to pain. We do not stand in judgment of it. We keep others in our circle of love even if they scare, dislike, or fail us.
- We do not look down on those who act irresponsibly or deleteriously. We feel compassion for those who are so caught up in ego or addiction that they lose their reason and jeopardize their happiness. They are brothers and sisters, not inferiors. We look for ways to support their recovery and share information with them.
- We do not give up on others or ourselves. To think they—or we— "will never change" is a form of despair, a choice that cancels possibilities and closes us to unexpected miracles. We dare to persevere with a subversive faith in life. As the Hindu teacher Nisargadatta Maharaj says, "The unexpected will certainly happen, while the anticipated may never come."
- Our heart practice does not emerge from moralism and rules but from an inalienable lovingkindness. We are born with it, and/or we learn it by practice. It is a generous inclination, a genuine caring about others, a capacity to be touched by suffering as Buddha was. In fact, his compassion for other people's suffering was what started him on his path to awakening.
- We hold an abiding commitment to serve others while not claiming to have answers to life's dilemmas and contradictions. The best

response comes from action not from intellect. For example, we may hear this question: "If love rules the world, why do children starve?" Our answer is simply "We feed hungry children." "Why do so many good people die painful deaths?" becomes "We work with the dying." In other words we find the meaning of our life by living it. When we realize our abiding and intense interconnectedness with everyone and everything, compassion is our only possible response. Our every thought, word, and deed leads to and exudes compassion no matter what. Shakespeare describes this process in *King Lear*, "A most poor man, made tame to fortune's blows, / Who by the art of known and feeling sorrows / Am pregnant to good pity."

- We will not despair of love but work toward it. Our human journey seems to be about love, finding out what it is and then learning to give and receive it. In the course of reading and working with this book, we have a richer sense of what love is and have become more skilled at sharing it in an adult relationship.

- Free of fear and desire, we can receive, and once we receive, we can also give. The giving-receiving of intimacy now has a greater purpose. Rising in love is that destiny and all it takes is refusing to fall and choosing to dive in.

There is only one question left for the reader as this book comes to an end: *Am I getting better at loving?*

> These two
> Imparadised in one another's arms,
> The happier Eden, shall enjoy their fill
> Of bliss on bliss! . . .
> Add love, . . . then wilt thou not be loath
> To leave this Paradise, but shall possess
> A Paradise within thee, happier far.
>
> —MILTON, *Paradise Lost*

Appendix:
The Steps and Shifts
of Mindful Grief

We must in tears
Unwind a love knit up in many years.
—Henry King

Mindful grief means mourning and letting go of the past without expectation, fear, censure, blame, shame, control, and so forth. Without such mindful grief, neither past nor person can be laid to rest. When we grieve mindfully, we mourn every one of the disappointments, insults, and betrayals of the now irrevocably lost past. We mourn any abuse—physical, sexual, emotional. We mourn for how our parents just did not want us, did not love us, or could not get past their own needs long enough to see us as the lovable beings we were and allow our unique self-emergence. We mourn every way they said no to the gift we sought to give them: full visibility of our true self, not the self we had to manufacture to please or protect them. We mourn all the times they saw how scared, forlorn, and sad we were and yet did not respond, relent, or apologize. We mourn because even now, after all these years, they still have not admitted their abuse or lack of compassion.

Why mourn for what we never had? Because we had an instinctive sense of the five A's of good parenting and of their absence in our lives. We grieve our loss of birthright. We mourn because our parents had that same sense and somehow ignored it. We mourn because we were hurt by those who loved us: "Look at how I was wounded in the house of those who loved me" (Zech. 13:6).

Mourning is a process. It goes on all our lives as we discover new levels in the pain and losses we felt in the past. One lifetime will not suffice to let it all go. It is enough to do our best at releasing our pain so that the energies fixated in the past can be reinvested in the present.

Grief's favorite position is piggyback. If I am abandoned in the present and allow myself to grieve the abandonment, all the old abandonments of the past, which have been waiting their turn, jump onto my grieving shoulders. Also included in the piggybacking are the griefs of the human collective, what Virgil calls "the tears in things." These are the givens of relationship: the sense of something missing, the fugitive intimacies, the inevitable endings. We carry sensitivities to all those in our hearts, and our personal griefs evoke them. What a way to find out we are not alone! We carry the heritage of the archetypal past and enrich it continually with our personal experience.

Jung suggests that working on our childhood issues is a necessary first step toward spiritual consciousness. As he puts it, the "personal unconscious must always be dealt with first . . . otherwise the gateway to the cosmic unconscious cannot be opened." The steps outlined in this appendix were designed and then revised in accordance with my work with many clients and in many classes on grieving the losses and abuses of childhood. They can also be adapted for grieving death, the end of relationships, or any other losses we may suffer in the course of life. We cannot make up for losses, but we can learn to tolerate them and contain them. This is what the soulful journey of mourning is about. "Our souls are love and a continual farewell," wrote W. B. Yeats.

Mourning is an action not a transaction. It is our personal responsibility, so we do not do it with the perpetrators of our losses, including our parents. *We interrupt our own healing as long as we still have to tell our parents how bad we think they were.* It is, however, appropriate to ask our parents for information about what happened to us. If you do tell your parents about your grief work, be sure you are telling to share information, not trying to convince them they were wrong, hurt them, or get back at them.

Some of us are not yet ready to face what really happened to us; we suspect or even know that we do not have the strength to follow the process through to its painful conclusion. It is important to respect this hesitancy and honor our own timing. Some tears may be shed today, some next year, some in thirty years. The inner child of the past tells her story a little at a time, lest we have too much to handle all at once. "Hurry or delay is interference," D. W. Winnicott says. The fact that grief takes so long to be resolved is not a sign of our inadequacy. Rather, it betokens our depth of soul.

Step One: Allowing Ourselves to Know or Remember

> To show what good came from my experience I have to tell of things that were not so good.
>
> —DANTE, *The Inferno*

Though the haunting memory of past events always remains in our psyche, it is not always easily retrieved. A feeling or intuition about something that happened (traces of the memory) is enough to begin the process of grief work. Remembering any one way in which our needs were not met is sufficient. If no specific memory arises, then a feeling of sadness is enough.

Having remembered a cause of grief, we can then discuss it with someone we trust. "You do surely bar the door upon your liberty if you deny your griefs to your friends," as Rosencrantz tells Hamlet. Recitation of past abuses authenticates our experience, and like all testimony, it requires a witness—not the perpetrator of the abuse but some fair, alert, and trusted person, a therapist or friend—who can hear the story mindfully (that is, without having to judge, fix, maximize, or minimize it). Discussing our memories with such a person can lead to mirroring: the loving responsiveness of others who understand, accept, and permit our feelings. Such mirroring lets us know that our feelings are legitimate and frees them from shame or secrecy. When our parents did not mirror our griefs, later griefs will feel destabilizing, overwhelming us and throwing us off center. Now we reclaim the unmirrored feelings by having them mirrored to us at last. It is another journey, this time from abandonment to communion.

One further note on remembering: A cognitive recounting of the past may only be a memory of a memory unless it is connected strongly to a bodily feeling, because every cell in our body recalls every event that impinged upon us in childhood. The body, more than the mind, is the real human unconscious, storing both the memory of pain and our attempts to avoid it. The work, then, is to find the accurate sense of what we felt and not necessarily a story line of exactly what happened. In fact, the content of the memories is less crucial than the conflicts they represent and the reenactments we are still caught in. These are the true targets of grief, not the memory of what happened.

Actually, we may never know what truly happened in our past, not because it is so lost in oblivion but because it is continually shifting in our memory. At each phase of life, it rearranges itself to fit our new sense of ourselves and the world. Memories are selections from the past. Thus, our goal is not so much to reconstruct memory but to restructure our overall *sense* of the past to fit our changing needs. Mark Twain quipped, "The older I get, the more clearly do I remember what never happened."

PRACTICES

MOVING INTO THE PAST • Raise your right hand high, then extend it out horizontally. Now do the same with your left. Repeat each of the four movements slowly with your eyes closed, imagining one of these childhood experiences in each of the four hand positions: (1) An adult is holding my hand as I cross a street; (2) I am reaching across the table for more food; (3) I am asking a question in class for the first time; (4) I am reaching out to my first friend.

As you remember each of these experiences, notice how you feel. Were the original experiences associated with pain or nurturance—for example, were you dragged across the street, helped by being handed food, shamed in school, rebuffed by a prospective friend? Look for the effects on your present level of self-esteem and on your present relationships.

RECALLING • Some of the abuses of early life are too overwhelming to be dealt with directly or safely. Thus, we may have dissociated ourselves from the abuse (forgotten it, numbed ourselves to it), a useful tool when we were victims, powerless to alter our condition. The first step in the healing of memories is to reassociate ourselves with our past by drawing on our adult power to look at our pain so that we can get through it and let go of it.

Do this by locating a setting from the past and picturing yourself in it. Then begin describing (aloud or in writing) what happened, how it all looked, where you sat or stood, what you remember saying, what was said to you, how you were treated, what was allowed or prohibited, and so on. In every reminiscence, keep talking or writing until you get to how you felt. Then notice when in your present life you feel the same way. This will show you how the original hurt still hurts you. In the past you were powerless to change the thing that hurt you, but now you can change your reactions to situations that resemble those that once caused you pain.

For example, suppose you remember being ridiculed for "asking too many questions." Now you still fear rejection if you inquire too deeply into people's statements or behavior. You do not give yourself permission to ask assertively for the information you want. You act as if you were still a child afraid of a rebuke. Pull the childhood and adult experiences together and express the feeling that emerges: anger, sadness, fear, or all three. Express these feelings to someone who will honor them. You do not have to blame the perpetrator, only to express your present feeling freely. By granting yourself this freedom of feeling, you reverse the original abuse and the silencing. First, you show that you do not need anyone's permission; second, you show the feeling instead of hiding it; and third, you let go of it by expressing it (instead of holding on to it by repressing it). You have moved from being told by others what you should feel to telling others what you really feel.

Here are some hints that may be helpful at this stage:

- Tell your story over and over. This is the normal way a shock is absorbed. If it is not easy for you to tell about your experience in words, draw or make a collage expressing what is hard for you to say or write. Also, take a cue from any resistance you feel. It may be your psyche's way of telling you the time is not right for this kind of work. Honoring that message is healing in itself.

- Your present distress is the horse on which you can ride into the past. Ride every present distress to a past distress.

- Treat reminiscence as an admission of something to yourself, something whose extent or seriousness you were once afraid to admit to yourself or anyone else. Reminiscence means baring the abuse not bearing it. It is an admission to yourself of what happened and what you felt about it. It does not matter whether you are accurate in your recollection. You are working on subjective impact not on historical precision.

- Avoid concern with why abuse happened. Such inquiries lead us back to the thinking mind, the ego trickster who will perform his usual "D&C"—distraction and consolation. Instead, change every "Why?" to a "Yes." Meister Eckhart said, "The only way to live is like the rose: without a Why."

- Distinguish between a parent who was anxious and neurotic and took out his distress on you and the parent who was malicious, mean, or cruel and took pleasure in seeing you hurt. The latter inflicts a deeper wound and leaves a more serious scar on your ability to trust in later relationships.

  In these first stages of remembering and feeling, do not let your parents off the hook ("They didn't know any better back then," "It's different now"). True compassion and forgiveness follow anger.

  Remembering evokes a disturbing and perplexing question: "What was I paying for?" What pain in my parent(s) was I being forced to atone for? Am I enduring torture to pay for the defects of my ancestors? Is my whole adult life a post-traumatic-stress syndrome in reaction to childhood?

- It is best to work in therapy on establishing inner safety before working on past memories directly. Moreover, the grief work that follows here is geared to those who did not experience severe abuse or trauma. That experience requires even more preparatory work on establishing inner safety before you begin the processing and healing of memories.

- A wound does not destroy us. It activates our self-healing powers. The point is not to "put it behind you" but to keep benefiting from the strength it has awakened.
- Contemplate photos of each of your parents before they met one another. Place the photos side by side. Speak aloud or in writing to each of them about some of what is in store for them that they could never have guessed—for example, divorce, abuse, you and your story with them. Then tell them the positive things that were to happen. Notice how compassion for their story may arise.

The first step is the only one we really have to take. The later steps will follow on their own. Full feelings will arise and with them instinctive replays of events, compassionate forgiveness, letting go, and rituals to commemorate the process. Finally, when we notice ourselves recalling and mising the *good* things that happened to us, we are feeling nostaligia, the light grief that signals the sunset of griefwork.

Step Two: Allowing Ourselves to Feel

The feelings specific to grief are sadness, anger, hurt, and fear (even terror). In mindful grief, we become the landing strip that allows any feeling to arrive. Some crash, some land softly. Some harm us, but none harm us in a lasting way. We remain as they taxi away or as their wreckage is cleared away. We can trust that we will survive; we were built for this task.

Surprisingly, denial plays a role in healthy grieving. For an addict, denial provides a way of not facing the reality. But for people working through childhood grief, denial provides a healthy way of letting in the pain little by little, so we can handle it safely. It is normal to avoid the full onslaught of a loss and its implications. The *terrifying* grief is the one that does not permit that slowed-down intake of information—for example, the sudden news of a loved one's death—but leaves us powerless, defenseless, unshielded in face of unalterable and irreversible information about a loss.

Speaking of terror, a strong reaction to a particular situation, even in a film, may give us a clue that something in ourselves cries out for mending. I recall seeing a film in which a mother is told of her child's sudden death. I felt her terror powerfully, as a sinking, gnawing feeling in my stomach. A month or so later, perhaps an example of synchronicity, my son told me of two child clients of his whose mother had died suddenly. In my sorrow for them, I felt that same terror for myself that I had felt during the film. It was beyond compassion; the news of these deaths felt somehow personally threatening. "Why so strong a reaction?" I wondered. One morning, a day or two into this inquiry, I awoke with a conscious recollection of something I had always known from my family history. Before I was born, my grandmother had heard of the sudden death of her son, Blaise. Thinking of this, I felt the same painful reaction in the pit of my stomach. Then, focusing on that place in my body, I suddenly realized that my mother had heard the same news about her favorite brother *while I was in her womb.* She had always told me she felt depressed and cried uncontrollably for many weeks thereafter. In other words, I heard the news in some way, too, and my own health/survival was threatened by it. The psyche remembers all its hurts and losses. Could that incomplete, never-mourned pain in myself account for my reaction to the equivalent pain in others? Is the archetypal connection among us humans that strong? My terror and powerlessness about the shock others felt pointed me to unfinished work for myself.

PRACTICE

This is not about who I am but about what happened to me.

ALLOWING YOUR FEELINGS TO EMERGE • Working out our grief is mostly about the release of sadness, which we express primarily with tears. At any age it is appropriate to cry when instinctively required love is not forthcoming. This is not a sign of childishness, but a sign that we are allowing our inner child to feel authentically. The best way to grieve is to allow ourselves to feel sad not only for the past but also for our present losses. We grieve because we did not get the five A's from our parents or are not getting them now from our partners.

Also remember that, in addition to sadness, mourning can involve processing several other feelings. Unless it is expressed and processed, hurt becomes self-pity. Unexpressed anger becomes bitterness. Unexpressed sadness becomes depression. Unexpressed fear becomes paralyzing panic. These results continue the abuse, except that now we are inflicting it on ourselves.

Thus, in this step we admit each feeling and its total legitimacy. Then we express it in a physically emphatic way, for example, weeping, gesturing, changing our voice. To experience all your feelings fully leads to catharsis, or release. (Chemicals in the tears of grief have been found to reduce stress. Onion-induced tears have no such chemicals.) The less we can feel, the deeper the wound must have been. This is helpful to remember when it comes to our partner, too. We or that shut-down partner who rarely expresses feelings may be full of unprocessed grief from childhood.

The feelings connected with grief have sounds. These sounds are deep, guttural, even scary. They are loud and unpredictable, not cool and polite. Be sure you have the free space to let them all out. You have a right to all your feelings. They do not have to be justified or logical. But beware of a sense of rejection, disappointment, humiliation, abandonment, or betrayal. This is not a feeling but a judgment, a subtle form of blame, a visit from the ego trickster within, who whispers, "You are the one who is right" or "Don't let her get away with this," rather than "I am really hurting now and really scared!" It helps to locate the feeling behind the judgment. Behind disappointment, for example, may be sadness and the belief that all expectations are supposed to be met. Behind each of these judgments, in fact, is a quarrel with a given of life and a belief in our entitlement to special treatment. As adults who are free from childish ego, we take it for granted that we will suffer disappointments and rejections. We take them in stride as normal conditions of human relating. See how mourning challenges us to deflate and transcend ego! In this sense it is both psychological and spiritual work.

According to Greek mythology, wine originated as the tears of Dionysus, who was weeping for his dead lover, Ampelos. So joy will ultimately come from grief. Letting go of fear and anger in grief is a powerful way of finding serenity and adult freedom. The *Baghavad Gita* says: "What is at first a cup of sorrow, becomes at last, immortal wine."

Step Three: A Chance to Replay It

The third step toward the healing of memories is to replay in memory the original abusive speech or action, but this time to speak up and interrupt it. In this psychodrama, you place yourself mentally in the original setting and hear or see what was said or done to you. Then you proclaim your power and say no to the abuse. Do this vocally or as a dramatic action, with someone watching and listening. You can also do it in writing, drawing, dance, movement, clay modeling, or any other expressive medium. Do not attempt to change the abuser in your memory-drama, only yourself. Having said no to abuse, you are now no longer the victim of the scene but its hero. You have added a new ending to the original memory, and whenever it arises in the future, you will remember it with the new ending.

All this may seem useless because we cannot change the past. But the past that we cannot change is the historical past. We can change the past that we carry inside ourselves: We carry a fact (unchangeable), but we also carry its impact on us (very changeable). When we allow the original memory to become a mere fact, the charge is gone from it, and it ceases to hurt. Now when we recall the past, we also recall how we healed old pain. This reconstructed memory leads to serenity and resolution, just as the memory of a hurt becomes more bearable, even uplifting, when the person who hurt us apologizes.

Step Four: Dropping Expectation

The fourth step in the healing of memories is dropping any expectation that some other person will give you all you missed in childhood. Scan your lifestyle and your present life choices in search of any such expectations. Are you demanding that a partner give you what your parents did not? Are you training a partner to treat you as your parents treated you? Are you attached to a guru? Are you caught up in any fanatical movements? Are you addicted to a substance, a person, sex, or a relationship? Are you compulsive or obsessive about something that you cannot let go of? Are you, in effect, trying to get something or someone to give you now what you once got or hoped to get from your family?

We may sometimes imagine that we can find comfort, security, or peace of mind if our mother would only come through for us now and focus on us in all the ways she failed to do so before. We imagine that then we could let go of wanting that need fulfillment from her. Because we think this way, the key to our happiness remains tightly in her hand. How do we put that key into our own hands? By doing the work. When we use the tools of psychological health and spiritual practice to focus on ourselves, we become parents to ourselves and are no longer so needy for what parents or parent surrogates can give us. We still need others, but we are not needy for them. A need begins with the sensation that something is missing, is followed by a mobilization of energy toward fulfillment, and is resolved by fulfillment or by an acceptant recognition that fulfillment is not possible at this time or from this source. Neediness is an ongoing stressful state of unfulfillment, of unfulfillability, without resolution.

My own father left me when I was two and never came back, nor did he stay in touch with me. When I looked him up as an adult, I noticed how I kept trying, even then, to get him to be a father to me. But he would not come across the way I wanted him to. It was just not in him. This gnawed at me and created great frustration for me. It even obsessed me. I worked on this issue very intensely in therapy and with affirmations. One day I will never forget, I was crossing California Street in San Francisco, when suddenly I heard a new voice in my head. Instead of the usual "Why can't he _____?" it said, "He was meant to be a father to you in only one way, by contributing to your birth, and he did that perfectly." I stopped in my tracks in the middle of the street in shocked realization of that truth, and from that moment on I felt better about him; my craving for anything more from him ended.

Where did that voice come from? It was a grace I didn't plan or manufacture, the grace of the work I had committed myself to. My work all paid off in that one minute. We do the work to be free of illusion, and sometimes it truly pays off. On that day in San Francisco when I finally let my father off the hook and into my heart, I felt personally bigger. Then I knew that everyone in our lives has to find a place in our hearts before we can be complete.

Step Five: Thanking As a Practice

> If I defer the grief I will diminish the gift.
>
> —EAVON BOLAND

The fifth step in the healing of memories is to thank your inner Self (and/or higher power) that you survived whatever pain, abuse, or lack of need fulfillment you suffered in your childhood and that made you stronger. When you do this, you echo a theme of this book: that there is a positive dimension to everything that has happened to us. Identify some way the original abuse has led to a compensation in you. For instance, you may have learned how to handle pain, sometimes by flight, sometimes by direct confrontation—both legitimate and wise actions depending on your available strengths at the time. Locate the powers in you now that harken back to earlier pain or losses. This is what we are referring to when we say the hero is the person who has lived through pain and been transformed by it.

Compose an affirmation of thanks that what happened to you is what it took to make you the strong person you are now. You are thankful not for the pain you suffered in the past but for your power to handle pain now. "It took just such evil and painful things for the great emancipation to occur," Nietzsche said. He is also the one who said that what doesn't kill us makes us stronger.

Are you strong now? You are at least willing to face the pain of honestly grieving past abuses. Look how many ways there are for the past to reveal the present! It tells us what we need and why we need it. It reveals the origins of our assets and deficits. It actualizes potential. It is the inner blueprint of our adult lives. If we are only literate enough to read it, we will find a most touching story about our tender vulnerability and a most accurate account of our every yearning and fear.

My greatest joy is in the realization that I can still love. That capacity remained intact despite all the blows. That the love made it through means that I made it through.

Step Six: The Grace of Forgiveness

> My faith in the goodness of the human heart is unshaken. All
> the days of my life I have been upheld by that goodness.
>
> —HELEN KELLER

Forgiveness is a happening, not really a step. We cannot plan for it or will it. It is automatic compassion for and absolution of those who have hurt us. It means letting go of blame and anger while still acknowledging accountability. This is why it can arrive only after anger.

Compassion toward perpetrators of abuse means letting go of ego indignation long enough to see their pain. It means noticing that abusive people were themselves abused and that they never grieved their own unconscious pain, only perpetrated it on us. We see how wrong this was, but now we notice their pain consciously, perhaps for the first time, and we feel it with them. Forgiveness takes the burden of their pain away from us at last. It is truly unconditional love and promotes our personal, psychological, spiritual, and even physical health.

Forgiveness is a power, a grace that lets us exceed our own normal ego limits. The neurotic ego is often geared toward punishing and gaining revenge. Indeed, seeking revenge is a way to resist mourning. It substitutes power over the unjust for the vulnerability of feeling sad about injustice. Healthy grief, on the other hand, leads to a commitment to handle wrongs nonviolently, to seek reconciliation and transformation instead of vengeance and retribution. This is a way of *harnessing* power rather than being stampeded by it or using it to stampede others.

Forgiveness is mindfulness applied to our hurt. To feel forgiving and compassionate is a sign that we have transcended ego. If you feel forgiveness, assisting forces have blessed your work. It is a moment that integrates the psychological work achieved by will and the spiritual gifts received as graces that enhance and complete your exertions. Like the mythic heroes, we struggle and feel with all our might, and then a power greater than ourselves appears with gifts.

The ego imagines that forgiveness requires punishment as a prerequisite. But authentic forgiveness lets go of that eye-for-an-eye model in favor of pure generosity. Forgiveness is the highest form of letting go, because by forgiving we let go not only of resentment toward others but of our own ego. It is a spiritual Olympic event.

When my mother abused me in her out-of-control way, she would instill fear in me and then blame me for showing it, calling me a coward if I raised my hands to avoid blows to my head. I understand now that my mother did not enjoy beating me. She was caught in a compulsion to take out her own deepest shame and grief on me. When I grieve, I do not excuse this behavior, but I do notice my compassion for her trapped pain, and this compassion—unlike enduring resentment—does not distract me from my work of grieving.

Say this from time to time until it feels like it has all become true for you: "When I recall the hurts done to me by family members, I feel compassion for the inadequacies, ignorance, and fear that were behind them. I have no wish to retaliate or harm anyone or even to have them understand me. I shower my family with all-forgiving love. I rejoice in the fact that I am now free from having to change them. I no longer bring up my story to my family but only with friends or in therapy."

Step Seven: Healing Rituals

A ritual enacts a newfound consciousness, making its deepest reality proximate and palpable. It sanctifies the place we are in and the things we feel by consecrating them to something higher than the transitory. Design a ritual that takes into account the rituals of childhood but then expands on them. Find a gesture that enacts your intention and your accomplishment in the grief work you have completed. Find a way to show thanks for the spiritual gifts you have received. Rituals enlist our bodies. The hand and the eye have an ancient wisdom that works better than the mind in the process of integration.

Grieving the past is not only about family resentment but about finishing family work. Those who are gone or dead remain a part of our family system. No one is fully excluded, no matter how completely we rejected him or how much he rejected the family. When we honor and reinclude our excluded ones, they no longer dominate our psyche like restless ghosts. And relating to our own dusky past may not only heal us but also reach all the way back into our family's past and heal our ancestors, too. Perhaps we are here to work out some of the karma of our forebears. What did Grandma or Mother do that was never taken care of and healed? What did they suffer and then pass down rather than work out? Am I imitating their fate? A ritual works powerfully when it embraces our connection with the past and makes us the wounded healers of it.

PRACTICE

CREATE A GRIEF RITUAL • Plan a ritual with these four parts:

1. Acknowledging—Write a full disclosure of your painful experiences and an account of your mourning process.

2. Abolishing—Burn the pages on which you wrote these things and bury the ashes with seeds or under a tree.

3. Renewing—Use affirmations that acknowledge your letting go of the past, your resolution of your griefs, and your going on with joy and freedom. Recommit yourself to adult need fulfillment and freedom by shouting or singing about your powers at the beach or in the mountains or anywhere in nature that feels life-giving. Remember some good times from the past: If memories of trauma are painful and debilitating, then memories of safety and comfort are healing. Evoke one good memory for each bad one from now on. Include the memory of your grieving process, treating it as the final chapter of your childhood.

4. Giving Back—When a grief begins to ease, you will begin to feel joy, release, and healing. These feelings result from your work but also from grace. Return the gift in the form of a donation, a favor, volunteering your time, and so forth to any person or cause that reflects your own healing work—for example, abused or starving children, education, consciousness-raising. Give something to those farther back on your same path. This may be what W. B. Yeats meant when he wrote: "I was blessed and could bless."

Step Eight: Self-Parenting and Reconnecting

To say we have truly completed our grief work, we need to achieve not only catharsis of feelings but also self-nurturance and fearless intimacy with others. The pains of grieving are the labor pains from the adult self being born. To grieve is to pay attention to the weeping, frightened part of ourselves and to console it. When we do this, we parent ourselves, and we show the vulnerability that leads to healthy relating. As Saint Gregory of Nyssa wrote in the fourth century: "We are, in a sense, our own parents, and we give birth to ourselves by our own free choice of what is good."

Self-parenting means granting the five A's to ourselves: We pay attention to our pain and to our inner resources for healing. We pay attention to how our past has interfered in our relationships and how it has helped us find ourselves. We practice self-acceptance, embracing all our talents, virtues, failings, and inadequacies. We feel appreciation for our journey and the steps and missteps we have taken on it. We appreciate our parents and our partners for their contributions to our character, for better or worse. We love ourselves as we are and feel respect and compassion for our past selves and openness to our future. We allow ourselves to live in accord with our deepest needs, values, and wishes. No one can stop us; no one ever could.

Self-parenting also means opening ourselves to our inner resources and to a support system of loving, wise, and compassionate people. Pain and loss alienate us from others; grief work reconnects us with others we can trust. They may include those who hurt us, but they mainly come from the larger world, where many arms await us. Holocaust survivor Elie Wiesel says, "There is no messiah but there are messianic moments." We may not always have parents in our lives, but there are fatherly and motherly moments when someone who loves us—our biological parents or any supportive adult—comes through for us. Self-parenting includes accepting and cherishing these moments and the people who bring them. *Perhaps we were never promised full-fledged parent love but only parent-love moments, then and now, from actual parents and other adults. What we have been waiting for has come into our life many times, is it here now?*

The last step of mourning is the first step of intimacy. An inner nurturant parent empowers us to open ourselves to intimacy. As we become healthier, we look more consciously for a context in which we can safely resurrect our original thwarted attempts at finding mirroring. At the same time, we may fear that our original wounds may be reopened. We enter a relationship with both desire and fear, hope and terror, optimism and pessimism. Behind every wish from or complaint about a partner lies an unmet longing. All our lives, we go on requiring/seeking attunement to our feelings in the form of the five A's. Fear can be a flare showing us where the longing for the five A's is located within us.

Finally, to look at the bigger picture, grief work is completed by compassionate consciousness of similar anguish. For instance, the Jews' grief about the Holocaust may rightly lead them to feel outrage and resistance to the brutal oppression of the Tibetans by the Communist Chinese. Thus, grief is a path to the virtue of compassion and to world progress, something that retaliation has never been able to effect.

> Reciprocal tuning leads to delight and exuberance and sets the stage for trust. . . . The polarity to be harmonized in human development is between certainty that begets trust at the beginning of life and mature ability to negotiate life's vicissitudes. . . . in the face of uncertainty.
>
> —L. W. SANDER, M.D.

PRACTICES

Once my agony in the secret garden of my soul is finally permitted, witnessed, understood, and lovingly held, my own capacity to tolerate feelings, no matter how painful, expands freely. This allows me to attune to myself. Healthy intimacy helps me parent myself, to grant myself the five A's. As I mirror myself in the context of your mirroring me, my demands on you become more moderate, and I strike a happy balance between my need for nurturance from you and my capacity for self-nurturance.

ALLOWING YOUR FEELINGS • Notice your feelings. Before you try to fix them, let them happen fully. Only then can they be worked through thoroughly. Make room and time to tune in to what you are feeling. Then cradle it—that is, grant it legitimacy in a self-soothing way. Treat your feelings like babes in arms; you cradle them no matter how messy they become. Cradling is personal mindfulness, a granting of the five A's to oneself, a loving embrace of all one is. The alternative is self-contempt, no longer an option as we learn to love ourselves.

A cradling acceptance of ourselves makes us feel safe and empowers us. The father who stops what he is doing to listen to a whimpering child, squatting down to her level, tuning in, and hugging the child is being nurturant. The child feels better and runs off with more of a sense of power. We can do the same for the child within us.

Find the perhaps unfamiliar voice of empathy and acceptance inside yourself. It is the voice of the kindly uncle who cheers you up when he comes to visit. He tells your father not to be so strict. He points out all your good qualities. He gives you a dollar to buy candy. Affirm that you are that uncle for yourself. Affirm that you are in contact with the archetypal protector within. Recall that you have an inner child but also an inner strong and protective adult.

FINDING THE JOY • Samuel Taylor Coleridge spoke of what "might startle this dull pain and make it move and live." It is important to balance grief work with joyful play. Find ways to release your potential for fun and appreciation of life. Look at your relationships, your family life, your work, and your hobbies. When they become too serious or guilt-ridden, they inflict pain. How can you find some whimsy and enjoyment in each of them? Ask your partner and friends for suggestions. Integration happens when we transform what we have learned into art or fiction or humor or even a game we all can play. Inner potential can be activated if the conscious mind joins in with joy and alacrity. In fact, the unconscious is always waiting with a smile for consciousness to realize its unguessed powers.

CLEARING WITH YOUR OWN CHILDREN • If you have abused or neglected your children's needs, admit it to them. Ask them how you may have hurt or betrayed them. Inquire separately into their experience of each of the basic human needs—the five A's. *Our willingness to address and dress our wounds has equipped us to respond tenderly to others' wounds. Once we recognize our own hurts, we can never hurt others in the ways we were hurt.* We also let go of blame, the wish to punish, vengefulness, guilt, control, judgment, denial, hate, and bitterness. Letting go of blame is forgiveness; letting go of shame is self-esteem.

There is no shame in a parent apologizing to her or his children. I am a parent, and I apologize to my son for being controlling, manipulative, and demanding of him so often in our life together. I do it because I love him and because I want there to be an unimpeachable truth between us no matter how embarrassing. That is how, for any of us, the work and the practice make the first sentence of this book come true: Love is the possibility of possibilities.

MAKING A LIFELINE • Attentively contemplate all that has happened to you in the various chapters of your life. Write a lifeline decade by decade, making entries of the highpoints. Once it is complete, hang it where you can see it. Someday, when you are ready, bless and let go of each chapter by saying: "All this happened to me. I accept it as the hand I was dealt in life. It could have been better or it could have been worse. In this moment of serene compassion, I lay to rest any complaint, blame, or regret. I say yes unconditionally to all the conditions under which I lived. I appreciate them as providing just the lessons I needed to learn. I feel affection for myself and for all those who walked the path with me. I allow myself to go on as of now, without fear or clinging to the past or to any of its seductions or distractions. I line up all that has happened and simply say 'Oh, that *happened*. Now what?' Tragedy in life is not about any specific event but about losing our capacity to love. My life has been a history not a tragedy. May I and all those I have known become enlightened because of all that we went through together."

All thy old woes shall now smile on thee,
And thy pains sit bright upon thee.

All thy sorrows here shall shine.
And thy sufferings be divine;
Tears shall take comfort and turn to gems,
And wrongs repent to diadems.
Even thy deaths shall live and new
Dress the soul that once they slew.

      —RICHARD CRASHAW, *Hymn to Saint Theresa*

About the Author

DAVID RICHO, PH.D., M.F.T., is a psychotherapist, teacher, and writer who emphasizes Jungian, transpersonal, and spiritual perspectives in his work. He leads workshops at the Esalen Institute and throughout the United States. He lives and works in Santa Barbara and San Francisco, California.

He is the author of:

How to Be an Adult: A Handbook on Psychological and Spiritual Integration (Paulist Press, 1991)

When Love Meets Fear: How to Become Defense-Less and Resource-Full (Paulist, 1997)

Unexpected Miracles: The Gift of Synchronicity and How to Open It (Crossroad, 1998)

Shadow Dance: Liberating the Power and Creativity of Your Dark Side (Shambhala, 1999)

Catholic Means Universal: Integrating Spirituality and Religion (Crossroad, 2000)

Mary Within: A Jungian Contemplation of Her Titles and Powers (Crossroad, 2001)

David Richo gives workshops across the country, some of which are available on audiotape. For a catalog, send a self-addressed, stamped, legal-sized envelope to: DR, Box 31027, Santa Barbara, CA 93130.

Visit *davericho.com* for a complete listing of workshops, books, and audiotapes.